THE SOUL HYPOTHESIS

THE SOUL HYPOTHESIS

Investigations into the Existence
of the Soul

EDITED BY MARK C. BAKER
AND STEWART GOETZ

B L O O M S B U R Y
LONDON • NEW DELHI • NEW YORK • SYDNEY

Bloomsbury Academic
An imprint of Bloomsbury Publishing Inc

1385 Broadway	50 Bedford Square
New York	London
NY 10018	WC1B 3DP
USA	UK

www.bloomsbury.com

First published in 2011 by the Continuum International Publishing Group Inc
Reprinted 2011
Reprinted by Bloomsbury Academic 2013

Library of Congress Cataloging-in-Publication Data
A catalog record for this book is available from the Library of Congress.

ISBN: 978-1-4411-5224-4

Typeset by Pindar NZ, Auckland, New Zealand
Printed and bound in the United States of America

Contents

Acknowledgements

First of all, we are pleased to acknowledge the John Templeton Foundation for its substantial financial support of the project that culminated in this book. We owe special thanks to Paul Wason of the Foundation, who initially approached us about funding for our project and provided unwavering encouragement in seeing it through to its completion. Thanks also go out to all of the participants in the project — Robin Collins, Hans Halvorson, William Hasker, Daniel Robinson, Charles Taliaferro, and Dean Zimmerman — for their extensive contributions at group meetings, in personal conversations, and via email. It has been a pleasure to work together with these people more closely than is common for a work of this kind. A special word of gratitude goes to Dean Zimmerman for allowing us to bounce ideas off of him concerning just about everything regarding the book, and especially for helping with the Introduction, connecting pieces, and the Afterword. We are deeply indebted to Haaris Naqvi of Continuum Press for his interest in the book and his support in bringing it to print. We also thank Sara-May Mallett, the project manager, for her assistance with publication of the book. A word of sincere gratitude also goes to Michael Dello Buono for helping us put together the bibliography and to Yvon Kennon for her expertise in coordinating the logistics of our group meetings. Finally, we thank our wonderful wives, Carolyn and Linda, for having the soul to put up with our work on *The Soul Hypothesis*.

We dedicate this book to our children with love:
Catherine, Nicholas, and Julia Baker; Kathryn and Andrew Goetz.
Each is a unique kindred spirit and helps to convince us
that the existence of the soul is, in the end,
more than just a hypothesis.

Introduction

Mark Baker and Stewart Goetz

THE UNIVERSALITY OF A SOUL BELIEF

Most people, at most times, in most places, at most ages, have believed that human beings have some kind of soul.

Of course, it goes without saying that most people have also believed that human beings have some kind of physical body. In terms of their physical bodies, humans are subject to all the same forces and limitations that other physical objects are subject to. We are pinned down by gravity, we cannot pass through solid objects, and we cannot go from point A to point B without passing through intermediate points any more than a rock, or a leaf, or a frog can.

But when it comes to their thoughts and experiences, humans also seem to inhabit a rich world of beliefs and desires, goals and purposes, pleasures and pains, sights and sounds, joys and sorrows whose nature has little or nothing to do with ordinary physical objects and the forces that act on them. This second world is not unrelated to the first one. After all, pains and pleasures can be caused by dentists' drills and back rubs; beliefs and desires can be about sunsets and automobiles. But it does seem different from that first world, a world not enjoyed by rocks or leaves — perhaps not even by frogs. In short, then, most people have believed that a human being is a composite thing, made up of two distinct natures, a body and a soul. To use a technical term of Western philosophy, most people have been *dualists*. We refer to this belief as "the Soul Hypothesis."

No one seriously doubts how widespread belief in the Soul Hypothesis is. Its influence throughout the history of Western civilization

1

is undeniable. Greek philosophers such as Plato believed in a soul distinct from the body, and dualism (though not Platonic dualism) was also taken for granted by the authors of the Judeo-Christian scriptures.[1] It was thus a key point of agreement between these two founding sources of Western and European civilization, and most Western thinkers have thought in those terms from the beginning until (at least) the very recent past. The list of dualists includes thinkers such as Augustine, Aquinas, Descartes, Leibniz, Locke, and Kant, as well as hardcore scientists like Newton and Galileo. Even in the last century, the names of philosophers and scientists such as Karl Popper, Wilder Penfield, and Sir John Eccles appear on the list of well-known dualists.

Nor is belief in the Soul Hypothesis merely a quirk of the Western intellectual tradition. If it were, it could perhaps be blamed on the idiosyncratic influence of some charismatic but slightly whacky figure, a Plato or a St. Paul. But on the contrary, it is a long-standing result of cultural anthropology that such a belief is attested in almost all known human cultures. In a classic study in the anthropology of religious belief (1871), Sir Edward Burnett Tylor — one of the founding figures of scientific anthropology — identified "the doctrine of souls" as a basic belief underlying social and religious practices in all "primitive" human societies.[2] He admitted the theoretical possibility (attractive to him, given his views about the evolution of cultures) that there could be human tribes without any such notion, but said that in fact there was no evidence that such a tribe existed. In his own words: "Though the theoretical niche is ready and convenient, the actual statue to fill it is not forthcoming." He also discussed why various reports of human groups lacking any such belief were faulty, either based on prejudice, or on only superficial contact with the people in question, or indeed contradicted by the details reported in the very same ethnographic description that made the claim.

More recent anthropologists interested in universal features of human culture (and not just its many variable features) have agreed with this classic assessment. For example, George Peter Murdock, writing on "The Common Denominator of Cultures," presents a longish list of items that "occur, so far as the author's knowledge goes, in every culture known to history or ethnography."[3] In 66th place on his list (in alphabetical order) he puts "soul concepts" — just after religious ritual and sexual restrictions, and just before status differentiation and surgery. Similarly, C. F. Hockett writes that "acceptance of the soul-body distinction is nearly universal, though not quite."[4] He points out that "a few communities seem to have no interest in such matters," and his experience of various cultures leads him to note one true exception: "some very tiny segments of Western society reject the notion altogether."[5] We return to this unusual society below.[6]

Psychology joins the disciplines of history and anthropology in testifying to the robustness of the Soul Hypothesis. Recent studies in the area of developmental psychology use sophisticated experimental paradigms to explore the changing conceptual world of young children. This work has included probing children's beliefs about souls and the mental world, by researchers like Henry Wellman and Paul Bloom. Wellman sums up the modern developmental evidence by saying: "My own position is that young children are dualists: knowledgeable of mental states and entities as ontologically different from physical objects and real events."[7] Contrary to some reports, Wellman demonstrates that all children clearly distinguish the realm of physical objects from the realm of ideas and imaginary things. Along similar lines, Bloom observes that some children have been taught about brains in school, so that they know that the brain is important to thinking, but this interacts with their instinctive dualism to produce some odd conceptual confusions (from the point of view of their teachers). "They know that the brain is important for thinking, but they think of 'thinking' in a narrow cognitive sense of conscious problem solving. They still think that there are other things that THEY themselves do (although the brain might help). The brain is a useful, enhancing tool."[8]

Also relevant to these issues are investigations into children's understanding of death. For example, psychologists Jesse Bering and David Bjorklund asked children about a mouse that was eaten by a crocodile. Four- to six-year-olds knew that the mouse's *biological* functions would stop "now that the mouse is no longer alive."[9] It would not need to go to the bathroom, its ears wouldn't work, and neither would its brain. But the majority thought that the mouse's *psychological* properties would continue: it could still experience hunger, it would still have thoughts about the crocodile that ate it, and it would still have desires, such as the desire to go home.[10] This body of research shows that not only have all human cultures been dualists, at least in their origins, but also perhaps all human individuals have been dualists, at least in their childhoods.

In short, the Soul Hypothesis seems to be extremely natural, indeed almost inevitable, to the human mind and experience. On this, everyone seems to agree, both those who think that this belief is probably true and those who think that this belief is probably false. The question then arises: could so many people who agree on this basic feature of their lives and experience all be wrong?

A UNIVERSAL MISTAKE?

"Absolutely yes!" That is the answer given by many people within one particular culture that the reader no doubt has experience with — namely the contemporary Western intellectual culture that has grown up in part out of the production and consumption of books like this one. Indeed, prominent members of this culture say that the commonness and naturalness of this belief probably shows that the belief is false, rather than that it is true.[11] After all (they say), common-sense notions have been shown to be false — even radically false — in virtually every other domain in which science has had its say. For example, the common-sense notions of astronomy and cosmology that included the sun going around the earth were shown to be profoundly false by Copernicus, Galileo, and the others. Common-sense notions of physics have been shown to be radically false by modern science, particularly with the advent of relativity and quantum mechanics in the twentieth century. Common-sense notions about the nature of life and the relationships among animal species have been overturned by modern studies in biology. Indeed, on no other point has "common sense" been vindicated by scientific research, it is said.

To the scientifically minded, the bad history of common-sense notions is not really surprising. Within this framework, what we call "common sense" is the product of the evolution of the human animal, including its brain/mind. And evolution has no direct interest in what is true, only in what is useful for the purposes of survival and reproduction in some environmental niche. So the most that we should conclude from the ubiquity of the belief in souls, people say, is that the belief was useful to our ancestors — or perhaps it was a relatively benign side effect of other beliefs that were useful to them. We should not conclude that the belief is true. Rather, given the track record of common sense when it is opposed to scientific research, the smart bet would seem to be that common sense is wrong also when it comes to the Soul Hypothesis.

In this way, a belief that has remained common among the masses has slowly but surely all but disappeared in certain smaller circles. Beginning early in the last century and accelerating up to the present day, the idea of the soul has receded more and more into the background among the intellectual elite of scientifically informed people in Europe and North America, to the point that it has become almost extinct.[12] The explanations for this anthropological oddity are many in number and wide-ranging in nature. However, it seems fair to say that at the heart of the matter is an intellectual devotion to and fascination with science as the exclusive source of all truth. It is on purpose that we say an intellectual devotion to and fascination with science as the source of all truth — what one might call a doctrine of *scientism* — because we believe that there is nothing about science itself that should lead anyone to believe that there is something problematic about the existence of the soul. In other words, there is nothing inherently anti-scientific about the Soul Hypothesis being either acknowledged outright or used as a conditional hypothesis within an overall scientific project. Certainly the founders of modern science — people like Bacon, Descartes, Newton, Galileo, and Leibniz — detected no such incompatibility. Of course, it is worth considering whether scientific research might show that the Soul Hypothesis is false or at least that it seems incompatible with certain other pieces of evidence. But that is a very different matter from saying that it is intrinsically anti-scientific, and hence entirely out of bounds — a claim that has been made in many recent discussions.

WHAT IS SCIENCE?

In engaging these matters, it is important to keep track of just what one means by the word "science." Like every other word, this one can be used in both broad and narrower senses. In the narrow sense, science is characterized by close adherence to a particular method — one that involves controlled experiments, measurement of observables, testing predictions, replication by others, and so on. This is the justly famous scientific method. But there is also a much broader sense, in which the word "science" is almost synonymous with "rational inquiry"; it is simply a commitment to finding and using the best tools available to ascertain the truth of a given matter. And there is a continuum of intermediate senses that fall between these two extremes, determined by how large a role the core scientific method plays in the overall inquiry and how much it is supplemented with other techniques and considerations.

Now consider the question "Does the existence of human souls fit with science or not?" in the light of this range of meanings for the word "science." The correct answer to the question might very well depend on what sense of the word one has in mind. We believe that if "science" is used in a somewhat broad sense, the answer is "Yes, it does." Consideration of the soul's existence is perfectly compatible with the pursuit of the truth in the relatively flexible sense of using whatever intellectual tools give the most purchase on the topic in hand. We demonstrate this in various ways, from various different viewpoints, in the body of this volume.

If, on the other hand, one thinks of science in the narrowest sense defined by the classical scientific method, then perhaps we should concede that the Soul Hypothesis is not a scientific hypothesis per se. It does seem to be the case that the soul is not directly observable, cannot be measured numerically, and cannot be added into and taken out as the independent variable in controlled experiments. (Or at least no one has figured out how to do such things yet. But then neither are quarks or strings directly observable or manipulable.) Given this, it is quite possible that the narrow scientific method is not the right tool for finding out the whole truth in this particular domain.

But if this is what one means by science, then one must certainly abandon the claim of scientism that science is the way to discover all important truths. For example, historical truths cannot be established by the narrow scientific method: they cannot be manipulated in an experimental situation; they cannot be observed directly; and they cannot be replicated exactly. There is a truth of the matter as to whether Napoleon won the battle of Waterloo. Moreover, this truth is knowable to some degree of certainty by rational inquiry (science in the broadest sense). But it is not knowable simply by applying the scientific method per se — not by creating 50 battles of Waterloo, putting Napoleon in 25 of them, measuring how he fares relative to a control group, and analyzing the results statistically versus a null hypothesis. Narrow science might play a role in the inquiry — say by doing some kind of chemical testing to help evaluate the authenticity of relevant documents — but narrow science would not frame this inquiry as a whole.

Now what should be obvious in this case is also true in part of many sciences that are more obviously continuous with "real" "hard" science, but that also have an important historical component to them: fields like evolutionary biology, geology and cosmology — to say nothing of economics, anthropology, and the like. We do not conclude that the earth was formed x number of years ago by such and such a process purely by the narrow scientific method, any more than we conclude that Napoleon lost at Waterloo this way. We do not set up a giant experiment with gas clouds of different kinds in systematically varying conditions, and then measure directly in which ones the earth forms (and in how much time). Narrow science plays a crucial role in approaching this question, but by chipping away at its edges rather than by defining the inquiry as a whole.

In fact, it seems clear that the most common and useful sense of science these days is a medium-broad one, somewhere in between the two extreme senses that we originally staked out. Fields like evolutionary biology, geology and earth science, astronomy and cosmology have joined physics and chemistry as prestige sciences, and have been some of the most active areas of recent scientific endeavor. They are built on the foundation of the classical scientific method, and they continue to use this method as an important part of what they do. But they also crucially do other things — like observing unique objects that cannot be manipulated, controlled, or repeated, such as the fossil record, existing rock formations, and the structure of the universe as a whole. So these are medium-broad science, not super-narrow science.

But if one sets the bar for being science at "medium-broad," then we think that it is very likely that the Soul Hypothesis will count as a scientific hypothesis. We officially recommend simply leaving open (for now) just how much disciplined rational inquiry into the truth of this matter would have in common with familiar science in its various senses. But we would not be at all surprised if the answer turns out to be "quite a lot." We return to further discussion of this below.

FUNDAMENTAL CHALLENGES FOR MATERIALISM

Since non-dualists have become the majority in some circles of scientifically educated people in North America and Europe, we now often hear that there is a (near) consensus among scientists and philosophers that there is no such thing as a nonphysical human soul. But this alleged (near) consensus against the Soul Hypothesis arguably disguises a very wide diversity of views about how the purely materialist alternative can be worked out to explain all the phenomena. Among people who think seriously about such things, there simply is no agreement about *how* one can explain human beings without a soul. The field is splintered between so-called property dualists at one extreme and radical eliminativists at the other, with type-identity theorists, role-filler functionalists, perceptual concept theorists, and higher-order functionalists scattered in between (among others). While this is not the place to go into the defining characteristics of these various views, suffice it to say that they differ from one another widely, and contradict one another in various ways.[13] No one view is making obvious progress in terms of explaining particular results and winning adherents. Thus, it does not seem clear (to us) that there is truly a unified research program here, under the name of materialism. The apparent consensus could be something of a mirage, with the only thing holding it together being a denial of the Soul Hypothesis. If so, it begins to look more like a shared assumption than a shared discovery. And of course there can be consensuses based on fashion and the spirit of the age, as well as consensuses based on observation and reason. Even scientists must always be on guard to make sure they are part of the latter rather than the former. The honorable mantle of the scientist conveys no inherent infallibility in this regard.

We do not mean to imply by anything that we have said that the scientific disciplines that study human beings from a materialist point of view — for example, cognitive science, psychology and neuroscience — are all a sham. They have unquestionably made valuable, interesting, and important discoveries, within the domain of the physical world. This is entirely to be expected and hoped for, also from the perspective we are urging. After all, a proponent of the Soul Hypothesis in no way denies that we have bodies. (We are dualists, not idealists who believe in the existence of the soul but not the body!) Part of those bodies is a brain, and that is an important and interesting thing to study in its own right. It is no surprise, then, that discoveries can be made and have been made in these disciplines by scientists working with materialist assumptions. In principle, then, we dualists can perfectly well include almost anything that materialists include in their view of the material world, whenever the facts truly warrant it — perhaps with some adjustments to the details of our dualist theories (see below).

What we are seriously skeptical about, however, is the idea that the results of scientific work done with purely materialist assumptions will add up to a complete picture of the human mind, simply by accumulating the results of normal incremental science. In other words, we highly doubt that we will get a complete theory of the mind simply by doing more of what we already know how to do. Materialists may accuse us of being pessimists in this respect. (And indeed we all need to be optimists when looking for funding for our research, or when explaining ourselves to the media.) But there are some big problems, too, well-known in the relevant literatures. The successes of cognitive science and neuroscience come from solving little, localized, well-defined problems. These are typically problems that arise at the periphery of the human mind, concerning either input functions like visual perception and language, or output functions like motor planning. For larger scale problems at the center of the human mind — reason, will, conceptual thought, and so on — progress has been far more limited, and severe new questions about integration arise. Cognitive science so far has made essentially no discernable progress on many of these issues. The list of widely acknowledged outstanding problems includes the following.[14]

- What gives conscious experience its particular subjective character? How could electrochemical events in the brain (but not anywhere else, as far as we know) produce the taste of a lemon, the distinctive sound of a flute, or the pain of a toothache? (The problem of qualia.)
- How can our words and thoughts, understood as patterns of activity in the brain, be the sorts of things that have meaning, that refer to things we could never have direct contact with, that represent states of affairs that can be true or false? (By contrast, other naturally occurring things, like rocks, may bear the imprint of past events, but they are not true or false concerning those events; they simply are what they are. Of course, a rock can bear an inscription of some kind, which could be true or false, but we would only see it as that if we believed that it was put there intentionally, by something with a mind — not if it appeared "accidentally," as the result of ordinary physical processes.) (The problem of intentionality.)
- How can we act (or at least think we act) in a way that flows out of freely made choices, which are neither predetermined nor random, but freely chosen, so that we are rightly held morally responsible for the consequences? (The problems of free will and morality.)
- How can we understand the human capacity to reason in a way that is truly rational, managing to figure out what is relevant to a particular problem or issue in an open-ended and holistic way — even when there is no simple way to tell in advance what kinds of information might be relevant to the problem — all in a finite amount of time? (The problem of abductive reasoning, alias the epistemic frame problem; see Fodor 2000.)
- How can the specific perceptual properties that are "recognized" by individual neurons (e.g. colors, shapes, textures) be integrated together, first into coherent perceived objects (e.g. fuzzy blue squares), and then into a rich overall perceptual experience that takes in many objects perceived through different sensory modalities?(The binding problem, the unity of consciousness.)
- How can stable bits of abstract knowledge be represented by the ever-shifting flux of electrical activity that we observe in the brain?

To flesh out just one of these problems a little bit, consider the last one on this list. This all by itself should teach those who profess to believe in the near-completeness of our current neuroscientific theories some humility, since it looks like it *should* be a relatively simple one. It can be shown beyond reasonable doubt that an ant foraging for food, even though it wanders in a complicated path, always keeps track of the exact distance and direction back to its hive. As a result, whenever its mission is completed (say, it finds food) it can immediately and accurately go straight home by the shortest path. If it is picked up and moved to a new spot by a mean experimenter, it still heads straight to where its home ought to be (not thrown off by the different terrain), and acts confused when it arrives there to find no hive. This kind of behavior shows that the "mind" of the ant stores two numerical constants, which it continually updates: the distance to home, and the compass bearing to home. However, the dominant theories of neural computation cannot account for this.[15] These theories are built around idealizations of what we see going on in brains, and that is complex patterns of electrical activity, which are continuous in nature and always in flux. Theories that try to be realistic to the neurology in this way are exactly the wrong sorts of theories for representing discrete numerical values — like the distance to home. The disconnect between neural modeling and observed behavior here is so profound that neuroscientists have pressed a researcher we know who works on animal navigation to deny the facts, to say that ants do not know the distance and direction home. But their behavior clearly shows that they do.

This example of the ant is not an argument for the Soul Hypothesis per se. There is nothing spooky or supernatural about the ant's ability to navigate, nothing which points toward it having an immaterial soul. It is simply navigating by the method of dead reckoning, just as human sailors often do. We know very well how to record numerical constants like distance and direction in purely physical objects, such as logbooks and digital computers. But the ant is a stern reminder of the radical incompleteness of our current theories of how even very simple knowledge is stored in the brain. If neurological theory is missing fundamental ideas about how the ant can keep track of where home is, how can it claim to be anywhere near complete? And if it is so radically incomplete, how can it be so sure that there is no contribution for the Soul Hypothesis to make, especially when it comes to enormously more challenging issues like many of the others on our list? The Soul Hypothesis is certainly not alone in facing some fundamental challenges, and in needing some new ideas in order to move forward.

As a final point along these lines, we mention that those thinkers who want to keep things simple and unmysterious have generally not fared so well even in physics. No doubt much of the intellectual attraction of materialism as opposed to dualism is that it seems simpler, cleaner, and less mysterious. This is because it believes in fewer kinds of things (by definition). In science, less is more. Materialism should be the null hypothesis, the one that is believed unless there is compelling evidence to the contrary. Ockham's Razor gives dualism its fatal cut, we are often told. But as the physical sciences have progressed, the truth has not always come down on the side of the simpler, the cleaner, and the less mysterious. On the contrary, if we have learned anything about fundamental physical reality in the last 100+ years, it is that it is *really weird*. Spare ontologies and simple laws have not stood up. Einstein's theories of relativity are mathematically more complex than Newton's, and they are positively classical compared to the discoveries in quantum mechanics — to say nothing of more recent proposals in terms of superstrings and the like. It also turns out that there are many more than three elementary particles, and these particles undergo some highly unintuitive modes of interaction. If physics had really settled permanently into the idealized post-Newtonian vision that all that exists are tiny billiard balls in space, bouncing off each other in accordance with a few simple mathematical laws, maybe the view that "the simpler theory is always better" would have a kind of compelling force. But it hasn't turned out that way: the world is full of strange, wonderful, counterintuitive things — at least leptons and gluons, if not spirits and angels. Nor does it seem to be getting simpler and less mysterious as we go. In this brave new world, how can we say with any confidence that there is no room for souls, that such things could not be possible? Indeed, two of the chapters that follow take a look into modern physics from the point of view of these issues, and lay the charge that it is those who offer arguments for materialism who have not kept up with the physics, not the dualists.

A PLURALITY OF SOUL HYPOTHESES

By trying to win a new hearing for the Soul Hypothesis, we don't mean to deny that some forms of dualism are false. Some of them certainly are. This is a simple point of logic, given that there are various forms of dualism, and only one can be completely right.

A problem that besets dualists in the current climate is that people talk as if there were only one kind imaginable, namely pure Cartesian dualism. Such is the prominence of Descartes that this is the version that everyone thinks of, argues against, typically dismisses, and perhaps ridicules, calling it (in the words of the philosopher Gilbert Ryle) "the ghost in the machine."[16] But, like any other interesting hypothesis, the Soul Hypothesis can exist in many guises, which share some basic assumptions but not others.

One can think of the range of logically possible Soul Hypotheses in the following way. Ordinary material objects have a familiar set of properties, which we think we more or less understand. For example, material objects exist at a specific time, they occupy a specific region of space, they have well-defined physical properties like mass and charge, and they are particulars rather than universals. (Particulars are things that can be identical to one another in all their properties without being the same thing. For example, there are different cars, and different shades of red. But two cars could have all the same physical properties — size, shape, color, etc. – and still be different cars. In contrast, two shades of red could not be identical in every respect and still be two distinct shades of red. So a car is a particular, whereas a specific shade of red is a universal.) Dualism is the claim that humans have a part (the soul) that is not a material object. This amounts to saying that a soul has some properties that ordinary material objects do not have. But one could make different choices about which properties souls have that distinguish them from physical objects. For example, Descartes' view was that souls exist in time and are particulars, but he thought that they do not have any spatial location or proper parts. He also held that souls could exist entirely independently of the bodies they are associated with, to the extent that a person should actually think better when separated from a body than when linked to it. This counts as a relatively radical form of dualism, in that the soul has a number of properties that make it very different from a material object. One can also define other, somewhat milder forms of the Soul Hypothesis, which explore other combinations of features. For example, one might say that souls lack mass and charge, but do have spatial locations as well as locations in time. Or one might say that souls are distinct from brains but depend on brains for the energy to fuel them, or even for their very existence, in something like the way an electric field depends on a charge for its existence (see Chapter 8). In the limit, the milder dualisms might shade into slightly quirky materialisms. For example, if one thought that souls had all the same properties as physical objects, but only had a different combination of those properties — say they had the charge of an electron but the mass of a neutron — this might count as a minor variant of materialism rather than as a true dualism. But the point remains that there is a whole range of Soul Hypotheses that might be considered, to which the standard refutations do not apply and which may have important new explanatory advantages. Some of the chapters that follow explore different forms of dualism with this possibility in mind.

As dualists we do not (necessarily) deny that current research in brain sciences and related disciplines might pose some interesting new challenges to a dualist theory that includes the Soul Hypothesis as a component. For example, dualists have the specific challenge of sorting out in some detail which features of human mental life depend directly on the physical part (the body) and which depend directly on the nonphysical part (the soul). A particular researcher might have a theory that holds that some function or characteristic depends on the soul and not the brain — say personality/character, or reasoning ability, or consciousness, or the ability to make a decision. Obviously, there are specific results of current science that challenge these views, or even refute them. Such challenges are part and parcel of any inquiry that includes a scientific component, as this question does in our view. We do not mean to downplay or deny or avoid such challenges. On the contrary, we welcome being challenged, even strenuously, by scientists and philosophers working from a materialist perspective. One of the purposes of this book is to face some of these challenges, to the best of our ability, in some new and creative ways.

What we do take exception to is being declared out of bounds, non-scientific, anti-scientific, not deserving the opportunity to participate in the conversation any longer. If a simple or naïve version of the Soul Hypothesis is falsified by scientific research, then that might mean that dualism is false — but it might also mean that it is time to move to a richer, more thoughtful version of the Soul Hypothesis. This courtesy is routinely extended to other kinds of hypotheses; their proponents get the opportunity to revise and rethink in the light of new findings, as long as they can find new conceptual resources within the theory that they think are worth developing and testing.

How does one normally detect that the leading idea of a theory is (probably) false in scientific and philosophical research? Not just by showing that one preliminary version is false, but rather by showing that every version that has been seriously proposed is false. It can happen that an idea is proposed, then refuted, then rescued by adding auxiliary hypotheses, then refuted again, then rescued by adding still more auxiliary assumptions on top of the first set, only to be refuted once more. Once a hypothesis has been discredited through an extended process of this sort, it could be reasonable to give up on it, even if a few zealots still cling to it. But we claim that the Soul Hypothesis has not been given this chance in the last century. Rather, one old-fashioned version (Descartes') is summarily rejected, and that is taken to be that.

More generally, we claim that the Soul Hypothesis can function as a hypothesis in the sense of being an idea that is an integral part of a complex overall theory of the true nature of human beings (at least, and very possibly other animals as well). Like any high level hypothesis, its connection to observable empirical data must be real and not eliminable, but the connection will be complex and indirect. As such, no one experiment or kind of experiment can be expected to falsify (or confirm) the Soul Hypothesis per se, any more than it could falsify (or confirm) materialism. If the theory that includes the Soul Hypothesis happens to make a false prediction, or is incompatible with certain empirical results, the problem could be that there is something wrong with the Soul Hypothesis itself, or the problem could be with one of the other auxiliary assumptions that make up the theory as a whole. Even if the problem is with the Soul Hypothesis itself, it is perfectly possible that there would be another version of the Soul Hypothesis, some sort of refinement or variant of the original version, which preserved something of its essential character but did not make the false prediction. Ideally it would even make other, unanticipated true predictions. Another goal we have for this volume is to show that the Soul Hypothesis is by no means as powerless and defeated and without resources to face the challenges as many people allege. The Soul Hypothesis should be able to function the way that other scientific hypotheses do, through testing, refinement, developing alternatives, debating those alternatives, and so on. We will take a step forward along these lines in what follows.

TESTING A SOUL HYPOTHESIS

We made the charge above that the materialist consensus was not as firm as it seems, that it is held together more by its naked denial of the Soul Hypothesis than by a body of positive results. One might wonder at this point if the same charge couldn't be made about dualism. Is it really an inherently negative hypothesis, consisting only of a denial of the completeness of purely materialist theories of human beings? We admit that there is the danger of it degrading into this. It is possible that the essays in this book will not seem any more complete or self-consistent than those in a comparable collection of writings by various materialists would be. If so, we may need to beg some indulgence from the reader. One of our points is that not enough time, energy, and talent has gone into developing serious dualistic theories in the last few decades. We cannot claim to have the results of a mature new alternative consensus in the pages that follow. Our goal must be more modest: to take a few steps toward such an alternative, and by doing so to lend credence to the claim that the project is worth a serious try.

Even at this early stage, though, we want to do what we can to present positive dualisms, which have some ideas of their own and some prima facie evidence in their favor. Some of the contributions are primarily defensive in the sense of showing that the reasons many people have given for rejecting dualism are not as strong or compelling as many take them to be. But just as many of the essays also have a positive theme, trying to construct interesting new dualisms, pointing to positive evidence for dualism, showing the positive role that dualistic premises can play in scientific reasoning, and the like.

Could specific positive versions of the Soul Hypothesis really be tested empirically? We do not see why not. To illustrate this possibility in some detail, imagine the conceivability of the following experiment designed to test one version of the Soul Hypothesis.

The experiment could rest on the following assumptions. A proponent of the Soul Hypothesis might well claim that the immaterial soul can initiate a cascade of neural events that results in a voluntary bodily movement, such as blinking one's eyes (see also Chapter 4). A strict materialist would deny that any such thing happens. However, the materialist presumably admits that there are some random firings of neurons in the brain, given that all complex physical systems contain a certain amount of "noise," caused by random quantum fluctuations and similar factors. A complete brain science ought to be able to tell which neuron firings are caused by random factors, and which are predictably caused by other normal brain activity. The key question at stake, then, would be whether the apparently uncaused neuron firings are really (all) random occurrences, or whether some of them are caused by a so far invisible factor, the soul.

To test these two views, the experimenter brings into the lab both an experimental subject and a neurologist as a consulting expert. The neurologist opens up the subject's skull and places detectors at all the relevant locations in the brain necessary to get a comprehensive neurological description of what happens (ideally one detector in each neuron!). The experimenter then instructs the subject to blink voluntarily at various times chosen by the subject during a certain time frame, without informing the neurologist when he chooses to blink. During the same period, the subject will also presumably blink at various times as a result of his normal blinking reflex. As a further control, the experimenter might allow the neurologist to stimulate the subject's brain electronically from time to time, so as to cause the subject to blink at times chosen by the experimenter but not by the subject. Every blink is recorded. The subject reports to the experimenter which of the blinks were voluntary. Independently, the neurologist reports to the experimenter which blinks she caused directly by electrical stimulation, which blinks were fully caused by normal processes in the brain that she can identify (such as the firing of other neurons), and which blinks had random firings as part of the neural activity leading up to them. The experimenter then matches up the subject's reports of voluntary blink versus involuntary blink with the neurologist's categories of artificially caused neural event versus neurally caused neural event versus random neural event. The experimenter then does a statistical analysis of the results, looking for correlations and interactions.

We imagine that the dualist and the materialist might well make opposite predictions about the results of an experiment like this. Suppose that the blinks that the subject reports as being voluntary match at a very high rate those that neurologist identified as having a random component. Then the dualist can claim a success for the idea that there are causal factors at work that do not involve just the brain. (Some of) the neural firings that looked random to the neurologist were not truly random after all, but rather were caused by something that was not part of the neurologist's account of the brain, complete as it might have been in its own terms. On the other hand, suppose the blinks that the subject reports as voluntary are consistently among the ones that the neurologist declared to be entirely neurally caused. Then the materialist can claim credit for a successful prediction: a voluntary action might be caused by a pattern of neurons firing that is different from the pattern that causes a reflex action, but either way the significant events seem to be all brain events all the time. Finally, if the subject often reports as voluntary blinks that which the neurologist says she caused artificially by electrical stimulation, this would confirm experimentally the idea that our sense of purposeful action is only a kind of illusion — an-after-the fact rationalization of what we observe ourselves to be doing, not a true cause of the behavior, as the dualist believes.

Of course, an experiment like this would not truly decide the question between dualism and materialism. Either side could rethink some of their assumptions if the first round of facts came in against them. The materialists might realize that that the neurologist's description of neural interactions was not as complete as they thought. The dualists might realize that they were looking for the influence of the soul on the brain in the wrong place: perhaps it is not to be found in the *initiating* of a kind of neural activity, but rather in the *suppressing* of neural activity, or in *channeling* the neural activity in a particular way. But controversies like this over the interpretation of the results would not at all disqualify the experiment from being a scientific one that at least bears on the truth of the Soul Hypothesis. On the contrary, the fact that it raises such questions would tend to confirm its status as science.

Are there any principled grounds for denying that this investigation would count as science? Conceivably. It is true that the dualist who predicts that the subject's reports of "voluntary" will correlate with the neurologist's reports of "has a random component" is positing a theoretical factor that the experiment does not pretend to measure directly, namely the soul. It is also true that the experimenter is collecting a somewhat unusual kind of data: the subject's reports that an action was voluntary. This seems rather far from classic dependent variables like mass, velocity, length, and charge. We can therefore (barely) imagine someone saying that it is not a scientific experiment on these grounds.[17] But that seems like it would be a very narrow and unhelpful judgment. After all, the proposed experiment does include many other features of standard experimental design. For example, it includes certain controls, the data is collected in double-blind fashion (the subject not knowing what the experimenter is doing, and vice versa), there is statistical evaluation of the data, and so on. It seems to us that only the most narrow and doctrinaire view of what science is would exclude this as being an instance of science — a view according to which much award-winning science also would not count as such. We conclude that there is (in principle) room for a positive and constructive dualism within the bounds of scientific inquiry.[18]

We also believe that no full-scale experiment like this has been done yet. Perhaps the brain sciences are not yet advanced enough to distinguish reliably between neuron firings that are caused entirely by the firing of other neurons and those that are not. Even if the brain sciences are advanced enough to do this in principle, it may not be feasible to make this determination in practice, within a finite amount of time, at arbitrary locations in the brain. Indeed, it is conceivable that the brain is irreducibly so complex, and the ethical limitations of how one can experiment on humans are so strict, that we will never be able to do this experiment in practice. (We admit that we ourselves would be reluctant to volunteer for it.) If so, that will be a shame.

Nevertheless, one can imagine more modest experiments that

approximate the one we have outlined in various ways, which might be more feasible. Indeed, some of these have been performed, with results that we take to be encouraging for dualism. For example, some features of our proposed experiment are drawn from the research of pioneering brain scientist Penfield. Penfield discovered that by stimulating areas of patients' brains with an electrode he was able to produce the recall of certain memories and involuntary movements of their limbs. But he was unable to make them *choose* to move a limb, in a way that they felt to be voluntary. He wrote, "There is no place in the cerebral cortex where electrode stimulation will cause a patient . . . to decide [choose]."[19] Penfield himself interpreted this as evidence for some form of dualism. Our grander experiment is conceived as an upgrade of his that takes into account more factors.

There are also other experimental results which, while not conclusive evidence for dualism, at the very least are the sort of thing that a dualist would expect. For example, Mario Beauregard has recently reported experiments in which the electric activity in the brain produced by looking at very primal pictures of sex or violence is influenced profoundly by how the subject chooses to view the scene, whether as an emotionally engaged participant or as a detached impartial observer.[20] Beauregard makes a similar point about fears such as arachnophobia. Those who are afraid of spiders can make choices about behavior that reorganize their brains and lead to a reduction or elimination of their fear of the little creatures.[21] This is at least consistent with the claim that free choices made by the soul influence profoundly how the brain processes sensory information.

These seemingly free choices can even be observed in clinical practice. The neuropsychiatrist Jeffrey Schwartz has stressed the central importance of free will in treating patients with obsessive-compulsive disorders (OCDs).[22] OCDs are known to be rooted in the functional anatomy of the brain. Compared to the brains of normal persons, positron emission topography (PET) shows that the brains of OCD patients have hypermetabolic activity in the orbital frontal cortex, which is located on the underside of the front of the brain above and behind the eyes. This hyperactivity, caused by a biochemical imbalance, leads to the patient's belief that something is wrong (e.g. my hands are dirty and I must wash them), even though he knows rationally that nothing is wrong. Schwartz argues that if an OCD patient believes the prevailing orthodoxy that he is no more than a victim of the disease, then his chances of conquering his disorder are severely diminished. But Schwartz maintains that an OCD sufferer can *choose* as a free and active agent to redirect and focus his attention on ways of acting and living that prevent fulfillment of his OCD urges, hence greatly improving his chances of overcoming them. Schwartz claims that this chosen, redirected and sustained attention by the soul causally produces a rewiring of the sufferer's brain with the result that the OCD urges are greatly diminished, if not completely calmed. If he is right, then this is a tangible, clinically proven case that provides support for the hypothesis that the soul has the non-deterministic freedom to causally affect (even overcome) the brain. It is positive facts like these — not just the remaining gaps that we discern in purely materialistic views — that motivate us in pursuing the Soul Hypothesis.

CONCLUSION

The body of this book consists of nine essays, written by different authors. Each author explores some aspect of the Soul Hypothesis within the contemporary context, each from a different angle and conceptual background. While all of our authors have at least some philosophical background, several of them also have extensive training in one of the relevant sciences, including physics, neuroscience, psychology and linguistics. In this way, we hope to illustrate not only the viability, but indeed the potential fecundity of the Soul Hypothesis from several disciplinary perspectives with a level of expertise that would be very difficult to achieve in a single-authored book. At the same time, we have designed the book in two ways to try to prevent this richness and diversity of perspective from being unduly confusing to the general reader. First, we have carefully ordered the nine essays into a coherent sequence that we believe gives the clearest possible survey of the "lay of the land." Second, to aid the reader in his or her journey through the book, we have written brief introductions to each chapter. These should help prepare the reader for the topic to be discussed, and show how the chapter to come relates to the themes raised in the chapter or chapters that precede it. In this way, we hope to integrate the specific arguments that each author presents into an overall plotline, making it into a more cohesive and satisfying whole than many multi-authored books are. Our goal then is to knit the various pieces together into an overall case for the Soul Hypothesis that is even more than the sum of its parts. The book concludes with a brief afterword, in which we face the contentious question of what relationship the Soul Hypothesis might have with religious belief, as opposed to scientific and rational theory-building.

Throughout the book, we make the claim that consideration of the hypothesis that the soul exists both belongs to broad science (disciplined rational inquiry in pursuit of truth) and interacts in some respects with narrow science (the pursuit of truth by a particular method). More than that, we demonstrate that reports of the death of the soul have been exaggerated, and there are some very interesting things to be said in its favor from many different angles, even now in the twenty-first century.[23]

With these overarching themes in mind, we turn to our first essay: Charles Taliaferro's chapter "The Soul of the Matter." Taliaferro introduces for us several key concepts that are important for understanding subsequent chapters.

First and foremost among these is the distinction between the first-person and third-person perspective. The third-person perspective makes use of one or more of the five senses (sight, hearing, touch, taste, and smell) to acquire information about the external world. In contrast, the first-person perspective is introspective in nature. It provides us with a direct and unique awareness of our own thoughts, perceptions, pleasures, pains, choices, hopes and fears. For example, if I see Chris wince and draw her hand away from a sharp item and utter the word "ouch," I might infer that she feels pain in her hand. I say "Chris feels pain," and I know this from the third-person perspective. But I know that I myself feel pain in a much more direct way, because I feel the pain myself. I say "I feel pain," and I know this from the first-person perspective.

The unique first-person perspective provides much of the basis for what has become known as "folk psychology." Folk psychology is an informal explanatory framework that is rooted in our introspective awareness of ourselves and is used to explain our everyday actions. We know by direct awareness that we feel and know certain things. We then use our desires and beliefs to make choices to act. For example, many of us regularly go to the supermarket. Our folk psychology explanation of this odd behavior (unique in the animal kingdom) is that we want to eat, so we want to have food on hand, while at the same time we know that the supermarket is located where it is and we believe that it has available the food that we want. When we put together these everyday desires and beliefs in the right way, we can explain why people do many of the objectively complex and arcane things that they do.

Taliaferro goes on to point out that those in philosophy and science who call into question the existence of the soul do so by adopting the third-person perspective on human experience and behavior at the expense of the first-person perspective. They are so suspicious of the first-person perspective and the related folk psychology that they seek to discredit *them and even dispense with them entirely. According to these researchers, science is the discipline that enables us to escape the subjective first-person perspective and remain entirely within the objective third-person perspective. It is based entirely on objective measurement and reasoned inference, not on imagining what it feels like to be (say) an electron. It seems to be because science proceeds in this way that it has made such incredible progress in curing diseases, controlling our environment, and generally improving our quality of life. The remaining task, then, is simply to complete the revolution, and come to see ourselves in the same third person light in which science has taught us to see other things.*

Taliaferro explains why he is skeptical of most of the claims of these philosophers and scientists. His most basic point is that science itself is necessarily engaged in and practiced by persons acting from the first-person perspective. There simply would not be any science unless its practitioners were beings with desires and beliefs, hopes, fears, and purposes. For example, medical science works hard to seek cures for diseases because those diseases cause pain and suffering, which are ultimately first-person phenomena. Theoretical science seeks to find answers to unanswered questions because those questions induce curiosity and finding the answers produces intellectual satisfaction — and those are also ultimately first-person phenomena. When scientists seek new discoveries, then, they are seeking to improve the quality of our first-person experience.

Along with bringing up the word "quality," we want to introduce to the readers the related Latin term "quale" (plural "qualia"), which occurs in many of the following chapters. A quale is best defined by example: an experience of pleasure is a quale, as is an experience of pain, the smell of a flower, the taste of an apple, and the color of a sunset. Talking about qualia allows us to go beyond the naked fact that someone sees a certain object and points us to the nearly ineffable quality of their experience of seeing the object — what the object really looks like to them, its special shade of blue that is so hard to describe, and its glossy sheen. Qualia are the raw material of which the first-person perspective is made up, and what distinguishes it from the third-person perspective; it is that qualitative aspect of my pain that you cannot really feel, even if you may sympathetically say that you feel my pain. On the positive side, pleasant qualia are among those things that most of us would rank right up near the top on a list of what is most valuable to us in daily life. They are literally the smelling of the roses.

Despite their immediacy and their subjective value to us, Taliaferro points out that the prevailing orthodoxy among philosophers and scientists who advocate scientism is that qualia are not really real, incredible as that may sound. Science does not explain qualia because they do not fit into scientific theory, so science suggests that qualia do not exist — or so the story goes. Qualia are some kind of myth or illusion. But Taliaferro points out that if qualia are not real, then it is hard to understand how and why science itself exists. After all, science is supposed to be based on careful observation, and observation involves perception, and perception is made up of qualia. How could the scientific perspective lead us to think that there are no qualia, when science itself depends on their existence.

One way to understand Taliaferro's essay, then, is to see it as posing the following overarching question: How wrong could we be about the nature of ourselves and still be right about science? Given that science cannot call into question qualia without undercutting its own existence, one cannot help but wonder if its attack on dualism is unwarranted, even anti-scientific. These are the broad concerns that Taliaferro engages in his chapter.

CHAPTER 1

The Soul of the Matter

Charles Taliaferro

INTRODUCTION

Most of us believe that we think, feel, act, and have desires, purposes, and experiences. To sum up what should not be a shocking thesis: most of us believe that *we are conscious, thinking, acting persons*. In fact, this belief we have about ourselves as persons seems to be the most certain of all the claims we might make about reality. If we begin thinking about human nature from what we know consciously and attentively in our own experience, we have a great deal of data to bring to the natural sciences — and the brain sciences in particular — in forming an overall theory of human nature. The natural sciences can serve to complement what we know in the first-person, contributing to our understanding of ourselves as conscious, purposive beings. This approach to a philosophy of human nature has been the most widespread in the history of modern philosophy.

Despite this heritage, this common-sense and natural approach to human nature faces a strong and radical challenge today. Philosophers Daniel Dennett, Paul Churchland, Stephen Stich, Susan Blackmore, Richard Rorty, Georges Rey, and others have proposed that we should instead begin with what we know in the physical sciences and only then should we look for a place to locate consciousness, experience, purposes, desires, and so on. Rather than taking "first-person," subjective experience as a starting point, we need to begin with what some of them call the "third-person" perspective of science, in which we can verify and test hypotheses through external observation and experimentation. It is their shared view that if we begin with ordinary, so-called "common sense" about our experiences we risk falling into a dualism of mind and body, an outcome that they believe to be unscientific and fraught with insurmountable philosophical problems. For if we do, indeed, have first-person awareness of sensations, desires, conscious undertakings, and so on, it is not at all clear how these states could be the very same thing as brain states or neurological events and other physical processes. After all, it seems that one can observe brain states and other physical processes without thereby observing what a subject is actually sensing, thinking, desiring and the like. If all I know of you is your bodily states, it appears that I will not know of your thinking and feeling unless I know how to correlate your bodily states with thinking and feeling. Obviously everyone believes that the mental and physical are deeply intertwined — a brain injury can cause mental distress, loss of consciousness, and emotional conflict can generate deep anatomical problems. But it isn't obvious to everyone how first-person mental states (my thinking about writing you an email) could be numerically identical with certain neurons firing.

Should we abandon the first-person point of view or only accept it if we are compelled to do so on scientific grounds? In this chapter, let us consider this new move to avoid dualism by beginning our study of human nature with the natural sciences. After building up a picture of this new method, with some liberal use of quotations so that its advocates can speak for themselves, I then argue that the new, third-person-point-of-view move is deeply problematic, if not incoherent. This chapter will therefore build a case for beginning our thinking about human nature from the standpoint of our own conscious awareness, experience, and action. If this leads us toward dualism, and the soul, so be it.

THE THIRD-PERSON, SCIENTIFIC POINT OF VIEW

Many, but by no means all, philosophers working on the mind-body relationship today assume that the mind (or self, soul, or subjectivity) is either the same thing as the body or some bodily process like brain activity. The more hearty philosophers even go further, claiming that subjectivity and the self are illusions and do not actually exist. Common to all these philosophers is a commitment to physicalism, the theory that all that exists is either physical or determined by physical things and events. Frank Jackson offers a succinct statement of physicalism: "If mental nature is not an addition to physical nature, then the physical way things are necessitates the mental way things are. Fix the physical way things are and you have done enough to fix the mental way things are. There is no more to do."[1] D. M. Armstrong spells out the bedrock physical strata:

What does modern science have to say about the nature of man? There are, of course, all sorts of disagreements and divergences in the views of individual scientists. But I think it is true to say that one view is steadily gaining ground, so that it bids fair to become established scientific doctrine. This is the view that we can give a complete account of man *in purely physico-chemical terms.* . . . I think it is fair to say that those scientists who still reject the physico-chemical account of man do so primarily for philosophical, or moral or religious reasons, and only secondarily, and half-heartedly, for reasons of scientific detail. . . . For me, then, and for many philosophers who think like me, the moral is clear. We must try and work out an account of the nature of mind which is compatible with the view that man is nothing but a physico-chemical mechanism.[2]

Rorty provides a representative version of the physicalist project: "Every speech, thought, theory, poem, composition and philosophy will turn out to be completely predictable in purely naturalistic terms. Some atoms-and-the-void account of micro-processes within individual human beings will permit the prediction of every sound or inscription which will ever be uttered."[3]

One of the reasons why materialists like Armstrong, Rorty, and others embrace such a reductive program is that they believe that only such a reduction will be able to provide a genuine explanation (scientifically and philosophically) of the existence of our mental lives. If our mental lives are somehow not fully accounted for in terms that are non-mental, then mentality or psychology or consciousness will stand as an irreducible, in some sense independent reality, and we are stuck with dualism or pluralism. Rey puts the point succinctly:

Any ultimate explanation of mental phenomena will have to be in *non*-mental terms, else it won't be an *explanation* of it. There might be explanations of some mental phenomena in terms of others — perhaps *hope* in terms of *belief* and *desire* — but if we are to provide an explanation of all mental phenomena, we would in turn have to explain such mentalistic explainers until finally we reached entirely non-mental terms.[4]

Lots of explanations we rely on are mentalistic. To the question "Why did you text message Pat?," we are more likely to understand the answer "To get a date," rather than an answer in terms of purely physico-chemical activity in the parieto-insular cortex (a reply that makes no reference whatever to beliefs and desires). But by Rey's lights, a thorough explanation of the mental must dig down to a physical account that is not itself mental. To motivate this project, Rey, Rorty, and others directly challenge the portrait of self-awareness that we considered at the outset. Can we be so sure that we are immediately aware of our own experiences, states of mind, consciousness and the like?

Some materialists like Churchland, Dennett and Stich refer to the ordinary beliefs we have about ourselves — our mental states and consciousness — as *folk psychology*. Basically, folk psychology includes beliefs that have proved useful historically and are employed by ordinary persons with practical success today. But why be confident that our folk psychology is sound when our ancient, early folk beliefs about the physical world have turned out to be false? Churchland writes:

> Our early folk theories of the structure and activity of the heavens were wildly off the mark, and survive only as historical lessons in how wrong we can be. Our folk theories of the nature of fire, and the nature of life, were similarly cockeyed. And one could go on, since the vast majority of our past folk conceptions have been similarly exploded. All except folk psychology, which survives to this day and has only recently begun to feel pressure. But the phenomenon of conscious intelligence is surely a more complex and difficult phenomenon than any of those just listed. So far as accurate understanding is concerned, it would be a miracle if we had got that one right the very first time when we fell down so badly on all the others.[5]

Stich concurs:

> Folk astronomy was false astronomy and not just in detail. The general conception of the cosmos embedded in the folk wisdom of the West was utterly and thoroughly mistaken. Much the same could be said for folk biology, folk chemistry, and folk physics. However wonderful and imaginative folk theorizing and speculation has been, it has turned out to be screamingly false in every domain where we now have a reasonably sophisticated science. Nor is there any reason to think that ancient camel drivers would have greater insight or better luck when the subject at hand was the structure of their own minds rather than the structure of matter or of the cosmos.[6]

Rey, Churchland, and Stich then go so far as to claim that contemporary natural science is a far better source of knowledge than our own self-awareness and experience. Dennett articulates his position on the primacy of science in bald terms in response to a philosopher (David Chalmers) who thinks we can and should recognize the undeniable reality of experience. Dennett (famous for his irony and humor) likens

Chalmers case for experience to someone claiming that the property *cuteness* exists:

> We can see this by comparing Chalmers' proposal with yet one more imaginary non-starter; cutism, the proposal that since some things are just plain cute, and other things aren't cute at all — you can just see it, however hard it is to describe or explain — we had better postulate cuteness as a fundamental property of physics alongside mass, charge and space-time. (Cuteness is not a functional property, of course; I can imagine somebody who wasn't actually cute at all but who nevertheless functioned exactly as if cute — trust me.) Cutism is in even worse shape than vitalism. Nobody would have taken vitalism seriously for a minute if the vitalists hadn't had a set of independently describable phenomena — of reproduction, metabolism, self-repair and the like — that their postulated fundamental life-element was hoped to account for. Once these phenomena were otherwise accounted for, vitalism fell flat, but at least it had a project. Until Chalmers gives an independent ground for contemplating the drastic move of adding "experience" to mass, charge, and space-time, his proposal is one that can be put on the back burner.[7]

This confident reversal of appealing to experience first and then considering science is played out in an influential introduction to philosophy of mind, *Matter and Consciousness*, by Churchland. Churchland offers the following portrait of a neuroscientist who has a thorough, clear understanding of the body and its physical processes, but she is perplexed about whether there is anything more going on in persons than what is disclosed in terms of electrochemical events:

> Put yourself in the shoes of a neuroscientist who is concerned to trace the origins of behavior back up the motor nerves to the active cells in the motor cortex of the cerebrum, and to trace in turn their activity into inputs from other parts of the brain, and from the various sensory nerves. She finds a thoroughly physical system of awesome structure and delicacy, and much intricate activity, all of it unambiguously chemical or electrical in nature, and she finds no hint at all of any nonphysical inputs . . . What is she to think? From the standpoint of her researches, human behavior is exhaustively a function of the activity of the physical brain.[8]

The line of reasoning is in some sense elegant. Assuming that you can get an exhaustive, purely physical explanation going, why posit *some additional reality to do any work*? Churchland and Dennett both apply Ockham's razor: if there is no need to posit something in addition to the body and its physical states, do not do so. According to Dennett, dualism is the view that "an enlargement of the ontology of the physical sciences is called for"; dualism adds "something above and beyond the atoms and molecules that compose the brain."[9] If we can get a successful account of persons in the brain sciences or in the natural sciences more generally, it would be anti-scientific to be a dualist. Dennett sums up a view deeply shared in the current philosophical literature: "Dualism is to be avoided at all costs."[10]

Churchland further argues that when we consider our mental states of sensing, and so on, we are not on reliable grounds in terms of understanding the true nature of the world or what we are sensing. Dualists wind up assuming that "inner observation or introspection reveals things as they really are in their innermost nature."[11] This assumption, however, should not be made:

> This assumption is suspect because we already know that our other forms of observation — sight, hearing, touch, and so on — do no such thing. The red surface of an apple does not look like a matrix of molecules reflecting photons at certain critical wave lengths, but that is what it is. The sound of a flute does not sound like a sinusoidal compression wave train in the atmosphere, but that is what it is. The warmth of the summer air does not feel like the mean kinetic energy of millions of tiny molecules, but that is what it is. If one's pains and hopes and beliefs do not introspectively seem like electrochemical states in a neural network, that may be only because our faculty of introspection, like our other senses, is not sufficiently penetrating to reveal such hidden details.[12]

Churchland proposes that the natural sciences are able to reveal the hidden structures of the world and its states more accurately than introspection or self-observation.

Dennett's case against subjective states of awareness is as radical as Churchland's. Dennett takes particular aim at our apparent awareness of ourselves as subjects. The idea that we are substantial individual subjects who endure over time and experience the world in different ways is problematic. Dennett thinks there is nothing physical in the brain or the body as a whole that can play the role of such a substantial, individual subject. "The trouble with brains," writes Dennett, "is that when you look in them, you discover that there's nobody home."[13] Dennett contends that the person is best viewed as a coordinated series of functions and that there is no self who acts as a subject. "Conscious minds are more-or-less serial virtual machines implemented — inefficiently — on the parallel hardware that evolution has provided for us."[14] Dennett thinks that our tendency to believe that we have subjective appearances (what he calls "seemings") is because we implicitly assume some form of dualism. If there is a soul or self as a nonphysical subject, perhaps that self can be the subject of experience; Dennett describes dualism as positing a little person (a homunculus) in the head who beholds a screen on which are projected pictures of the external world. He describes the little person as occupying a Cartesian theatre. But, according to Dennett, a proper explanation of the self needs to dispense with "seemings" and the Cartesian theatre. Dennett does not go so far as to deny that people form judgments, but he does deny that persons have experiential states in which the world appears to us in different ways:

> Perhaps the Cartesian Theatre is popular because it is the place where the seemings can happen in addition to the judgings. But . . . postulating a real seeming in addition to the judging or "taking" expressed in the subject's report is multiplying entities beyond necessity. Worse, it is multiplying entities beyond possibility; the sort of inner presentation in which real seemings happen is a hopeless metaphysical dodge, a way of trying to have your cake and eat it too, especially since those who are inclined to talk this way are eager to insist that this inner presentation does not occur in some mysterious, dualist sort of space perfused with Cartesian ghost-ether. When you discard Cartesian dualism, you really must discard the show that would have gone on in the Cartesian Theatre, and the audience as well, for neither the show nor the audience is to be found in the brain, and the brain is the only real place there is to look for them.[15]

The reasoning here seems to be that if we must recognize that subjects have experiential states (and presumably this includes an awareness that a light seemed to move along a path in a person's visual field) that are not themselves cognitive judgments, we have to posit a self. There is no self in the brain and the brain as a whole does not constitute a unified self. Therefore there are no such experiential appearings.

In a very useful book, *Consciousness: A Very Short Introduction*, Blackmore endorses Dennett's rejection of the substantial self, and she offers the following portrait of three choices in philosophy of mind. Either one can embrace a dualist outlook (which is hopeless) or adopt a form of materialism that simply asserts that the brain is conscious of itself (which she finds problematic), or one can deny the substantial self:

> Having rejected the Cartesian theatre, [Dennett] also rejects its audience of one who watches the show. The self, he claims, is something that needs to be

explained, but it does not exist in the way that a physical object (or even a brain process) exists. Like a centre of gravity in physics, it is a useful abstraction. Indeed he calls it a "center of narrative gravity." Our language spins the story of a self and so we come to believe that there is, in addition to our single body, a single inner self who has consciousness, holds opinions, and makes decisions. Really, there is no inner self but only multiple parallel processes that give rise to a benign user illusion — a useful fiction. It seems we have some tough choices in thinking about our own precious self. We can hang on to the way it feels and assume that a persisting self or soul or spirit exists, even though it cannot be found and leads to deep philosophical troubles. We can equate it with some kind of brain process and shelve the problem of why this brain process should have conscious experience at all, or we can reject any persisting entity that corresponds to our feeling of being a self.[16]

Blackmore thinks "our feeling of being a self" is unreliable, and she rejects the idea that we are persisting selves. She acknowledges that this is not easy personally, but there are good intellectual grounds for the denial of a substantial self:

> The trouble is that it is very hard to accept in one's own personal life. It means taking a radically different view of every experience. It means accepting that there is no one who is having these experiences. It means accepting that every time I seem to exist, this is just a temporary fiction and not the same "me" who seemed to exist a moment before, or last week, or last year. This is tough, but I think it gets easier with practice.[17]

BEGINNING AGAIN, THIS TIME WITH THE FIRST-PERSON, SUBJECTIVE EXPERIENCE

The first question to raise in response to the above radical materialist proposal is whether one can make any sense of "the third-person" point of view at work in science (and in ordinary, nonscientific reflection) without there being a first-person perspective of self-aware, conscious subjects. Dennett claims to be more certain about mass, charge and space-time than he is of experience, but how might we have any idea at all of mass and charge or any science at all unless there are scientists who have experiences of the world and can reason about those experiences? Dennett's construction of science without experience (or a science that can construe experience as "a back burner issue") is a radical departure from the understanding of science from Copernicus and Galileo to Einstein and beyond which sees science itself as a purposive activity being carried out by subjects who record observations, engage in predictions, construct theories, and so on (all of which are presumed to involve experiences).

The difficulty with Dennett's attack on experience comes to the fore when considering Drew McDermott's defense of Dennett. McDermott thinks that declaring the existence of experience to be basic and indisputable is akin to an insane person declaring he is Jesus Christ:

> Suppose a lunatic claims he is Jesus Christ. We explain why his brain chemicals make him think that. But he is not convinced. "The fact that I am Jesus is my starting point, a brute explanandum [or a non-further-explainable reality]: explaining why I think this is not sufficient [to undermine or discredit the reality of this basic fact]." The only difference between him and us is that he can't stop believing he's Jesus because he's insane, whereas we can't stop believing in phenomenal experience because we're not.[18]

The analogy is wide of the mark because it radically underestimates the role of experience as well as consciousness. One might be able to explain the falsity of one's belief that one is Jesus Christ, but *unless one has experiences and is conscious*, one cannot have any beliefs at all, either sane or insane, and explanations of or refusals to explain something. Hence, explaining away the basic reality of experience or consciousness is not at all like explaining the falsity of a belief. (McDermott's "defense" of Dennett also seems a little odd, because he appears to concede that we are not insane when we acknowledge the existence of experience.)

What about the charge that confidence in the first-person point of view is akin to folk astronomy and the like? Why assume that we should be confident about our psychological states when we have been so wrong in the past with our beliefs about the world? Two replies are in order. First, how far off the track were the "folk" ideas in the past? Arguably, if the majority of the beliefs our ancestors had about food, work, safety, trade and travel had not been reliable, then they would not have survived. Moreover, many people today overestimate the ignorance of the past, as has been exposed by books like *Inventing the Flat Earth: Columbus and Modern Historians* by Jeffrey Russell,[19] which points out that many pre-Columbians going all the way back to Aristotle knew what we know: the earth is round. But second, and more importantly, conscious awareness and experience is simply too fundamental to not be confident that for as long as people could reflect on experience, they knew they were having experiences. A person in severe pain in ancient Babylon may have been confused about the cause of pain, and the pain may even have been induced by wildly false beliefs, but it is hard to believe that the subject might have been mistaken that he was feeling pain. It seems, instead, profoundly implausible that persons in the past were mistaken when they treated each other as having experiences of pain, pleasure, anger and love, and so on. This is not to say that progress has not been made to develop more accurate concepts and devices for describing and explaining experience, but it is difficult to hold that people were wrong in thinking they have experiences. John Searle offers this forceful reply to Dennett: if Dennett even concedes that it appeared to people in the past that they had experiences, then they had experiences:

> But someone might object: Is it not possible that science might discover that Dennett was right, that there really are no such things as inner qualitative mental states, that the whole thing is an illusion like sunsets? After all, if science can discover that sunsets are a systematic illusion, why could it not also discover that conscious states such as pains are illusions too? There is this difference: in the case of sunsets science does not deny the existence of the datum, that the sun appears to move through the sky. Rather it gives an alternative explanation of this and other data. Science preserves the appearance while giving us a deeper insight into the reality behind the appearance. But Dennett denies the appearance to start with.

But couldn't we disprove the existence of these data by proving that they are only illusions? No, you can't disprove the existence of conscious experiences by proving that they are only an appearance disguising the underlying reality, because *where consciousness is concerned the existence of the appearance is the reality*. If it seems to me exactly as if I am having conscious experiences, then I am having conscious experiences. This is not an epistemic point. I might make various sorts of mistakes about my experiences, for example, if I suffered from phantom limb pains. But whether reliably reported or not, the experience of feeling the pain is identical with the pain in a way that the experience of seeing a sunset is not identical with a sunset.[20]

Searle's point may be bolstered by considering how peculiar it would be for you to be working with a dentist who claims that, despite your appearing to be in agonizing, mind-shattering pain, this is merely an appearance and you are actually not feeling any pain at all. The dentist might accurately point out that the pain is being caused by tooth decay or certain nerve damage or perhaps the pain is brought on by your anxious anticipation of a root canal operation, but when it comes to pain itself, for a subject to be in agonizing pain is to feel agonizing pain. There seems little room to avoid "mentalistic" terms here and to substitute talk of pain with talk of purely physico-chemical processes.

To bring to light the larger difficulty of simply beginning with what Churchland and Dennett understand to be our scientific, third-person view of the world, let us return to Churchland's description of the neurologist. Churchland describes a neurologist who finds "no hint at all of any nonphysical parts." She does, however, seem to be studying "sensory nerves" and so we can assume that her work includes some explanations of a subject having this or that sensation. Imagine the neurologist is trying to find the neurological conditions that are causing a subject acute pain. Using acute pain as an example of a sensory state, consider this question: is the acutely painful sensory state of the subject the very same thing as the "unambiguously chemical . . . activity of the physical brain"? Arguably, if the neurologist were only able to study the electrochemical properties of the brain as an unambiguous physical reality, she would not thereby be studying the sensation of acute pain. Presumably she could only learn that the subject is in pain based on the subject's testimony, behavioral signs (moaning), or correlating analogous chemical activities in other subjects who testify to pain or provide us with reliable behavioral signs. Simply to observe the electro-chemical activity of the brain does not seem to amount to observing the acutely painful sensory state. If she treats the electrochemical activity as pain, then isn't that a matter of her adopting a theory of physicalism according to which sensations are brain states, rather than her making an empirical observation? I suggest that, strictly speaking, when the neurologist refers to pain states, it is far from clear that these states are to be treated exhaustively in terms of brain activity. As Richard Swinburne observes:

> My sensations are no doubt *caused* by brain-events, but they are not *themselves* brain-events. My having a red after-image or a pain or a smell of roast beef are real events. If science describes only firings of neurons in the brain, it has not told us everything that is going on. For it is a further fact about the world that there are pains and after-images, and science must state this fact and attempt to explain it.[21]

Might it be the case, however, that what we experience in the first person simply is the very same thing as brain activity, though it is seen through different frameworks or concepts? After all, the same person (Muhammad Ali) might be known under different names

('Cassius Clay') and some people might even think two persons are involved, rather than one (The person called 'Muhammad Ali' is a different person than the one called 'Cassius Clay'). But Muhammad Ali is identical with Cassius Clay. Similarly, someone may understand water as H_2O and another person who lacks knowledge of atomic theory may simply know water as a colorless, odorless liquid. Yet H_2O is identical with water. Analogously, some philosophers propose that the first-person perspective is only a different framework or conceptual vantage point on what can be properly identified as non-mental, physico-chemical processes from a third-person, scientific point of view.

One problem with this reply is that the different perspectives in the cases of Muhammad Ali/Cassius Clay and water/H_2O are both species of the third-person framework. Hence, they share a common spatial-temporal framework within which to locate and identify "two" objects as one. With some investigation and reflection, you can come to understand how the one called 'Muhammad Ali' is identical with the one called 'Cassius Clay,' and similarly with water being H_2O and a colorless, odorless liquid. But the first-person and third-person perspectives are themselves different frameworks, and while goings-on in one can occur at the same time as goings-on in the other, issues of spatial location are not so straightforward. Consider an experience of pain that seems to be in one's foot. Physicalists say that the pain is identical with a brain event. But surely this is ultimately no more than declaration by fiat and not at all like discovering that Muhammad Ali is Cassius Clay. Moreover, while water is liquid, which makes intelligible its identification with spatial rearrangements of atomic entities, pain seems to lack any kind of structural property that would make intelligible its identification with something neuronal in nature.

A second problem with this reply can be illustrated by considering Churchland's identification of warmth with mean molecular kinetic energy, quoted earlier in this chapter. It is true that if "temperature" ("warmth") refers to molecular motion in some inanimate object, then heat is mean molecular kinetic energy, but if "temperature" refers to *feeling hot* (a subjective state), it has not been "long established" that *feeling hot* is the very same thing as *molecules in motion*. It may be that there would be no feeling of heat without molecular motion, and it may be plausible to see molecular motion as the cause of feeling heat (in a being with a healthy nervous system and brain), but there is no evident identity between sensation and molecular motion. You could know all the facts about a human or nonhuman animal's molecular composition and activity, but without knowing how to correlate the molecular processes with something more (the *feeling* of heat), you would not know the mental states of the subject. And the same is true for Churchland's other cases: it is not obvious that seeing red is the same thing as a matrix of molecules reflecting photons; the molecular motion may (once it impacts a person's retina and stimulates the visual cortex) cause a person to see red, but the molecular motion is not necessarily the seeing itself. A musician may use a flute to cause a sinusoidal compression wave train in the atmosphere, but that is not clearly the same thing as the sensation of hearing music, which occurs only when the wave train stimulates the ear canal, and initiates an elaborate process involving the tympanic membrane, the stapes, the cochlea, the auditory cortex, and so on. All these give rise to a person's hearing the music as a sensory, conscious experience. Churchland can simply assert the contrary position that temperature (sensory feelings included) is mean molecular kinetic energy, and so on, but this would not count as an argument for the truth of his position.

As for Dennett's elimination of the self as a substantial individual, known from a first-person point of view to have experiences and so on, his position is very difficult (as Blackmore concedes) to consistently embrace in practice as well as in our ethical reflection. In a book that is on philosophy of religion (*Breaking the Spell*) and not philosophy of mind, Dennett seems to be very comfortable with asserting our privileged awareness of our own mental states. In the following passage, Dennett seems to think that each of us is an "insider" when it comes to our own self-awareness but an "outsider" when it comes to other persons.

> When it comes to interpreting religious avowals of others, *everybody is an outsider*. Why? Because religious avowals concern matters that are beyond observation, beyond meaningful test, so the only thing *anybody* can go on is religious behavior, and, more specifically, the behavior of *professing*. A child growing up in a culture is like an anthropologist, after all, surrounded by informants whose professings stand in need of interpretation. The fact that your informants are your father and mother, and speak in your mother tongue, does not give you anything more than a slight circumstantial advantage over the adult anthropologist who has to rely on a string of bilingual interpreters to query the informants. (And think about your own case: weren't you ever baffled or confused about just what you were supposed to believe? You know perfectly well that *you* don't have privileged access to the tenets of the faith in which you were raised. I am just asking you to generalize the point, to recognize that others are in no better position.)[22]

Elsewhere in the same book Dennett seems to be fully committed to the reality of selves and the first-person point of view and to shed his skepticism about being a complete outsider to other's states of mind. Consider this passage in which Dennett seeks to comfort his daughter:

> One's parents — or whoever are hard to distinguish from one's parents — have something approaching a dedicated hotline to acceptance, not as potent as hypnotic suggestion, but sometimes close to it. Many years ago, my five-year-old daughter, attempting to imitate the gymnast Nadia Comaneci's performance on the horizontal bar, tipped over the piano stool and painfully crushed two of her fingertips. How was I going to calm down this terrified child so I could safely drive her to the emergency room? Inspiration struck: I held my own hand near her throbbing little hand and sternly ordered: "Look, Andrea! I'm going to teach you a secret! You can push the pain into my hand with your hand. Go ahead, push! Push!" She tried — and it worked! She'd pushed the pain into Daddy's hand. Her relief (and fascination) were instantaneous. The effect lasted only for minutes, but with a few further administrations of impromptu hypnotic analgesia along the way, I got her to the emergency room, where they could give her the further treatment she needed. (Try it with your own child, if the occasion arises. You may be similarly lucky.) I was exploiting her instincts — though the rationale didn't occur to me until years later, when I was reflecting on it. (This raises an interesting empirical question: would my attempt at instant hypnosis have worked as effectively on some other five-year-old, who hadn't imprinted on me as an authority figure? And if imprinting is implicated, how young must a child be to imprint so effectively on a parent? Our daughter was three months old when we adopted her.)[23]

In reply, Dennett may claim that these sorts of narratives are merely narratives and do not reflect or presuppose the reality of himself or his daughter as subjects who endure over time as real beings as opposed to being a posit like (to use Blackmore's language) a center of gravity or a useful fiction. But the above case illustrates how difficult it is in practice to foreswear what we seem to grasp in the first-person. Dennett's own reported practical experience gives us some reason for thinking that the existence of the self and first-person point of view is something that needs to be recognized and scientifically explored (what are the neuro-logical conditions enabling us to manage pain, and so on) rather than denied or explained away.

A MODEST NOTE ON THE BODY AND SOUL

Other chapters in this book will address the soul and space does not permit further building-up a positive case for dualism and the existence of the soul, a project that I have done elsewhere.[24] But what I do want to stress at the end of this chapter is that materialist critics often exaggerate and caricature dualism as holding that the soul-body relationship must be like the relationship of someone (the soul) and their container or vehicle or (as Dennett has proposed), the person is a tiny subject in a theatre located in the head. Must dualism land us with the idea that the body is like a mask or machine that a nonphysical ghost-like soul controls? I have argued elsewhere that it does not.[25] In a healthy, fully functioning human being there need be no bifurcation of person and body. To see me writing is not to see a soul controlling a body; it is to see an embodied person. Dualism is best seen (in my view) along integrated lines. In healthy conditions, mind and body, the mental and physical, function as a unit. But under different conditions, in the case of death, for example, the body may perish but, if a person is more than his or her body, death may not mark the end of the person or soul.

The philosophers we have considered in this chapter who disparage the first-person point of view fail to appreciate that what we know in our own experience and what we know of ourselves as selves is foundational for any inquiry. Without first-person awareness, it is difficult to know how one might begin to have third-person points of view. Scientific inquiry can and should be used to explain the nature of our embodiment, not to explain it away. As Swinburne observes, "Detailed scientific discoveries are relevant . . . to showing more about what souls are like — e.g. that they have free will — not in showing that there are no such things at all."[26]

Taliaferro stresses the dependence of science on observation, hence on qualia, hence on the first-person perspective that is also a primary source of our belief in the soul's existence. Hans Halvorson will once again draw our attention to the importance of observation in science in a more technical context, in his chapter on the measurement problem in the puzzling world of quantum physics (Chapter 6).

For now, however, we keep our feet firmly planted in more ordinary life with a chapter by Daniel Robinson, in which he continues and develops the theme of the relationships between science, dualism, and everyday experience. Indeed, he is particularly well placed to highlight these relationships. He has served as a consultant to a number of governmental and private organizations, including the National Science Foundation, the National Institutes of Health, and the Department of Health and Human Services. He was principal consultant to the Public Broadcasting Service for its award-winning series, The Brain, and again to the Public Broadcasting Service (PBS) and the British Broadcasting Corporation (BBC) for the sequel, The Mind. In 2001 Professor Robinson received the Lifetime Achievement Award from the Division of the History of Psychology of the American Psychological Association and, in the same year, the Distinguished Contribution Award from the American Philosophical Association's Division of Theoretical and Philosophical Psychology.

On one dimension, Robinson's essay is narrower than Taliaferro's: he focuses more specifically on one particular kind of science, namely the history and development of the brain sciences. In this vein, Robinson makes it clear that the brain sciences are older than many people realize, with a history that goes back to ancient Greece. Brain science is thus not just a recent phenomenon that has arisen simply because of developments in modern technology, even though new technologies have certainly expanded and accelerated this area of inquiry. Science writers often give the impression that, whereas it may have been reasonable (or at least excusable) to believe in an immaterial soul in earlier ages, now that we can do a Positron Emission Tomography (PET) scan or functional Magnetic Resonance Imaging (fMRI) we know better. But in fact even the ancients and the medievals knew more about the brain than we give them credit for, through (for example) careful observation of people with different kinds of head injuries. And yet they were dualists. Robinson thus points out that it is far from clear that we do in fact know things that other generations did not that are substantively more relevant to questions about the existence of the soul, with the result that we need to change our answers to the mind-body problem.

Conversely, Robinson also questions whether we know as much as we now think we know about the mind and the brain, simply because we have published large amounts of neurological data. He looks at the quality of evidence for the materialistic conclusions that many brain scientists have drawn from this data, and finds it shaky and overstated on certain points. Most significantly, Robinson shows that these materialistic conclusions are all too often based on observations that are heavily colored by the expectations, desires, and even prejudices of the researcher. They have been ideas that the researchers have brought to their research at least as much as they have been ideas that researchers have derived from that research. Robinson traces this trend from the classical results of Pierre Broca in the nineteenth century into the present day.

Robinson goes on to point out some inherent limitations to the methods of the brain sciences — the ways in which they need to go about their business given the kind of things they are studying (typically living people). These limitations cause the brain sciences to be correlational rather than explanatory. Brain science as it is normally practiced may often discover systematic pairings between a neural event and a psychological event. It cannot, however, tell us in general whether it was the neural event that explains the occurrence of the psychological event, or whether it was the psychological event that explains the occurrence of the neural event.

While the kind of science discussed in Robinson's essay is narrower than the science discussed in Taliaferro's, Robinson's essay broadens a concern raised by Taliaferro on another dimension. Whereas Taliaferro concentrates on our perceptual experience, Robinson puts common-sense folk psychology in a much broader context — that of all the richness of "lived life." For Robinson, this is a realm that includes relationships among family and friends, the pursuit of marriages and careers, moral achievements and failures, and aesthetic experiences like the enjoyment of an evening at the theater. According to Robinson, we study the brain in relationship to lived life primarily for the purpose of improving the quality of that life. The "heavy traffic," he says, is in the significance and meaning of the various elements of our lives. The brain sciences ultimately can only make sense and have a purpose within this broader framework of purposefulness.

As a simplistic analogy of Robinson's point about the centrality of lived life and its relationship to brain science, consider the following item:

Liberty

One can look at this as a physical object and describe in arbitrary detail its exact shape and constituency as such. One can give a precise chemical characterization of the ink and paper that it is composed of, and a geometrical description of exactly how the ink is distributed on the page, accurate to as many significant figures as you like. Once you have done so, the account of it as a physical object is in one sense complete. But in another, very important sense, you have said absolutely nothing about this item yet. You have not even hinted at the fact that these marks on the paper spell out a word, that the word means something, that people care about and typically value the thing referred to by the word for various complicated and cultural reasons, that they have all kinds of complex associations with it — and so on, and so on. In short, the exhaustive physical description of the item does not get at its meaning at all. In Robinson's view, there is much the same kind of disconnect between the brain sciences and the normal healthy human lives they are supposed to explain. The brain sciences might provide an exhaustive and sophisticated description of a complex human body that approaches completeness along one dimension, while completely missing the more important facts about the life of the person whose body is being described — how that life works on the level of symbols and culture and understanding and value. Robinson's ultimate point about "lived life" is that this kind of issue arises with virtually everything we do or care about, and so the brain sciences as such miss the whole point of it all.

CHAPTER 2

Minds, Brains, and Brains in Vats

Daniel N. Robinson

FOLK PSYCHOLOGY AND BRAIN-SCIENCE

Perhaps the best way to begin this chapter is with a diary entry or meditation. Months ago I was asked to prepare a chapter for a book defending the concept and reality of the soul. Considering what might be said on the subject, it was my belief that many of the criticisms advanced against that concept and reality were insufficient. Agreeing to the assignment I was hopeful that I might do justice to the subject. Moved by certain convictions and fortified by certain judgments, I decided to accept the challenge.

Or did I? Suppose instead that my summary of these events was associated with a lesion in the brain. There is after all a syndrome displayed by some patients with abnormal functions of the cingulate gyrus. Among other symptoms are the patient's failure of memory and the presence of confabulation or pseudoreminiscence.[1] Thus, my recollections may include some accurate items but these may well have been laced into an overall story radically at variance with what actually was the case. Of course, not every instance of damage to the cingulate gyrus leads to confabulations. Nor does every instance of confabulation involve the cingulate gyrus. In rare instances the predisposing condition is multiple sclerosis. More common are confabulations arising from alcoholic Korsakoff syndrome, where the distortions of memory are autobiographical in nature.[2] Note, however, that even under these conditions, it is only the first-person account that can provide the necessary side of the equation that is somehow to be balanced with data obtained from studies of the central nervous system. For there to be confabulations there must be a story. Furthermore, it must be someone's story, and it is no less a story for being false or for being causally affected by a pathological condition in the brain. This much said, it is important to keep clear as to what is not said: That events in the brain may lead to confabulation does not mean that confabulation is "in the brain." That my diary entry in the first paragraph is accurate and true owing in part to a normal and properly functioning brain, does not mean that my diary entry is in a normal and properly functioning brain. More generally, propositions of the sort, A *is a necessary condition for B* are entirely different from propositions of the sort, A *is B*, or B *is within the set of A*.

The first two paragraphs above are readily understood by anyone competent in the English language. All of the key terms in the passage are drawn from what is often dismissively referred to as "folk psychology," a term intended to connote innocence, credulity, and pardonable ignorance.[3] Keener and modern residents of the world of thought know better. For to speak of preparing, believing, agreeing, hoping, judging, recalling and holding convictions is to speak in the *patois* of an older age — the age before the brain sciences! Accordingly, if the first paragraph in this essay is to be rendered consistent with the scientific world view, all references to mental, emotional and motivational states must be recast to match up with brain states. But thus translated, the opening paragraph is instantly stripped of the very terms that convey meaning to English speakers. The allegedly improved rendition now requires them to learn a radically different language and to think in radically different terms. To impose such a burden surely calls for a justification. And to accept such a burden certainly calls for any number of pragmatic and conceptual deliberations. Why on earth should I stop talking about my motives and aspirations, and start talking about neuronal discharges and synaptic networks? What is gained? What is lost?

If the critics of folk psychology are to be believed, the gains are considerable. It is no longer necessary to enter something they routinely refer to as the Cartesian theater where an audience of one sits on a little chair and looks at the projections of the external world on to the screen of the alleged "mind." Instead, what? As one does look at the external world, how should the result be conceptualized? Whether one is a direct or a representational realist,[4] the account will still be rendered in terms of oak trees, sunsets, and cups of broth. So by the criteria of intelligibility and realism, nothing is gained. Moreover, the phenomena of interest are lost. This is not only a great cost but an impermissible one within the accepted standards of scientific theory. The business of science is to explain and not ignore phenomena. The business of science is to *save the phenomena.* The phenomena briefly sketched in the opening paragraphs include motives and aspirations, judgments and commitments, beliefs and plans. The notion that these might be correlated with certain events in the brain (not to mention with events elsewhere in the body) predates Hippocratic medicine. The very grounding of that notion, however, is folk psychology. Were there no judgments, hopes, feelings, etc., there would be nothing with which to correlate events in the brain and the body. There would be no better reason to undertake studies of mind-brain relations than to examine mind-spleen relations or mind-kidney relations. Actually, renal disease is associated with significant cognitive deficits. Accordingly, had science been restricted in its methods to the study of the functions of the kidney there would sooner or later have been a "mind-kidney problem" introduced into the literature on philosophy of mind.[5] To put the matter all too briefly, the so-called brain sciences are entirely parasitic on folk psychology and are unimaginable in its absence. Properly understood, therefore, it is not folk psychology that is put on notice by the facts of mental life, but some entirely different language and perspective drawn from levels and contexts of observation utterly foreign to lived life. Properly understood, then, the more searching question is why one has any reason whatever to study brain function in order to understand more fully the mental, moral, social and aesthetic dimensions of *lived life.*

One now popular answer to this question is that *lived life* is, as it were, nothing more than the brain's life. On this account it is brains that write constitutions, build houses, and take on the task of composing essays in philosophy of mind. Whether one is shocked or amused by such accounts, all will agree that they are eerily removed from reality. Presumably, a brain maintained in a vat, properly nurtured and stimulated, might in some sense ground perceptions and intentions and even thoughts. But it surely would not ground a lived life. Nor would the fact, were there some way of verifying it, put the larger issues to rest, for it would still be perplexing as to just how the physico-chemical processes of the brain in the vat were somehow generative of thought, perception and feeling.[6] Perhaps a more modest contention can be framed: The brain, not isolated in a vat but located appropriately in the cranium of an intact person, is the causal entity by which thoughts, perceptions, etc. become possible and actual. However, except under some hopelessly reduced Humean notion of causality, an account of this sort faces great and grave difficulties generally subsumed under the heading, *the explanatory gap.* Events in the brain are entirely physical, whereas the events to be explained are entirely phenomenological. The gap between the former and the latter seems unbridgeable. In any case, once the phenomenological is granted, some species of dualism (if merely linguistic) is unavoidable. The materialist who grants the linguistic form explains it as a residual of ignorance and superstition made useful by habit. How this proved to be so useful and habitual, however, is never made clear. As it happens, granting the "linguistic" form of dualism is a revealing sign of resignation in the face of the facts of life.

If the metaphorical theater is to be useful, let us think of it as consciousness itself. Motives, thoughts, feelings — these are somehow held within the theater of consciousness. Every motive is someone's motive. It is by way of consciousness that this possessory relationship comes about. The relationship is personal, for consciousness is the state of a given person. In a widely cited essay published thirty-four years ago, Thomas Nagel asked what it is like to be a bat.[7] There he claimed that, "No matter how the form may vary, the fact that an organism has conscious experience *at all* means, basically, that there is something it is like to *be* that organism."[8] On this construal, it is in virtue of Jack's and Jill's consciousness that questions of the sort, "What is it like to be Jack?" or "What is it like to be Jill?" are meaningful and to some extent answerable.

It is useful to stay with Nagel's thesis, at least briefly. He chose the bat because it is a creature whose perceptual contact with the world is based on principles that are utterly different from those that operate in us. The bat navigates by sonar. We might imagine ourselves sleeping upside down in dark caves, and even having bodies covered with fur. But nothing in our experience, or even in our means of representing the external world, would allow us to *know* what it is like to identify objects in that world in terms of their reflection of high-frequency pulses of sound. We cannot know what it is like to be a bat, nor can the bat know what it is like to be us. Nagel extended this to instances in which one human being might not know what it is like to be another, where one of them happened to be born blind and deaf. To be sure, if we are so taxed when trying to discern what it is like to be a bat, I should think our situation is hopeless if we are required to discern what it is like to be a brain.

What was it like to be Solomon Veniaminovich Shereshevskii? He was the tormented mnemonist[9] studied over a course of decades by Alexander Luria.[10] Plagued by an especially intrusive form of synaesthesia, the patient (dubbed "S" by Luria to preserve anonymity) would convert words to sounds; could picture and read off the entries in a large matrix of numbers after but momentary exposure; could perspire at will by picturing himself running after a bus on a hot day. An expression of the sort. "It's raining cats and dogs" would result in 'S' experiencing a torrent of falling animals. To say something about trumpets or drums would result in their being heard. No inquiry into the structural or functional details of S's brain would deliver these facts to an observer. Without S's account, the findings from studies of his brain would be useless except as facts about brains. To know what it might be like to be 'S' is, among other things, to have accounts from S about what he takes to be salient facts drawn from his own life.

The larger point and one that Nagel wished to defend is that *reductionistic* (and especially *eliminativist*) strategies are not likely to be productive, predictive or explicative in attempts to comprehend the nature and sources of mental life. Nagel argued that we and bats are conscious of a world of objects, but the means and mechanisms by which this is achieved are too different for such consciousness to be reduced to a common set of physical causes. I concur with that conclusion, but on grounds that overlap only slightly with Nagel's. To the extent that consciousness is, indeed, widely distributed among different animals, it cannot serve as the unique identifying mark of our humanity. In this I am sure Nagel and many others would concur. Apart from that, the very question, *What is it like to be something?*, admits of just too many possibilities. It leaves unsettled the nature, the metric, the very criteria of likeness. It isn't even helpful at the level of first-person reflections. Ask yourselves what is it like to have consciousness in your own case. I doubt you will unearth an especially informing answer or even any answer at all. You would be rather like the fish, wondering what it is like to live in water. To offer an informing account of what it is like to be conscious calls for a distinction between being conscious and something else. But nothing else can be *known*, for first-person epistemic claims require consciousness. It is doubtful in the extreme, therefore, that much would be generated by the question, *What is it like to be in a particular brain state?*, for here there is simply no knowledge at all. This all follows from Nagel's argument, but there is a more fundamental objection to the entire reductionistic strategy; viz., it eliminates the very phenomena it would purport to explain, a point to be developed throughout this chapter.

My objective here is to invite colloquies rather than to summarize a doctrinal position. If there is a guiding maxim it is the caveat that attends any and every purely correlational form of inquiry. As the principal mode of inquiry in the "brain sciences" is correlational, it is clear that only a very limited explanatory resource can be brought to bear on the findings. In light of such limitations, I will illustrate the worrisome degree to which the theoretical prejudices of investigators have shaped and shaded their selection of data and the essentially rhetorical uses to which the findings have been put. This rhetorical element has been habitually prominent in the brain sciences, perhaps owing to the seeming intransigence of the ordinary percipient to regard meaningful life as something fully explained by physics. First, however, it is useful to consider the methods available to the brain scientist, for in these very methods at least a hint of their explanatory limitations is conveyed.

THE CORRELATIVE METHODS OF THE BRAIN-SCIENTIST

Historically and at present, there have been five main approaches in addressing the question of the relationship between mental life and brain function. As distinct modes of inquiry, each is based on both explicit, and, to some extent, hidden assumptions. Each has its own special assets and liabilities. To use headings that are all too broad, we might subsume the five modes of inquiry under surgical, pathological, electrophysiological, radiological and neurological. Common across these approaches is the presence (or the experimental creation) of one or another neurological impairment sufficiently debilitating to warrant study. It is not "lived life" that fills out the ample tables of correlations. Rather, it is typically a gross and significant loss of function rendering the animal or patient incapable of living a form of life characteristic of healthy members of the species. This point is not to be set aside as some sort of technical problem likely to be solved with the inevitable advances in technology. The methods by which diabetes or pneumonia or ulcers are detected do not separately or in combination establish *health*, let alone the quality of life. Similarly, the mere combination of separately assessed "functions" is not productive of accurate and meaningful accounts of mental life. Specific structure-function relationships are not additive. The diabetic patient, the patient suffering from pneumonia or from ulcerations, will present specific symptoms, each of them readily associated with tissues and organs subject to direct observation and assessment. There is, however, no tissue or organ or even combinations of these that in some additive manner serve as "health" where this term is intended to convey an overall and enduring state. A lesion in the occipital cortex may be reliably associated with visual impairment but it would be simplistic to say that Smith's attitude toward art is the result of his not having a lesion in the occipital cortex. Briefly put, what I refer to as *lived life* does not lend itself to an assembly of modules, each of them being in either a normal or pathological state.

Surgery on the cranium appears early. One or another form of trephination can be dated to the stone age some seven thousand years ago.[11] Long before the period of modern medical science there was widespread recognition of mental or psychological disturbances arising from injuries to the head. The Smith papyrus, discovered in 1862 and dating to the sixteenth century BC, presents some 48 cases of which more than 30 describe neurological deficits traced to injuries of the skull, the brain and the spinal cord. For example, the papyrus associates both aphasia and loss of hearing with skull fractures in the area of the temporal cortex.[12] The point is that recognition of the special relationship between the brain and various sensory, motor and cognitive powers occurs quite early in the history of disciplined observations. What might be called *experimental* neurosurgery did not begin until the second century AD when Galen sectioned the recurrent laryngeal nerve of pigs to test the hypothesis that vocalization is localized in the throat.[13] Pathologists, too, entered early in the development of the brain sciences. The Hippocratic texts of ancient Greece note that traumatic injuries to one side of the brain have behavioral effects on the contralateral side. A century later, the great anatomist, Herophilus, identified the brain as the organ of cognition and perception and even distinguished between sensory and motor nerves.[14] His now lost works were cited as authoritative by Galen. The modern history of experimental neurosurgery begins early in the nineteenth century with attempts to test the theories advanced by Gall and the phrenologists (*vide infra*).

This rich tradition has yielded highly developed investigative tools. Routinely, post–mortem examinations of the nervous system now permit pathologists to determine the extent to which observed symptoms are associated with the most subtle pathological changes in neural tissue. Electrical stimulation and recording from the brain developed later and required still other advances in technology. With these advances it became possible to record not only the gross electrical activity of the brain (as in the case of the EEG or electroencephalogram), but also activity in small populations of cells and even in single neurons. The same technology permits direct stimulation of nervous tissue to establish reliable relations between specific sites in the nervous system and specific sensory, motor, affective, and motivational functions.

Radiological forms of inquiry, once confined to X-rays, now include such modern techniques as Computerized Axial Tomography (CAT) scans, and the previously mentioned PET scans and fMRIs. These add to the large body of correlational data linking neuroanatomy and psychological processes, though the linkage is far from neat and the contexts are limited, episodic and (in all relevant respects) unrealis-tic. Among the more striking departures from textbook accounts of structure-function relations are those studied over a course of years by the pediatric neurologist, John Lorber. Taking CAT scans of hundreds of persons who had survived hydrocephaly at birth, Lorber showed that normal cognitive function is present in some persons with negligible brain mass. So surprising were the findings from Lorber's studies as to raise in a serious way the question, "Is your brain really necessary?"[15] Last but not least is that most venerable of the methods, the neurologi-cal examination, which at one time was the sole means of diagnosis and which now is employed in conjunction with all the rest. But for all the extraordinary advances, it was those Hippocratic physicians, studying the effects of brain damage on movement and sensibility, who exemplify the *correlational* mode of inquiry characteristic of the full range of methods.

At a superficial level, all of the experimental sciences might be clas-sified as correlational in that research is designed to identify the effects on one set of variables given systematic manipulation of another set. Such general laws as $F = ma$ are correlational in that they specify (in this example) what a given force must be in order to impart a desired acceleration to a body of given mass. In the developed sciences, such relationships enter into ever more general accounts as the merely con-tingent fact of a relationship comes to be replaced by credible *causal* explanations based on an understanding of the functions served by the relevant variables. The contractions of cardiac muscle are reliably related to the thumping sounds made by the heart, but the *function* served by these contractions is the pumping of blood, not the produc-tion of sound. Note, then, that the explanatory potential immanent in mere correlations is set by the precision with which the participating variables are specified and controlled by the larger conceptual frame-work within which piecemeal relationships are functionally integrated. Whatever the future may bring, at this juncture it should be obvious that the specification of "mass," "acceleration," and "force" is drawn from conceptual and mensurational domains patently different from those in which we find "cognition," "emotion," and "memory." The implications to be drawn from this will be considered again later when attention is turned to the ordinary affairs of life and the place of *meaning* in comprehending these.

Historically and currently, neurological examinations are attentive to lateralized symptoms. The diagnosis of neuropathologies proceeds economically when a physician observes one drooping eyelid, or a left side hemiparesis, or a tongue that deviates to one side. As noted, the

Hippocratic texts reported such relationships and offered the earliest guide to neurology's defining mission. The functional geometry of the nervous system being what it is, the well-trained clinician is able to associate even slight sensory, motor, or cognitive deficits with specific regions of the nervous system, both peripheral and central. Success here can be attributed to centuries of such correlative investigations, which were supplying useful clinical information even before the general principles of neurophysiology had been established.

It was in the closing decades of the eighteenth century, and drawing on this long accumulating record, that the "science" of phrenology was advanced by Franz Josef Gall, a pioneer in neuroanatomy. By examining spontaneously aborted fetuses at various gestational stages, he contributed significantly to the field of human developmental neuroanatomy. Long before Paul Pierre Broca would become famous for identifying the so-called speech center in the brain, Gall had presented evidence that linguistic ability required the functional integrity of the anterior cortex. Gall's anatomical studies of criminals, mental defectives, artists, and presumed geniuses, led him to conclude that the intellectual and moral dimensions of life required for their normal expression the proper functioning of specific regions of the brain. He went so far as to lay down what he called the "incontestable truths" of phrenology. Chief among these was the claim that the mental and moral faculties are innate, and that each identifiable mental or moral faculty depended on a specific region of the brain — or what Gall referred to as specific *organs* of the brain.[16] It would not be an exaggeration to say that the modern "brain sciences" began with Gall's claims and with clinical and experimental attempts to test them. Nor is it beside the point to note that Gall's phrenology is very much a "modularity theory of mind."

In the two centuries since Gall's major publications, great strides have been made in both the gross and the microscopic anatomy of the nervous system. The development of specific stains has made it possible to identify specific cells and pathways within the brain. Techniques for electrically stimulating and recording from regions of the brain — including single cells — has made it possible to associate activity in specific regions of the nervous system with behavioral, perceptual, and cognitive functions. Imaging techniques, beginning with CAT and PET scans, to which MRI technology has been added, have evolved to the point at which real-time records of the human brain are available even as the patient or experimental subject participates consciously in the overall program of research.

OVERREACHING THEORY IN THE BRAIN SCIENCES

In a manner that seems often to be breathless, rampant speculation has attempted to keep pace with these technical advances. The results have been mixed. Many if not most persons active in this area would take it to be a sign of progress that psychologists, neurologists, and, yes, philosophers, not only read each other's specialty journals, but even serve as co-authors and co-workers. Truth be told, however, it is fair to say that, whatever it was about the mind-body problem that made it a philosophical problem in the first instance, developments in the brain sciences have done nothing to solve, settle, or eliminate it. The point here is not that, on a certain reading, Aristotle might be credited with a version of supervenience theory; or that Huxley's version of epiphenomenalism was as acutely articulated as more recent variants; or that Gall's brain "organs" did just the sort of work that Daniel Dennett would assign to various modules. Rather, traditional positions on the mind-body problem — from eliminative materialism to Cartesian dualism and Leibniz's psychophysical parallelism — are neither more nor less defensible after centuries of research and theorizing. At the level of theory and explanation, the use of an advanced technology and a correspondingly technical vocabulary has created something of an illusory effect. It has encouraged many to believe that some sort of mystery is soon to be solved, a Rosetta stone unearthed. The conceptual problem, however, never was at the level of technology; not even at the more fundamental levels of science. The problem is three-fold. First, there is the persistent misbehavior of human beings who reliably fail to confirm mere hunches that are nonetheless accorded the status of developed theories. Then there is that abiding "gap" separating the physical features of brain function revealed by an ever-improving technology and the (seemingly) non-physical features of mental life. Finally, there is the vexing fact that the available and even foreseeable findings can be applied with equal evidentiary force to such radically different solutions to the mind-body problem as interactionism, parallelism, epiphenomenalism, eliminativism, supervenience, etc. Note that dualism and non-dualism depend on the same law-like correlations. Thus, the more reliable the correlations, the more plausible are such theories as psychophysical parallelism, epiphenomenalism, interactionism, etc. It would seem that there is no *experimentum crucis* that will tell so thoroughly for one solution and against all the rest as to establish *the solution*. To the extent that a problem is a bona fide *scientific* problem if and only if there is some imaginable experiment that will settle it, the mind-body problem would have to be judged as falling outside the boundaries of scientific modes of verification. For this reason if for no other, little is gained by today's philosophical advocates who reach for one or another "finding" to support a pet conjecture. What is needed is not an enlarged data-base but a perspective enlarged to embrace the complexities of the case.

In referring to the misbehavior of human beings, I would draw attention to the well-known variations displayed by actual patients with specific neuroanatomical anomalies. Brains are not bones. The "growth" and "power" they achieve through experience — through the lived life — are different from anything taking place in any other organ of the body. The gross functional anatomy of the human nervous system certainly does permit precise structure-function relationships to be established and quantified. The accuracy and reliability with which this can be achieved increase as the functions themselves are of a narrower and more specific sort. But once the functions of interest are drawn from the realms of deliberation, language, emotionality, social adjustment, desires and real motives, the neat models featured in textbooks prove to be just so many pages of wishful thinking. Variations among patients and within the given patient over time leave the oracles speechless. That patients with lesions in parietal cortex are sometimes found to be unable to coordinate their movements in order, for example, to put on a jacket, is perhaps not unpredictable. That such dressing-apraxias arise from high altitude flying is! Again, the observed correlation of events is medically and therepeutically useful but the explanations are inevitably ad hoc. Similar symptoms may arise from radically different predisposing conditions.[17]

So be it. In science, however, especially high barriers are supposed to partition the world into what is the case and what is merely wished for. In this science — this recently dubbed "cognitive neuroscience" — the barriers were low and porous from the beginning. Impatient to get to the end of the story without tarrying over the thick intervening chapters, some (Gall's name jumps out as if out of a box!) would insert global theories between the clinician and the patient; inserted as might be a prism or colored transparency. The clinician, unmindful of the device or, alas, eager to make good use of it, thereupon proceeds to make "clinical observations" that, in fact, are not merely theory-driven but obeisant to a wider orthodoxy.

Note that the term "clinical observation" is different from, say, "measurement of core temperature" or "white cell count." No competent neurologist wastes time counting the hairs on the patient's head. There are some observations that really matter, others that are utterly irrelevant, and always a few that might fall in either category. It is clinical experience itself, both earned and derived from books, that equips the diagnostician with the essentials here. In time, observations become so reliable, exceptions so rare, that the trained neurologist enters the clinic armed with information approaching the lawfulness of physical phenomena. Again, all this (as of now) pertains to relatively narrow ranges of sensory, motor, affective, and cognitive functions. It is in the enlarged realm of human psychology that matters become less definite and incline theoreticians to reach beyond the actual findings, or to describe relevant findings in ways least embarrassing to a favored theory. Illustrations of this can be drawn from two of the most celebrated reports in all of the brain sciences; "Broca's area," and that most startling of cases, the case of Phineas Gage. It is useful to review these cases to assess how and by how much theory shapes observation, rather than the other way round.

In 1861, Broca reported that his aphasic patient, Mr. Leborgne (nicknamed "Tan"), was found on post-mortem examination to have a neurosyphilitic lesion in the third frontal convolution of the left hemisphere. For the better part of the century this area, long named Broca's area, received uniform treatment in textbooks. It was the official "speech area," confined to the left hemisphere, and associated with the ability to articulate words and form sentences.

In recent decades, however, a different picture emerges, still based on clinical observation and neuroimaging, but with a far more fully developed understanding of linguistic processes.[18] There is now a growing suspicion among specialists that the original position advanced by Broca and rendered nearly official for more than a century was the product of rather selective observations often systematically indifferent to counter-evidence and not fully informed as regards language itself.[19] Indeed, contrary to the older view that Broca's aphasia is specific to spoken language, there is now evidence indicating that lesions in this region of the brain are associated with comparable deficits in those using sign language.[20]

What should be clear at this point is that the once direct relationship between a specific area of frontal cortex and language has proven to be a rather more variable and diffuse set of associations between a fairly wide region of the anterior cortex and various syntactic, semantic and articulatory aspects of symbolic communication. This certainly does not warrant the removal of Broca's area from standard textbooks. If anything, improved imaging techniques and a larger body of clinical data confirm in a general way what Broca proposed over a century ago. However, the fuller picture leaves no doubt but that the original picture was not only too simple but also somewhat distorted.

Broca and other leaders of thought at the time adhered to specific theories regarding mental processes. Some were fully in the camp of Gall and the phrenologists whose theory required of each definable mental function the activity of a specific "organ" within either the cerebral cortex or the cerebellum. In light of this, it is less than surprising that they would expect a direct relationship between language at large and specific cerebral regions. Others, such as Broca and Alexander Bain, were committed to associationistic theories of mental function. In light of these theoretical attachments it is no surprise that the symptoms of aphasic patients were described and understood in terms of *failures of association*. With today's emphasis on linguistics, it is common to find the same neuropathological conditions understood in syntactical and semantic terms. Thus, a patient qualifies as relevantly aphasic or dysphasic not simply in virtue of failing to associate the right word with an object but when observed to assemble words in a manner lacking in grammatical structure and/or meaningfulness. Granting that presuppositions influence diagnostics, there is little doubt but that the anterior cortex — the *left* anterior cortex in all but a handful of cases — is functionally associated with "language" in the wider sense of the term. It is equally clear that there is no current and adequate neuropsychological theory of language that can claim consistent empirical support. Truth be told, there is no current and adequate neuropsychological theory that establishes just how any set of processes in the nervous system might constitute an *explanation* of language. Correlations are everywhere; *causal* explanations nowhere to be found. Left ignored at this point is the more fundamental question as to whether the right model of explanation here is in the form of causal accounts.

As for Broca's discovery, it is to be remembered that it did not take place in a vacuum. Already in place was a clinical and theoretical literature on the question of brain mechanisms and language. An early leader in this field was Jean Baptiste Bouillaud, one of the founders of the Phrenological Society in Paris. Faithful to Phrenology, Bouillaud insisted that aphasia arises either from a loss of memory for words or from deficits in the ability to articulate words. So confident was he of the adequacy of phrenological thought on this subject that he offered a reward to anyone who could present a verbally competent patient suffering from frontal lobe damage.[21] This was the general climate of thought by the time Broca entered the field and began to make his own contributions to it, presenting clinical findings taken as challenges to the phrenologists. He would become a figure of recognized importance a decade or two after Bouillaud's own celebrity was earned. An active member of France's Anthropological Society, Broca expressed his respect for Gall and phrenology, but proceeded to develop his own theory of localization, a theory seemingly supported by findings from "Broca's area."

At this same time, controversy surrounded the question of the right approach to such issues. Some defended an experimental mode of inquiry such as that developed by Pierre Flourens and requiring surgical destruction of specific regions of the brains of animals. Others, including Broca, advocated the clinical neurological approach, which, after all, was ideally suited to studies of human brain function. Broca's patient, "Tan," would be offered in support of a clinical methodology for which there was no "experimental" alternative.[22] As a veritable parade of instances and counter-instances made its way into the literature, the acceptance of "Broca's area" became more general. Nonetheless, the participants had to relax certain expectations regarding the specificity of linguistic functions, the criteria by which to accept these as lost or diminished, and the degree to which the dominant hemisphere was implicated. In all of this one recognizes the rich admixture of data, theory, and, to some extent, the politics of "professionalism."

As of now it is not even clear that "Broca's area" is a product of hominid evolution and is thus confined to human language users. The region of the brain designated as Broca's area falls within the inferior frontal gyrus and is typically more developed in the left than in the right hemisphere. A similar configuration has been found in three species of great apes, but with no evidence of linguistic function or ability.[23] Thus, Brodmann's area 44 is found in both human beings and apes but functions differently in both. This should be kept in mind whenever an "animal model" is proposed as representing aspects of human mental life.

I turn now to the case of Gage, one of the most cited in histories of neurology and the brain sciences. It offers yet another example of the lore that grows up around unusual clinical cases. Gage was a railroad foreman laying rail in Vermont. The fateful day was September 13, 1848, when an explosive charge he was using to shatter large rock foundations resulted in a tamping iron being blown up into and through his skull. With the force of a bullet, the three-foot tool, weighing more than 13 pounds, landed some 30 yards from Gage's fallen body. Although exact details are still conjectural, it is apparent that the point of entry was below Gage's left cheek, exiting then from the top of his skull.

He did not lose consciousness and in a matter of minutes was able to talk and sit erect on the cart returning him to his place of temporary residence. There he was attended by Dr. Harlow, whose records of the case continue to inform the literature surrounding "the American Crowbar Incident." Gage not only survived the trauma but was soon working again.

Thanks to Malcolm Macmillan, there is now an exhaustively researched account of just what happened to Gage, who he was, and what the actual findings were as made by the physician who took charge of the case.[24] What becomes clear, when comparing Macmillan's findings with the books and articles that have been based on the case of Gage, is that later commentators have given themselves fairly wide latitude; indeed, latitude so wide as to provide ample room for theoretical inventiveness of the wrong sort.

It is useful to begin with a widely cited article based on Gage and intended to outline and defend a theory about the psychological functions regulated by the brain.[25] The approach of the investigators was that of generating a computer model of Gage's skull. They availed themselves of existing X-rays and photographs of the skull. In a manner that must be described as theory driven, they then identified trajectories that they judged to be the most likely ones. Ruled out was a competing trajectory regarded as having lethal consequences. However, as Macmillan notes, the physician actually attending to Gage ". . . believed that precisely that damage had occurred: as he said, the abscess he drained on the 14th day 'probably communicated with the left lateral ventricle'."[26] Note that the trajectory ruled out by the computer model (on the grounds that it would have killed Gage) is the one that most closely matches the wound pattern reported by the examining physician. In fact, the more closely one examines the actual medical record in relation to the theory-driven and model-based generalizations by Damasio *et al.*, the clearer it becomes that these very generalizations and models rest on an entirely uncertain empirical foundation. Nor is the problem confined to identifying the actual trajectory. As Macmillan says, "Even were we able to resolve the uncertainties about the damage to Gage's brain, there are equally insurmountable obstacles to our relating the changes in his behavior to them."[27]

As for the behavioral changes, it would be necessary to know a great deal about a patient before such a traumatic incident, in order to determine the extent to which post-traumatic observed behavior can be properly traced to the trauma itself. The record here is thin. Thin though it is, the current literature has not been diffident in the matter of advancing highly specific areas to account for psychological changes allegedly resulting from damage to specific regions of Gage's brain. Thus, to the quite thin psychological profile of Gage, one adds uncertain neuroanatomical data and proceeds to generate a theory![28] The entire saga of Gage rests chiefly on a 160-word description provided by Dr. Harlow. In all, the current theoretical attempts to use this case to establish connections between rational and emotional functions within frontal cortex approach nearly mythical proportions. Quoting again from Macmillan, "Carelessness aside, the supposedly scientific representations are either the result of ignorance of the true nature of their subject or are distortions generated by a theoretically driven vision of what Gage should have been like."[29]

A current example of an ideology driving an otherwise scientific field of inquiry is found in the recently published *Big Brain*, by Gary Lynch and Richard Granger.[30] The authors are accomplished figures in the brain sciences and surely are not latter-day phrenologists. The phrenologists produced a table of some thirty-five distinct faculties, each tied to a specific "organ" of the brain. In the matter of intelligence, Lynch and Granger regard the unit of consequence to be not a specific organ but the overall mass of the brain. Human cognitive powers on this account arise from ". . . no shockingly new circuit types — just more of the same in outlandish excess."[31] In light of this, the authors focus on the *Boskops*, a race or tribe so named owing to the discovery in 1913, in Boskop, South Africa, of a very large skull fragment. The skull's estimated volumetric capacity was calculated to be 1800 cc. of volumetric capacity, which is 25 per cent greater than the average human skull.

Presumably the Boskops, these alleged precursors of *Homo sapiens*, had a native superiority owing to cognitive powers generated by their larger brains. They could think faster and more efficiently than we. The fact is chastening: "The Boskop skulls represented an important affront; a direct challenge to the presumed 'upward' trajectory and ultimate supremacy of present-day humans."[32] The authors note that "Human brains . . . are qualitatively the same as those of other primates; the primary difference is that they are enormous."[33] The conclusion reached by the authors is that an earlier race of beings was superior to us as we are superior to the balance of the animal economy in virtue of having big brains. Moreover, neuropharmacology holds within its powers the ability to produce offspring with Boskopoid brains.

All this aside, one insistent question is why the cognitively superior Boskop race disappeared. The authors offer two hypotheses. First, as the Boskops were probably peaceable, our kind was likely to have exterminated them. Then again, on the matter of surviving, "Perhaps they didn't want to . . . Perhaps the Boskops were trapped in their ability to see clearly where things would head."[34] As it happens, however, the Boskops did not disappear, for they never appeared in the first place! Regarding the original discovery of 1913, further study exploded the myth of a vanished tribe. The skull unearthed in 1913 was not complete. Its thickness was an obstacle to precise calculation of cranial volume. By the early 1950s Ronald Singer at the University of Cape Town had thoroughly explored the area, retrieving thousands of artifacts. Based on large and carefully measured samples of skulls, Singer was able to place the "Boskopoids" comfortably within the established metrics for the Hottentot and the Negro.[35] When two accomplished scientists devote an entire volume to the implications arising from the size of brains — and offer as decisive evidence in support of their thesis what turns out to be nothing less than a case of mistaken identity — it is clear that ideology is driving science.

I emphasize that criticism of such work is not drawn from a wider skepticism about the relationship between brain function and psychological processes. Rather, too much in the contemporary "brain science" literature takes the form of special pleading, a kind of *apologia* for a larger materialistic psychology otherwise indefensible at the level of actual data. Habitual in this literature is the ascription of psychological predicates to biological tissue. On this account, it is the brain that (somehow) thinks, perceives, plans, feels, and otherwise lives a life more or less accidentally surrounded by the rest of the body and that fictive entity, the *person*, whose life this presumably is. Bennett and Hacker have drawn attention to all this in a closely argued treatise on the philosophical errors and misapprehensions now so common in cognitive neuroscience.[36] It is sufficient here to call readers' attention to their important contribution.

The issues under consideration here can be illustrated in still another way. Consider the manner in which epilepsy has been understood historically. As early as the fourth century BC the Hippocratic physicians were content to regard the condition as a result of brain pathology. They rejected the orthodox view that epilepsy is in some special sense a "divine" illness. In a properly droll manner, they were all too willing to accept that the gods caused *all* illnesses, but surely epilepsy no more than any other. By AD 70 a different theory is advanced. According to the Gospel of Mark (9:14–29), Jesus Christ cast out a devil from a young man, here the devil being the cause of epilepsy. We next move to the official handbook for the detection, trial and execution of witches — the infamous *Malleus Maleficarum* of 1494. Now seizures are evidence that the defendant is a witch. With the progress of understanding, this all gives way to a different theory which, as recently as the early 1900s, led some US states to forbid marriage or childbearing by epileptics, some going so far as to require sterilization.

It should be obvious that the symptoms observed by the Hippocratic physicians of the fifth century BC were virtually the same as those observed by medical officers in various states in the United States in the twentieth century. The symptoms were surely the same in Inquisitorial courts in the sixteenth century, these guided by a theory according to which seizures are evidence of satanic possession. Unless brains were radically different between the fifth century BC and the early twentieth century, we must agree that the relationship in the past between epileptic symptoms and activity in specific regions of the brain was pretty much what it is known to be now. We can say, then, that the brain-behavior relationship has been stable over a course of many centuries but with colossal variations in the pet theories advanced to account for the observed facts. One might object here on the grounds that, unlike these scientifically less developed ages, we really do now have developed and precise knowledge of the physiology and neurochemistry associated with epilepsy. This is knowledge that the past surely could not claim for itself. In the absence of a developed science, theories are fairly free to range widely and wildly. But even with what we take to be the developed brain sciences of the late twentieth century, there are still quite remarkable and shifting differences of opinion as to how patterns of behavior and, e.g. emotions, motivations, desires, etc. are to be understood. Twenty years ago, the official diagnostic manual of the American Psychiatric Association classified homosexuality as a treatable neurotic disturbance. The most recent editions of that same work make no such claim. Needless to say, brain function has undergone no such variation; nor have the associated emotions; nor have the associated desires; nor has the associated behavior. Instead, the passage of time has hosted fundamental alterations in perspective. Not every instance of seizure is "epilepsy," nor is the absence of overt signs of seizure evidence that the patient is free of the disease. Such changes in our perspective on disease and normalcy are often responsive to practical needs and considerations. At other times the combination of cultural values and political expediency result in new "insights" into what was long judged to be a settled matter.

What of settled matters? Perhaps none enjoys more widespread support, and even enthusiasm, than that pertaining to the ultimate nature of all reality. Reduced to a maxim, the settled position is that *physics is complete.* It is a bold and spare ontological claim. It requires one to accept that, at the end of the day, each thing and all the things that might lay claim to real existence can have no property that is not a physical property. Support for this conviction is everywhere within the developed sciences — but nowhere else! It is a long conjectural stride to move from the certainties surrounding the dynamics of balls rolling down an inclined plane — or even the certainties associated with the scientific foundations of the space program — to the busy, hectic, shifting, noisy, variegated world of lived life. Outside the philosophy seminar room, there really is no good reason to make such a move. Much can be said on behalf of ontological economy, but it is far too costly if the price is self-delusion. In this connection, it really does no good to cite the conservation laws in physics, or note the incompatibility of "mental" and "physical" concepts, for this does no more than rehearse the maxim itself. It cannot be a limitation of mentalistic terms and concepts that they fail to match up with ergs and ions. Indeed, if it is lived life that it is the object of interest, the limitation seems to be quite in the other direction. Radical physicalism is drawn from the same shelf that contains all radical metaphysical propositions. The more radical the proposition, the greater the weight of evidence and argument that must be adduced in support of it. There is nothing radical about dualism. It matches up very well with common sense, which, as warrants go, is robust in and of itself. It matches up further with the phenomenology of lived life, and if it is that life that physicalism would explain, it must do so in a manner respectful of that very phenomenology.

Is it those eerie qualia, then, that pose the major obstacle? The seen world is as it *seems to us*, and this is a world of colors and shapes, patterns and forms, movements and contexts. All of these phenomenal features — these qualia — resist reduction to physics and are regarded as perhaps the only major obstacle to physicalism. But the obstacle is far more formidable than red roses and sweet candy. The days of actual persons are filled with purposes and aspirations, emotions and attractions, fancies and riveted attention. In most instances, these same days are filled also with social interactions explicable only in terms that are at once personal and cultural. Whether friends are swapping stories or gifts, the heavy traffic is in the form of *meanings*, not mere motions. Meaning is constructed; it is constructed out of the rich resources of language, which itself is constructed out of the seemingly limitless resources of the active life. No philosopher or theologian of note has ever doubted that a body — the actual material, corporeal body — is the instrumental *sine qua non* of such undertakings. But how this complex instrument brings about — that is to say *causally* brings about — that very active life, is a question that remains to be clarified before one might even hope to have it answered.

Causation, however, is not a univocal concept. The activity of the active life is typically in response to *reasons* for acting, rather than causes of action. There is all the difference between muscles contracting and "going to the theater" even if the latter depends on the former. It is important to be clear on this point. There is all the difference between a behavioral "event," a behavioral "act," and the "action" undertaken by an intending and competent agent. Restless sleep might result in the right hand moving up over the right eyebrow, fingers extended. Bright sunlight might cause the right hand to be positioned over the right eyebrow in the same fashion. An Army private, passing an officer, is found moving the same right hand up above the eyebrow with fingers extended. The first is a mere event, taking place without deliberation, based on no convention and having no meaning. The second is a defensive "act," not unlike adjustments routinely made throughout the animal economy. It is stimulus-bound and unaffected by cultural norms and rules. An observer can understand what the behavior achieves, but there is no semiotic ingredient to be deciphered. Saluting an officer is, of course, entirely different and stands as an ineliminably cultural datum. It is in the full sense an action. Going to the theater is a species of *action*.[37] Not every identification of brain-behavior dependency establishes a *causal* dependency of the right sort. The sense in which an infant depends upon the solicitude of parents is quite different from the sense in which the rate of descent depends on the angle of inclination of an inclined plane. The sense in which movement of the right hand depends on the functional integrity of motor nerves on the contralateral side, is different from the sense in which a salute depends on the appearance of a senior officer. It would be odd and needlessly distracting to say that what makes the movement a "salute" depends on the left side of the brain.

Nor does the problem become simpler by invoking one or another version of double-aspect theory allowing us a choice in the matter of description and explanation; a reality taken in one "aspect" (e.g. the mental) or another (e.g. the physical). On this understanding, there are two accounts available for just what it is that results in Smith being at the theater. One account can be rendered in exclusively neurophysiological terms. The second account can be rendered purely in motivational and rational terms. The problem here, of course, is that the first rendering has nothing to do with "going to the theater." We know what it means to be like someone going to the theater. We have no idea what it means to be in any given brain state. To say that being in a given brain state is *like* going to the theater is simply meaningless, for there is no clue as to the measure of implied similitude.

CONCLUSION

Stripped of uninforming rhetorical adornments, science has great appeal. It tends to be down-to-earth. Where it finds itself correcting some enduring ignorance or immoderate habit of thought, it usually does so by explaining just what it was that gave rise to the ignorance or odd thinking in the first instance. Typically, it is not the scientific explanation that is disturbing or shocking; it is disturbing and shocking that we were ever so convinced in our ignorance as to require the scientific correctives. With very few exceptions, the required instruction is in the form of defeating a theory chiefly by replacing it with a better one. One theory is better than another when it can subsume a greater number of phenomena and do so with the economy achieved by general laws. However, the phenomenology of lived life is not theoretical. *It just is what it is.* It is not to be explained by way of laws more fundamental than this very phenomenology, for the basic reason that the phenomenology is itself the most fundamental level of explanation. The arena within which psychological theories compete for acceptance is, when all is said and done, a cognitive and cultural arena. Whether one account is more economical than another is a matter that appeals at the level of aesthetics — the level of judgment, where what is judged are aspects that go well beyond the merely quantitative. It is in this respect that the foundational science of human nature just is folk psychology. That it must be refined through criticism and analysis there is no doubt. The methods and perspectives of science must always figure in that criticism and analysis. But these methods and perspectives are themselves cultural artifacts. Accordingly, they, too, require criticism and analysis. In the end, the relationship between an authentic science of human nature and the physical sciences is not one of causality, but of dialectic.

What, then, of souls? As Aristotle notes:

> To say that it is the soul which is angry is as inexact as it would be to say that it is the soul that weaves webs or builds houses. It is doubtless better to avoid saying

that the soul pities or learns or thinks and rather to say that it is the man who does this with his soul.[38]

Substituting *brain* for *soul* we have a useful corrective for what has become something of political speech in philosophy of mind. The thoughts and actions of persons are somehow associated with their brains, the strength of the association to be determined by systematic study. That the spiritual dimension of life is not amenable to study of the same sort establishes only its special nature, not its unreality. It is the dimension that impels significant actions, grounds nothing less than life itself, gives meaning and direction, answers aching questions — not for all but for many. It comes with its own special phenomenology, different from pains and colors but, like them, resistant to reductions to some other ontological level.

The wise course of action is to examine how the spiritual side of life affects life itself. The clumsy course of action is to assume this is all covered by what, in the end, is the philosophical form of quack medicine, promising a cure for what is not a disease in the first place.

Like Robinson, Mark Baker considers aspects of the history of neuroscience — both its successes and its gaps. But he reflects on these issues as they play out in a specific domain: that of human language. Baker is a prominent practitioner of a relevant science, namely linguistics. In 2007, he was made a fellow of the American Association for the Advancement of Science for his distinguished contributions in this field. He was also awarded a Rutgers University Board of Trustees award for excellence in research, in recognition of his outstanding contributions to the field of linguistics.

Baker poses the question of what it would be like to approach the subject of language from an explicitly dualist perspective. How might one's research agenda and one's interpretation of results be different if one were serious about the possibility that souls exist? Part of the answer, Baker suggests, is that dualism invites one to consider which aspects of the human mind depend primarily or exclusively on the human brain, and which depend primarily or exclusively on the human soul.

Of course, there need not be a particularly interesting answer to this question, even within the dualistic perspective, even if the Soul Hypothesis is in fact true. It could perfectly well turn out that both the brain and the soul are crucially involved in practically every aspect of every mental function that we can imagine: both are involved in language, in memory, in perception, in reasoning, in attention, in personality, in learning, and in action. In that case, research will not discover any significant differences among these various mental functions or their parts along these lines.

But it is equally imaginable to the dualist that there are significant differences to be discovered here. There is, after all, little reason to entertain the Soul Hypothesis unless the soul makes some important contribution to our mental lives. Some people have taken the view that what we think of as a soul is merely an epiphenomenon that is caused by brain activity, and it plays no initiating role within the human mind. But that is hardly a full-fledged dualist view. Assuming then that the soul does play a crucial role in the human mind somewhere, it is easy to imagine that it might not play exactly the same role, or an equally large role, in every aspect of the human mind. And if there are differences of this sort, then it is reasonable to think that scientific investigation and reflection could identify them. The goal of learning the truth about this matter (one way or another) is thus a natural part of a dualist's research agenda, making it somewhat different from the research agenda of a materialist, Baker contends.

Baker pursues this question by two kinds of inquiry. First, he presents a sort of functional analysis of language in general, where the different logically necessary components of speaking are identified and distinguished. In this, he draws on certain classic distinctions in the conceptual foundations of modern linguistics, distinguishing the vocabulary of a language, the grammar of that language, and the power and will to employ both in actual concrete acts of speaking and understanding speech. Then, with this standard conceptual analysis of language in hand, he turns to the domains of neurolinguistics, genetics, and comparative biology to see if there is evidence that all three components of language are equally dependent on the brain.

The findings that Baker reviews suggest that in fact they are not. Grammar and vocabulary can be selectively affected by specific brain injuries and genetic anamolies, but the power to use these resources to speak purposefully apparently is not. Similarly, a trained chimpanzee can acquire a rudimentary vocabulary and grammar, but apparently cannot acquire the power to use them beyond isolated words or rote-learned utterances. Within the dualist framework, then, it seems reasonable to infer that the vocabulary and grammar aspects of language depend on the brain in a crucial way, but the capacity to use them in a particular way is primarily the result of our having souls as well as bodies. This amounts to a specific illustration of a general point that was made in Robinson's essay: narrow and peripheral cognitive functions map onto brains much more neatly and convincingly than more general functions do. Using one's vocabulary to name an object or to pronounce a word is an example of the former kind, which can be accurately correlated with structures in the brain, whereas speaking in coherent and meaningful sentences newly constructed for the occasion is an example of the latter kind, which cannot be accurately correlated with brain structures.

Toward the end of Baker's essay, he also develops in a different way Robinson's observation that, when it comes to the human mind, "The heavy traffic is meaning." Baker considers the great hope of cognitive psychology, which is that the mind-brain can be fully understood as a powerful computer, which does what it does by manipulating symbolic representations in complex but systematic ways. Digital computers are those things we know of which seem to be both quite smart and entirely material. We know that they are (can be) smart because they can calculate square roots and play chess better than we can; we know that they are entirely material because we know how we built them, and what we used to do it. If then the human brain can be analyzed as a kind of computer, one can understand how it too could seem smart while still being entirely a material physical object.

But yet, Baker rehearses an argument that this plausible sounding approach could very well have started off on the wrong foot. Built into the very definition of a computer is the notion that they perform operations based on the form and structure of their input, but not on the meaning of that input. For example, one can program a computer to systematically replace one symbol with a combination of other symbols if and only if the first symbol is immediately followed by some third symbol. However, one cannot program a computer to systematically replace one symbol by another if and only if the original symbol happens to be one that refers (in this context) to one particular person. The trick to effective programming is to get around this limitation by carefully constructing and interpreting inputs so that their forms happen to correspond well enough to the meanings one is interested in. But in general there is no simple correspondence between something's form and its meaning. (The sentences "The sky is blue today" and "The boss seems blue today" have the same form, but quite different kinds of meanings, for example, and the rational creature will draw different conclusions from them.) Given then that the human mind (and the human life) is shot through with meaning from first to last, computation might simply be the wrong idea about how large parts of the human mind work.

Baker concludes that there is an intriguing match between what computers cannot do in principle and those aspects of language that the history of neurolinguistics suggests do not depend directly on the brain. Perhaps then cognitive science is correct to look at the brain as a sophisticated kind of computer, capable of performing complex computations — but at the same time fundamentally incapable of doing other sorts of things that are crucial to the way we speak. This aspect of the human mind might necessarily involve something else, Baker suggests. There is thus plenty of room in what we know for aspects of language to fall under some explanatory principle other than computation, an explanatory principle that is rooted in concepts of rationality and will — as the traditional Western notion of a soul in fact is.

CHAPTER 3

Brains and Souls; Grammar and Speaking

Mark Baker

FRAMING AN EMPIRICAL INQUIRY INTO THE SOUL

Suppose that we consider it an open question whether there is a non-physical aspect of human beings that contributes somehow to their mental lives — something akin to the traditional notion of a soul. On the one hand, we might not necessarily be twentieth-century Cartesians, who consider the existence of our souls to be immediately evident on the basis of the conscious experience that we enjoy, full of sights and sounds and thoughts and decisions. And we might not necessarily think that the existence of souls is crucially entailed by any religious or quasi-religious beliefs that we have about matters like the origin and infrastructure of the universe. But on the other hand, we might not be as certain as some people seem to be that all that exists is atoms in motion, and that the fewer things one believes in the better. We might find ourselves somewhat skeptical of claims that a few fundamental equations of physics ultimately tell us everything there is to know, especially when we find ourselves wondering about many other things — whether the economy will implode, whether people love us, which movie to go see. This is roughly where the current author finds himself, in any case. Ockham's razor is all very well, and it has its place as a useful tool, but I for one do not want to cut my throat with it and bleed to death.

Suppose, then, that we start from the position that whether or not people have souls could go either way. It is something like a 50/50 bet, with neither view on the matter having an especially high burden of proof to meet with respect to the other. Beginning from this neutral position, it is natural and appropriate to treat the question about souls as the Soul Hypothesis — as something that could play a role in guiding scientific research and other forms of rational investigation. In particular, we can ask what sorts of empirical facts might bear on the truth or falsity of the Soul Hypothesis, making it more likely or less likely to be true. And we can ask more specific research questions as well, such as which aspects of our mental life depend primarily or exclusively upon a person's physical part (especially the brain), and which depend primarily or exclusively upon a person's non-physical part? (Let me go ahead and call the non-physical part a soul, for directness and convenience, even though I leave open exactly what sort of thing it might be.)

In advance of consulting any facts, one can imagine different answers to this question. For example, it could turn out that both the body and the soul are crucially intertwined in every mental activity that we can identify. At least for broadly conceived activities, that is very likely to be true: every sight we see might involve both the optic nerve and the experience of the seer; every voluntary action we perform might involve both the nerves and muscles and the decision of the willer. Still, if there is such a thing as a soul, then there is the logical possibility that there could be some mental processes that depend more or less exclusively on the soul, the brain playing little direct role in that particular process. If so, then rational/scientific inquiry might be able to identify those processes. If such inquiry does make worthwhile discoveries about which mental processes are primarily dependent on the brain and which are not, those discoveries will redound to the credit of the dualist hypothesis that inspired us to look for them. In contrast, if there is no such thing as a soul distinct from the body then no such discoveries will be forthcoming: if human beings consist only of bodies, then all their mental processes must depend on the body alone. Hence failure to find mental processes that do not depend on the body could be interpreted as lending some support to the non-dualist view.

Of course neither empirical result will count as decisive proof for or against the Soul Hypothesis until the presumably far off day when our understanding of mental phenomena is complete. Until then, the committed dualist can say that it is mental processes we have not thought to isolate yet that depend on the soul but not the body. At the same time, the committed non-dualist can believe that any unexplained mental functions depend entirely on the body, we just haven't figured out how yet. Neither response will be unreasonable. Nevertheless, it is still worth seeking empirical evidence now that bears on such matters as best we can. Doing so gives us educated guesses as to what the final answer will be that are better than nothing, and it helps push us ahead in the search for those final answers. We have no chance of arriving at final answers unless we are willing to seek tentative and intermediate answers along the way.

BEGGING THE QUESTION

It is my strong impression that the soul question is almost never investigated as a hypothesis in anything like the way that I have outlined. Many popular science books about the mind give the impression that the research project has already been carried out, and that the Soul Hypothesis stands completely refuted. For example, leading psychologist Steven Pinker writes: "One can say that the information-processing activity of the brain *causes* the mind, or one can say that it *is* the mind, but in either case the evidence is overwhelming that every aspect of our mental lives depends entirely on physiological events in the tissues of the brain."[1]

This is a very strong claim, confidently stated in bold words. But a little reflection shows that the vast bulk of the work Pinker has in mind (if not all of it) has not been framed as an empirical test of the Soul Hypothesis, where the results could turn out either way. Rather, in virtually every case the research starts by presupposing (usually implicitly) that the soul plays no essential role in the matters under study. And all of us are strongly prone not to see (or not to report) what we do not expect or imagine that we will see.

To unveil the presuppositions behind this research, consider what would normally be involved in proving Pinker's claim. The quotation above makes it sound like psychologists and brain scientists are in possession of an exhaustive inventory of every aspect of our mental lives. Given such an inventory, they can use it as a checklist, taking the aspects of mental life one by one and investigating for each one whether it depends entirely on physiological events in brain tissue. But where did this list come from, and how sure are we that the list is correct and complete?

In fact, there is no such list, beyond very rough and ready outlines. That is not how these investigations really go at all. Instead neuroscientists generally go off into a long and impressive list of the many things that brains can do, and how bad it is to have a defective brain. Such discussions are not entirely to the point. It can certainly be shown that brains do a lot, and that every part of the brain does something. But no amount of research framed in that way is enough to substantiate the sweepingly universal claim of the anti-dualist, as a point of logic. To see why, imagine that a person comes to you claiming to know everything that there is to know about baseball statistics. He then offers to prove his claim to you by quoting baseball statistic after baseball statistic, probably exhausting your attention span for such things. There is still no reason to believe his boast unless you yourself have an independent list of all the baseball statistics and can test him on arbitrary facts from that list which are chosen by you. We have complete and detailed maps of the brain, and these can presumably be used to defend the claim that every part of the brain contributes to mental life. But we do not have complete and detailed maps of the functional architecture of the mind which can be used to prove that every aspect of mental life depends on the brain.

What then would it be like to do research into this area that did not presuppose the truth or falsity of the Soul Hypothesis, but treated it as a live option? To make the topic more manageable, let us focus in on one particular aspect of human mental life: the domain of language. This is a very important and distinctive part of human mental life; indeed, most of us are immersed in language for most of our waking lives. Even when we are not talking to anyone or listening to anyone, many of our private thoughts are presented to us in the form of language — phrases and sentences formulated in (in my case) English. Hence, language does not just concern input (perception) and output (action), which obviously depend on the body — the ears, the tongue, and those associated parts of the brain. Language also plays a role in pure thought, which might not depend on the body in the same way. Language also happens to be a part of mental life that has been studied rather intensively by linguists and researchers in allied fields. We can ask, then, if there is an inventory of mental functions and resources related to language that has emerged from linguistic analysis. If so, that inventory can be used to test sweeping anti-dualist claims like Pinker's.

The goal of this chapter, then, is to explore what is known about these issues with respect to language. I begin by reviewing how contemporary linguistics divides our language ability into three distinguishable components. I then review some empirical evidence from neuroscience, genetics, and the study of other primates. I show that there is good evidence that two out of the three components of language involve the brain in a crucial way, but there is a striking lack of comparable evidence that the third component depends on the brain in the same way. Moreover, the component of language that shows the least evidence of depending on the brain is also the component that has the most in common with the traditional notion of the soul. I interpret this as showing that the research project that emerges from entertaining the Soul Hypothesis is well-conceived and feasible to carry out to some degree.

ISOLATING ASPECTS OF THE HUMAN
LANGUAGE CAPACITY

What, then, are the component parts of the language faculty? Noam Chomsky, the founder of modern linguistics and one of the founders of the broader field of cognitive science, proposed a first-pass answer to this question back in the 1950s,[2] and most of the successes in this field over the past 50 years arguably depend on his answer. Chomsky distinguished three components to the human language faculty: the lexicon (a list of words), the grammar (a set of rules for combining words), and what he eventually came to call the "Creative Aspect of Language Use," or CALU for short.[3] When he divided up language in this way, he was making a practical and methodological decision; he was trying to separate those questions that were open to meaningful inquiry given the then-current state of knowledge from those that were not. His claim was that grammar could be investigated, but the CALU could not, at least for the foreseeable future.[4] The goal for linguistics, then, was to explain what sentences like "Harmless little dogs bark quietly" and "Colorless green ideas sleep furiously" have in common — the property of being *grammatically* well formed — and not to try to explain why a person might say one rather than the other.[5]

Chomsky's three-way distinction can be made clearer with an analogy from the construction industry. The lexicon of a language is like a warehouse of bricks and mortar; it provides the basic pieces that can be used in construction. The grammar is like a set of building codes and engineering principles; it specifies the ways in which the raw materials can be combined to make larger units such as walls, roofs, rooms, and buildings. We have a reasonable hope of understanding these two facets of the language faculty, according to Chomsky. But the construction industry needs more than just raw materials and building codes. It also needs architects to decide where the walls should go in particular cases to achieve the desired results, and contractors to actually assemble the raw materials in ways that are consistent with but not determined by the strictures of the building codes. In the same way, the human capacity for language must consist of more than a lexicon and a grammar; it also includes the ability to choose which words to use and assemble them in ways that are consistent with the grammar to make actual sentences. It is this capacity that Chomsky refers to as the CALU.

Chomsky's decision to factor the language faculty in this way may seem obvious, even trivial in retrospect, yet it was a radical proposal back in the 1950s. It constituted a clear break with the earlier behaviorist tradition, which did not distinguish the CALU from other aspects of the language faculty. As a direct result of their failure to factor the topic in this way, the behaviorists never made much headway in the area of human language. In contrast, Chomsky's conception has helped make the study of language a very productive area of research in the cognitive science era.

MORE ON THE CREATIVE ASPECT OF LANGUAGE USE

Chomsky's fullest discussion of the CALU is in his book *Cartesian Linguistics*, where he reviews with approval some of Descartes' observations about human language expressed in *A Discourse on Method*. Chomsky says that the CALU is the human ability to use linguistic resources (vocabulary items and syntactic rules) to produce and interpret language that simultaneously has the following three properties: it is (i) unbounded, (ii) stimulus-free, and (iii) appropriate to situations. Descartes was interested in this constellation of properties because he believed that behavior that had all three could not be explained in purely mechanical terms, within a theory of contact physics. Descartes observed that no animal had communicative behavior that had this set of properties, nor did any automaton that he knew of or could imagine. Descartes wrote:

> Of these the first [test] is that they [machines] could never use words or other signs arranged in such a manner as is competent to us in order to declare our thoughts to others: for we may easily conceive a machine to be so constructed that it emits vocables, and even that it emits some correspondent to the action upon it of external objects which cause a change in its organs; for example, if touched in a particular place it may demand what we wish to say to it; if in another it may cry out that it is hurt, and such like; but not that it should arrange them variously so as appositely to reply to what is said in its presence, as men of the lowest grade of intellect can do. . . . For it is highly deserving of remark, that there are no men so dull and stupid, not even idiots, as to be incapable of joining together different words, and thereby constructing a declaration by which to make their thoughts understood.[6]

For Descartes (and Chomsky), it was easy to imagine machines that utter a limited number of words or set phrases. These words or phrases could be uttered deterministically, whenever a certain stimulus is experienced, or they could be uttered randomly, with no tight connection to the environment. My sister had a doll like that: you pulled its cord, and it said one of about ten sentences. What is special about human language behavior is first that we "arrange [words] variously," in an unbounded way, not limited to ten sentences but able to construct an infinite variety of sentences as the situation may require. Moreover, human language behavior is not determined by stimuli in an automatic, reflex-like way, but neither is it random. Unlike my daughter's doll, we speak "so as appositely to reply to what is said in [our] presence" and to "construct a declaration by which to make [our] thoughts understood." In other words, we can speak in ways that are neither random nor determined by stimuli, but *appropriate.*

That our language use is unbounded is not enough by itself to make it "creative" in the sense that Chomsky and Descartes were interested in. It would not be creative, for example, to repeat back unchanged an infinite variety of sentences that we hear in our presence, the way a recording device might. That our language use is stimulus-free is also not enough by itself to make it "creative": it is not enough to utter words randomly, as a doll might. Nor is it sufficient that language simply be appropriate: it is not "creative" to produce the three utterances "Danger: snake," "Danger: eagle," and "Danger: leopard" in suitable circumstances, as vervet monkeys do.[7] But behavior that is simultaneously unbounded, not determined by stimuli, and yet appropriate to situations, is something special. Displaying that sort of behavior is what Descartes took to be evidence that a creature has a mind, and what Chomsky said must be put aside if one is to make progress on understanding other aspects of language using existing mathematical notions such as recursive rule systems.

Indeed, Descartes's intuition that human-like linguistic behavior goes beyond the bounds of what can be achieved by a mechanical device has proven to be remarkably accurate even hundreds of years later. Despite vast changes in technology, Descartes' prediction that no mechanical device could be like humans in producing an unbounded range of sentences not determined by stimuli but as appropriate responses to circumstances has turned out to be accurate. In contrast, the founder of computer science, Alan Turing,[8] famously predicted that by the year 2001 we would have computers whose linguistic behavior would be indistinguishable from that of humans. Turing was wrong about this. We are now several years past 2001, and we have computers that play chess as well as the fictional computer Hal did, but computers that converse as well as Hal did are nowhere in sight. There really is something very special about the ability to talk in a way that is simultaneously unbounded, stimulus free, and appropriate.[9]

The distinction between the CALU and the grammar/vocabulary is found in the work of psychologists as well as linguists. Willem Levelt has developed one of the most comprehensive psychological models of language production.[10] Levelt identifies three distinct "processors" that are involved in language production, which he calls the conceptualizer, the formulator, and the articulator. Vocabulary and grammar are resources accessed by the formulator, whose job is to transform "messages" into "inner speech." But before the formulator kicks in, the conceptualizer must take thoughts and intentions (which may not be expressed in language-like formats at all) and create sentence-like semantic representations called preverbal messages, which constitute the input to the formulator. Levelt's conceptualizer has the signature properties of Chomsky's CALU: it produces messages that are novel, undetermined by stimuli, and appropriate to situations. Levelt ends his discussion of the conceptualizer with a review of an experiment by Ehrich in which people were asked to describe how furniture was arranged in a simple room. He observes the following.

> But all of these are tendencies, not iron laws. A speaker is free to choose one perspective rather than another. And indeed, the ways in which the same scene is described by different subjects are surprisingly variant. When one looks over Ehrich's protocols, one is struck by the fact that no two descriptions of the same furniture arrangement are identical. Each subject added a personal touch in terms of the objects, the relations, the qualities attended to, and the choice of perspective.[11]

The subjects' productions are clearly unbounded and stimulus free, with the result that even tightly controlled stimuli and a narrow task-definition do not guarantee a small range of results. Yet the variations do not strike the researcher as being random; rather, they are interpreted as "adding a personal touch," as expressing something. The productions are thus also appropriate in the sense that, with all their variations, the subjects were cooperating with the task that was assigned to them. The CALU thus shows up in Levelt's psychological research too, albeit under a different name.

So far I have reviewed lines of thinking that show that people have a CALU/conceptualizer and this is something different from having a vocabulary or knowing the grammar of a particular language. However, it leaves unresolved the question of what relation the CALU might have to other aspects of the human mind. We have the ability to act in many other ways, not involving language. These nonlinguistic actions are also "creative" in that they are not determined by our immediate circumstances, are chosen from a huge if not infinite space of possibilities, and are appropriate in the sense that they are guided by rational goals. In traditional terms, we (seem to) exercise free will in a wide range of contexts (see Chapter 4). The question arises, then, whether what I am calling the CALU is simply what we call our general capacity for free will when it happens to be applied to actions of speaking as opposed to actions of other sorts, or whether the CALU is a distinct component of the human mind. Put in terms of the analogy from the construction industry used above, the question is whether our minds contain architects and contractors that have special expertise in building linguistic constructions, or whether they contain a kind of "jack of all trades," which can do the equivalent of building a house one day, repairing a car the next, and cultivating a field or skinning a deer on the third, all with roughly equal facility.

In fact, this is a highly debatable matter, with considerations pointing both ways. Some cognitive scientists favor domain-general approaches to cognition on general grounds, and it makes intuitive sense that our ability to speak freely and purposefully is not something entirely independent of our ability to act freely and purposefully. But other cognitive scientists are equally adamant in favoring a highly modular approach to cognition, in which our minds have many specialized subsystems for dealing with different domains. Such researchers think that the best chance of solving the overall problem of giving a naturalistic account of intelligence is to break it up into lots of small problems of being intelligent in a narrow domain, because then one can take maximum advantage of the particular opportunities and limitations that are inherent in that domain.

One sliver of evidence in favor of the second view, in which the CALU is a distinctive aspect of the mind specialized for acting linguistically, comes from comparing the abilities of humans with those of other animals. Animal minds and human minds seem to be similar, even continuous with one another in many respects, and these need to be kept in mind when formulating dualist theories (see Chapter 8). One such similarity is that higher animals seem to be able to make purposeful choices with a degree of "creativity" when it comes to tasks like navigating through a complex environment, adopting foraging strategies, or manipulating fellow members of the species.[12] However, we see no such continuity when it comes to the ability we have to create sentences freely and purposefully; that is something even the great apes just cannot do (see below). The fact that otherwise intelligent animals, which show cleverness and resourcefulness as well as purposefulness in many ways, cannot apply their intelligence to the particular domain of language suggests that some additional capacity is involved in that. If so, then CALU is a particular part of the language capacity and not just domain-general freedom of will.

Fortunately, we do not need to have complete answers to these difficult and loaded questions in order to proceed with the investigation at the level of discussion adopted here. The fact that the CALU is a feature of the human mind that can be distinguished from the vocabulary and the grammar is enough to proceed. What its exact relationship is to some kind of general purpose "central processor" (if there is one) can be left open for current purposes, even though the exact empirical expectations that go with the two views on this are in some cases rather different.

TAKING STOCK

Moving forward on this basis, we now have a rudimentary checklist of mental faculties related to language, which includes the vocabulary, the grammar, and the CALU. We can then go on to use this list to test universal statements about the mind's dependence on the body, such as the one from Pinker quoted above. Is it true that evidence shows that each of these three aspects of our mental lives depends entirely on physiological events in the tissues of the brain?

In fact, I believe that the data we have points to a dissociation: our materialist theories of neuroscience, genetics, and evolutionary biology might make a significant contribution to theories of the vocabulary and the grammar, but there is astonishingly little evidence that they contribute anything to the understanding of the CALU. Someone who considers that the "Soul Hypothesis a viable option", then, is well-justified in thinking that the CALU is a function of the soul more than the body. Let me survey what each of the three principal contributors to the materialist synthesis has to say about this. More specifically, let us ask whether there is evidence that the CALU is embodied neurologically, that the relevant neural structures are coded for in the genome, and that the relevant genes were selected for through evolutionary mechanisms.

NEUROSCIENTIFIC EVIDENCE FROM APHASIAS

I begin with neuroscience, since that is the most concrete of these fields of study, and probably the best understood. There is no doubt that the CALU capacity is dependent on the brain in the trivial sense that a person without a functioning brain will not be able to display that capacity. This by itself may not be any more significant than the fact that a person without a tongue (and with paralyzed arms) will not be able to display the capacity. The more interesting and less obvious issue is whether there are particular neural circuits that serve this function, such that having those circuits intact is both necessary and sufficient for having the CALU capacity. Circuits of this sort have been found for many aspects of perception, motor control, and language. The question is whether there is evidence for a CALU circuit of this sort.

The oldest and perhaps the best branch of neuroscience is the study of aphasia — the effect of damage to the brain on language. This has a history that goes back centuries, with its modern phase beginning with Paul Broca's work in the 1860s.[13] During this extended history, clinicians have developed a relatively stable typology of 7–10 aphasic syndromes. The standard classification has its origins in a paper by Lichtheim published in 1885, which proposed a complete enumeration of all the aphasic syndromes. Geschwind revived Lichtheim's typology in the 1960s, and Benson and Geschwind's major textbook of neurology adopts Lichtheim's classification, adding only three additional syndromes, which are largely combinations of the original seven.[14] Benson and Geschwind show that all of the important classifications of aphasia since Lichtheim's differ from his only in terminology, not in substantive descriptions of syndromes or in how those syndromes relate to areas of the brain. It still forms the basis of the most popular clinical classification of aphasias in North America.[15] Some controversies exist, surely, but they concern the details; there is remarkably little disagreement on the general lay of the land, on what is — and what is not — affected by brain damage. The question, then, is whether any of the classical aphasic syndromes seems to be the result of a CALU circuit having been knocked out while other neural circuits that relate to language have been spared.

At first glance, the answer seems to be yes. The hallmark of CALU is language use that is simultaneously unbounded, stimulus-free, and appropriate. A syndrome known as Wernicke's aphasia seems to be characterized by language production that is unbounded and stimulus free, but lacks appropriateness. Here is a sample of speech from a

Wernicke's aphasic: "His wife saw the wonting to wofin to a house with the umblelor. Then he left the wonding then he too to the womin and to the umbella up stairs. His wife carry it upstairs. Then the house did not go faster thern and tell go in the without within pain where it is whire in the herce in stock."[16] The impression that we are witnessing a random string of words is pretty strong. This could be a population that really does say the equivalent of "Colorless green ideas sleep furiously" or any other grab bag of words that occurs to them, because their CALU has been destroyed by brain damage.

But this is not an accurate interpretation of Wernicke's aphasia. Wernicke's aphasics clearly suffer language disruptions that have nothing to do with the CALU per se. In particular, they have serious problems understanding words presented in isolation. Goodglass and Kaplan write about this syndrome that "The impairment of auditory comprehension is evident even at the one-word level. The patient may repeat the examiner's words uncomprehendingly, or with paraphrasic distortions. At severe levels, auditory comprehension may be zero . . ."[17] This deficit is thus not a problem with putting words together; it is a problem with the words themselves. More specifically, the associations between the sounds and meanings of words seem to be disrupted, so that the patient cannot reliably retrieve the right meaning when he hears a given sound, or find the right sound for a particular meaning that he has in mind. Wernicke's aphasia must be some such disruption of the vocabulary component of language, not (or not just) a disruption of the CALU component. Given that the vocabulary is affected in Wernicke's aphasia, scientific parsimony leads us to ask whether this deficit is enough to explain the characteristic speech production of these patients, or whether we must assume that the CALU is affected too. In fact, the vocabulary deficit is entirely sufficient. One can perfectly well imagine that Wernicke's aphasics have reasonable sentences in mind originally, but they often pick out the wrong word forms to convey the meanings that they intend. That problem by itself would be entirely sufficient to create the effect of random-seeming strings of words. In fact, a vague and wandering plotline can be discerned underneath Wernicke aphasic speech once one factors out the malapropisms, as in the sample above. This type of aphasia shows us that the vocabulary component of language is dependent on brain tissue (at least in part), but not that the CALU is. Similar remarks hold for the other so-called fluent aphasias, including the rather rare Transcordical Sensory Aphasia.

The second major category of aphasias includes Broca's aphasia. The problem with the speech of Broca's aphasiacs is not its appropriateness, but rather its boundedness. In severe cases, patients speak only one word at a time. Here is a sample conversation:

Interviewer	What did you do before you went to Vietnam?
Patient	Forces
Interviewer	You were in the army?
Patient	Special forces.
Interviewer	What did you do?
Patient	Boom!
Interviewer	I don't understand.
Patient	'splosions.
(More questions)	
Patient	Me . . . one guy
Interviewer	Were you alone when you were injured?
Patient	Recon . . . scout
Interviewer	What happened; why are you here?
Patient	Speech
Interviewer	What happened?
Patient	Mortar[18]

One might think of this as a loss of the CALU circuit, with the effect that patients no longer have the ability to string words together into sentences.

But again this is not the only language problem that typical Broca's aphasics have. They also have severe articulation problems and their speech is slow and effortful, even when they are saying only one word. There are also syntactic problems (agrammatism), in which inflectional suffixes on words are lost and only the most primitive grammatical constructions are used. "While he [the Broca's aphasic] may try to form complete sentences, he has usually lost the ability to evoke syntactic patterns, and even a sentence repetition task may prove impossible from the grammatical point of view."[19] The Broca's aphasic thus has problems with articulation and grammar that do not directly concern the CALU, since they affect even one-word utterances and repeated sentences. Parsimony again bids us ask whether these deficits are enough to explain the behavior without the CALU itself being affected. And again the answer is yes: if saying words is so effortful and details of grammar do not come easily, it is plausible to think that Broca's patients have complete sentences (or sentence-like thoughts) in mind, but these complete sentences get reduced down to one or two-word utterances because of the great difficulty in producing the sentence. In Levelt's terms, their conceptualizer could be intact, even though their formulator is damaged. This interpretation is also consistent with the fact that Broca's aphasics are said to be relatively good at understanding new sentences — an ability that also draws on the CALU. Broca's aphasia thus tells us that grammar can be affected by brain damage (as well as articulation), but there is still no evidence that the CALU is directly affected.

What would an aphasia that targeted the CALU directly be like? Patients with such an aphasia would be good at naming objects and recognizing words, showing that their vocabulary is intact. Their speech would be fluent and free from grammatical errors when they are repeating a sentence or reciting a known text like a song or the Lord's Prayer, showing that their grammar and articulation is intact. But the patients would fail to put together words spontaneously into phrases, and/or they would put them together in a seemingly random, purposeless fashion. All these individual symptoms exist, but this particular combination does not seem to cluster together as an identifiable syndrome. Perhaps then it is not true that brain damage can directly affect any mental function one can imagine; the CALU itself is not disrupted.[20]

In fact, this conclusion reflects a classical view in neurolinguistics. Back in 1885, Lichtheim proposed a model of the language faculty that featured three distinct "centers": the motor center (production), the auditory center (perception), and the conceptual center.[21] These centers were connected to each other by neural pathways, and the motor and auditory centers were also connected to the organs of speech and hearing, respectively. Lichtheim explained the range of aphasias observed by proposing that any center or pathway could be disrupted by brain injury — *with the striking exception of the concept center.* As already mentioned, the classification of aphasias that emerges from this view has stood the test of time very well. The anomaly that Lichtheim's system had one crucial component that was not prone to disruption by injury has been treated as a conceptual flaw by subsequent neurologists (such as Caplan) — but these neurologists have not discovered the missing syndrome or proposed a reconceptualization of the domain so that the gap does not appear. Lichtheim's "concept center" is that aspect of the language faculty that is the last step in comprehension, the first step in production, and is not involved in simple repetition. Thus it is plausibly the same as the faculty I have been calling the CALU. The upshot of 140 years of neurological research, then, is that there is no evidence that the CALU depends on dedicated brain tissue.

As an aside, it is worth noting that when I described what a CALU-destroying aphasia would be like, I did so purely in terms of which language-oriented functions would be disrupted and which language-oriented functions would be spared. I said nothing in the description about whether the patient would also show deficits in nonverbal behaviors or not. The possibility of framing the matter in this way is what gives us the luxury of not taking a stand on whether the CALU reduces to a more general capacity to act freely or not. If the CALU is a distinct module of the mind and it is realized in brain tissue, we might expect to find patients with the serious language deficit I described, but who otherwise have no appreciable difficulty in acting in "creative," purposeful, unscripted ways. In contrast, if the CALU is simply a central processor acting in one particular way, and it is realized in brain tissue, we might expect to find patients with the serious language deficit I described, and those same patients would have very serious problems acting purposefully in nonlinguistic modes as well. But in point of fact, we do not observe the sort of aphasia in question, so the issue is moot. We can conclude that the CALU seems not to be directly dependent on the brain in the way that many other interacting functions (like vocabulary and grammar) are, and that holds true regardless of what its relationship to other, nonlinguistic capacities might happen to be.

GENETIC EVIDENCE FROM LANGUAGE IMPAIRMENTS

Next let us turn from neuroscience to a second pillar of the materialistic synthesis, namely genetics. Is there evidence that the CALU is coded for in the human genome? Is there a CALU gene (or a set of CALU genes) lurking somewhere in the human DNA? If so, then one might expect to find developmental disorders traceable to genetic abnormalities that affect the CALU in a differential way. The classification of so-called "Specific Language Impairments" (SLI) does not have as long and stable a history as the classification of aphasias has, but it has been the subject of intensive research in the last thirty years or so. Standard classifications come from Bishop[22] and Rapin and Allen.[23] Bishop tentatively identifies four types of SLI: typical SLI, severe receptive language disorder, developmental verbal dyspraxia, and pragmatic language impairment. The first three are clearly irrelevant to the CALU: typical SLI affects the grammar component; severe receptive language disorder is a problem with auditory processing; developmental verbal dyspraxia is a problem with articulation or perhaps with the more abstract representation of sounds. Children with SLIs of the first and third types are capable of speech that is unbounded, stimulus-free and appropriate — it is just grammatically flawed or phonologically deviant.

The one type of SLI that might bear on the CALU is Bishop's Pragmatic Language Impairment (called Semantic-Pragmatic Disorder by Rapin and Allen). This is described as follows: "The child with early language delay goes on to make rapid progress in mastering phonology and grammar and starts to speak in long and complex sentences, but uses utterances inappropriately. Such children may offer tangential answers to questions, lack coherence in conversation or narrative speech, and appear overliteral in their comprehension."[24] Rapin and Allen say that despite these children having what seems at first glance to be "good language," "there is a severe impairment in the ability to encode meaning relevant to the conversational situation, and a striking inability to engage in communicative discourse."[25] This sounds like a CALU deficit: their speech is unbounded, stimulus free, but not appropriate.

We must, however, be alert to what the word "appropriate" means in the descriptions of this kind of SLI. In describing the CALU, Chomsky and Descartes use the term "appropriate" in tacit opposition to "random": it is the characteristic of speech that responds to a situation in a way that is neither deterministic nor merely probabilistic. Repeating Descartes's words, it is the ability to speak "so as appositely to reply to what is said in [our] presence" and to "construct a declaration by which to make [our] thoughts understood." Children with Pragmatic Language Impairment are capable of speech that is appropriate in this specific sense. What Bishop, Rapin, and Allen seem to be describing is more along the lines of speech that is on its own wavelength. It is purposeful, but the purposes do not mesh perfectly with those of their conversational partners. Rapin and Allen's example is instructive: "For example, the question 'where do you go to school?' was answered by one of our children with 'Tommy goes to my school because I see him in the hall everyday, but we have different teachers, and I like arithmetic but Tommy likes reading.'"[26]

The child's response is inappropriate in that he did not answer the question. But it is a perfectly coherent and meaningful response to the situation when taken in its own terms. The child gives every appearance of successfully making his thoughts known. He may be lacking some social sensitivity, but he is not missing his CALU as Descartes and Chomsky defined it. Overall, then, there may be evidence in the literature on developmental disorders for a "grammar gene," defects in which produce Typical SLI, but there is little or no comparable evidence for a "CALU gene."

EVOLUTIONARY EVIDENCE: THE LANGUAGE OF APES

Finally, I turn to a third pillar of the materialist synthesis, evolutionary theory. What are the prospects for explaining the origin of the CALU in humans in evolutionary terms? Since we do not know how the CALU is embodied in neural hardware (if at all), nor how it is specified in the genetic code (if at all), the chances of constructing a detailed evolutionary account are slim to none. Of course it is easy to tell stories about why it is advantageous to survival and reproduction to have the capacity to freely express thought in a way that is appropriate to but not determined by situations, so the evolutionary paradigm can be applied to the CALU to that extent. But I take discussions that function exclusively at the level of "X is good, so X evolved" to be of limited interest — indeed, almost tautological. But despite these foundational concerns, it is interesting to consider briefly in this context the ever-contentious question of whether any nonhuman animal is capable of human-like language when raised in the right environment.

The answer naturally depends very much on what one means by "language," a vague word that has a range of different meanings. The question can be broken down into three more specific subquestions by focusing on the idea that the human language capacity consists of (at least) three components: vocabulary, grammar, and the CALU. Can our ape cousins acquire a vocabulary? The answer is apparently yes: apes raised by humans have been able to master a few hundred arbitrary signs, which function as their "words." Can apes acquire a grammar? Maybe. This has been taken to be the crucial question in much of the literature, both pro and con. Savage-Rumbaugh and her colleagues have argued that the bonobo chimpanzee Kanzi can understand grammatically complex sentences in English, and shows some very simple syntactic regularities in his own productions, including systematic ordering of verbs before direct objects (a grammatical principle that is characteristic also of English).[27] These claims are highly controversial, and can be interpreted in various ways.

But the crucial question for our purposes here is whether apes can manifest the CALU capacity. Here the answer clearly seems to be no. Even Kanzi, the most proficient of the apes, usually uses only one word at a time. Savage-Rumbaugh reports that only about 10 per cent of Kanzi's utterances consisted of more than one sign, and it was very rare for him to use more than two or three signs in one utterance. His behavior thus falls short of the CALU because it lacks the property of unboundedness.

Savage-Rumbaugh goes to some pains to explain that the shortness of Kanzi's linguistic utterances is not his fault. His vocal tract is not configured to speak longer sentences. His hands do not have fine enough control to sign longer sentences, because they have been toughened by being used in walking. His best method of communication is pointing to symbols printed on a chart. But this modality has an inherent limitation: once his vocabulary gets large enough to say an interesting range of things, it takes too long to find the sign he wants within the unwieldy array of symbols to demonstrate any kind of fluency. So a combination of practical factors has the joint effect of making it nearly impossible for an ape to produce unbounded speech in real time, according to Savage-Rumbaugh. This sounds suspiciously like a conspiracy to me. A simpler and more unified explanation consistent with the facts is that the apes lack the CALU processor that is present in the human mind, and this despite their ability to act with creativity and purpose in other respects (see above). Descartes was apparently correct that nothing like the CALU is attested in the animal kingdom apart from human kind.[28] Thus, there is no comparative evidence that the CALU developed by the gradual improvement or change in function of a preexisting capacity through natural selection.

PUTTING THE PIECES TOGETHER

Summing up the argument so far, I have reviewed Chomsky's claim that human language consists of at least three components: a vocabulary, a grammar, and "the Creative Aspect of Language Use" (Levelt's "conceptualizer"). There is reasonably good evidence that the physical brain is significantly involved in the vocabulary and the grammar. For example, people's grammar is differentially affected in a well-established neurological syndrome (Broca's aphasia), in a particular genetic disorder (Typical Specific Language Impairment), and has been mimicked (it is claimed) by at least one ape. But there is no comparable evidence that the CALU capacity to use vocabulary and grammar to create and understand an unlimited number of new and appropriate sentences is biological in nature. More specifically, there is no evidence from aphasia that it is neurologically embodied, no evidence from developmental disorders that it is genetically encoded, and no evidence that it evolved from something that we have in common with closely related primates. Seen with an openness to the Soul Hypothesis, it seems appropriate, then, to think that grammar and vocabulary depend at least in part on the body, but the CALU depends primarily upon another ingredient of human nature, the soul. The research questions that emerge out of entertaining the Soul Hypothesis turn out to be pursuable, and lead to some interesting and nontrivial results.

This conclusion might seem astonishing to some, depending on their ontological beliefs. And our ignorance is certainly great enough that it is possible to hide in it. One can say, for example, that the CALU is not a single mental capacity, performed in one particular part of the brain, but rather some large and complex capacity that is spread over many parts of the brain, emerging out of the interaction of those parts. That might explain why it does not seem to be disrupted by localized brain injuries, and why no one genetic defect prevents it from developing in a child. That was roughly Lichtheim's own view with regard to his "concept center," and most modern cognitive scientists seem to believe something similar when pressed. More generally, one can freely admit that we do not now understand the basis of the CALU in biological terms, while still hoping that one day we will, as the relevant sciences progress. There is thus no conclusive proof that we have souls distinct from brains to be found in this material. But this is very different from saying that we now know beyond a reasonable doubt that the brain is everything there is, as people like Pinker are fond of doing. The Soul Hypothesis raises the possibility that some mental capacities depend more on identifiable brain structures and functions and others less, and that view fits the known facts as well as or better than alternative hypotheses do.

LANGUAGE AND THE DEFINITION OF COMPUTATION

Should we be surprised that the CALU seems to be only tenuously connected to the biological sciences? Perhaps not. At its root, cognitive psychology is built on the idea that brains perform computations, much as computers do (although perhaps with a rather different computational architecture). Furthermore, we know that brains are extremely complex. Therefore, it stands to reason that brains could in principle perform virtually any computation we can imagine, no matter how complex. So surely there must be room for the CALU within the standard biological framework, even if we can't yet work out all the details, one might think.

But this false certainty loses its grip when we realize that uttering (or understanding) a novel sentence that is appropriate to the situation but not determined by it is *not* a computational process. Powerful and general as the notion of computation is, it has certain limitations built into it from its origins. There is a very precise mathematical definition of what computation is, due to Alan Turing, and Jerry Fodor points out the significance of this definition for cognitive science.[29] Fodor presses the point that the computational theory of mind has no account for *abductive* reasoning — forms of thought that involve inference to the best overall explanation, when there is no way of knowing in advance what facts are relevant. The transformations that a computer can do on an input — what we call "information processing" — must depend only on the formal, syntactic properties of that input, not on what it means. By definition, the computations of the most sophisticated computers transform strings of 1s and 0s into new strings of 1s and 0s in systematic ways, without any knowledge of what those 1s and 0s refer to. As a result, well-programmed computers are wonderful at deductive logic, telling us what conclusions follow because of the *form* of the premises. But they cannot reason abductively, telling us what conclusions follow because of the *meaning* of the premises.[30] The theory of computation thus gives us an excellent account of one aspect of rationality in terms of nonrational, mechanical processes. But it cannot give us an account of another aspect of rationality, almost by definition. Fodor thus identifies the question of how abductive thought is possible as the great mystery that hovers over contemporary cognitive science.

Fodor's point is relevant here, because the CALU is a blatantly abductive part of the human mind — perhaps our most clearly abductive capacity of all. This follows from the characterization of CALU as the capacity for behavior that is unbounded, stimulus-free, and appropriate. A Turing machine cannot, by definition, have such behavior. Each step in the computations it performs is determined by the syntax of the input it receives. The whole notion of what is "appropriate" is an abductive one. We judge that what someone says to us is appropriate not at all on the basis of the grammatical structure of what is said, but entirely on the meaning of what is said. So constructing and interpreting novel sentences that are appropriate is an intrinsically abductive process. Therefore, it is not a computational process. We thus have no assurance that the brain as a biological organ can perform it simply from the acknowledged facts that the brain is very complex and it can perform computations. There is thus an important convergence here between very general considerations about abduction as opposed to computation and empirical results from aphasia, dyslexia, and animal learning. Computation is important, but it is not everything when it comes to understanding rationality. Once we acknowledge that, we should be more open to a form of dualism — the idea that bodies are important, but not necessarily everything when it comes to understanding human persons.

ANOTHER PARADIGM FOR UNDERSTANDING THE CALU?

Finally, we can ask whether the CALU aspect of the human language ability fits any more naturally with the traditional notion of the soul than it does with the notion of computation. I think it does. There is of course no rigorous mathematical definition of the soul that we can appeal to which would be comparable to Turing's definition of computation. But the soul has, throughout the Western tradition, been seen as the seat of human rationality and free will (on the latter, see Chapter 4). And what is the CALU? It is the ability to speak in ways that are neither determined by circumstances nor random, but purposeful. In other words, it is a manifestation of our free will, within the domain of our mouths. The CALU is also the ability to speak in ways that are appropriate to situations, and to interpret others when they do. It is thus a manifestation of our rationality within the domain of our mouths and ears. Suppose then that a dualist theorist who accepts the Soul Hypothesis is able to develop and defend a category of explanation, distinct from physical explanation, that centers around rationality and choice. It should be no great surprise that the CALU would fall under this category of explanation, and not under the physical and computational one. It is thus reasonable to think that the CALU will fall out as the interaction between soul theory and the theory of language.

Baker's essay is, in part, a special form of an argument from free will. The "Creative Aspect of Language Use" or CALU capacity that he makes much of is roughly the human capacity to act freely and purposefully as it is manifested in language — specifically in the construction of sentences out of individual words. But our speech is only one particularly common and characteristic way in which human beings seem to exercise free will. Human beings also act freely and purposefully in many other ways: they stretch, they salute one another, they type, they go to the grocery store or the theater, and so on. In the next essay, philosopher Stewart Goetz takes up the general issue of free will and acting for a purpose, exploring its fundamental incompatibility with the materialist view.

Taliaferro's essay considered the deep conflict between our sense that we have perceptual experiences and the materialist-scientistic claim that there is no room for such things within the scientific image of the world. In a similar way, Goetz's essay faces the question of what needs to go, materialism or our sense that we act freely and purposefully. Engaging this topic from a general/philosophical perspective, he shows that the incredulity that many modern scientists and philosophers have had about nonphysical things (like souls) causing physical events (like bodily movements) to happen has not been developed in any noncircular way. When these researchers try to articulate more precisely their intuitions as to why a nonphysical thing cannot cause a change in a physical thing, Goetz finds that their statements simply amount to restating "It just couldn't." This begs the question at issue between materialism and the Soul Hypothesis, simply repeating the disbelief without substantially clarifying it or justifying it. At this level of discussion, the dualist can just as well respond "Yes, it can (obviously)." In philosophical parlance, Goetz identifies this as the metaphysical question concerning causal closure, since it concerns fundamental issues about what causation is and what can be involved in it.

Goetz also considers a more practically oriented version of the concern about whether souls can cause physical events to happen. Some writers have asserted that, irrespective of the absolute truth of the Soul Hypothesis, people must assume that dualism is false in order to proceed with doing science at all. The scientist must de facto assume that the phenomenon that he or she is studying — say, the firing of certain neurons in the motor cortex of the brain — has only physical causes in terms of the laws of chemistry if he or she is to make any progress in studying it as a scientist. This is the so-called methodological question concerning causal closure. Goetz shows that this assumption is justified in the context of science, as long as one recognizes science as being a rather specific enterprise, which only asks certain kinds of questions, and which is only a part of the broader range of activities which any human being would engage in (even a scientist). Scientists might indeed assume that on certain occasions a given type of event has only physical causes if what they want to study is either those physical causes or what a certain broad class of events taken as a whole has in common. But this need not deny that instances of the same type of event could have a nonphysical cause on other occasions, perhaps under different conditions. In this respect, Goetz's essay reinforces a theme also present in Robinson's, which is the inherent limitation of science (in the narrower senses) for understanding the whole picture of human life and activity.

Along the way, Goetz's essay also points out very gently another problem for the view that scientists must be de facto materialists in order to function. This is shown to be false simply by the fact that many great scientists have in fact been dualists. This is true not only of the founders of modern science in the sixteenth and seventeenth centuries, but even of some of the most famous, ground-breaking figures in brain sciences in the twentieth century, including Wilder Penfield and Sir John Eccles. It is hard to sustain the claim that entertaining the Soul Hypothesis is antithetical to doing scientific research when it is in fact possible to win a Nobel Prize in medical science while being a dualist. Indeed, in his book The Mystery of the Mind, Penfield presents his dualistic views as the result of a lifetime spent studying the brain and theorizing about it, not as an assumption that he brought to his scientific program or something that was independent of his research, coming from his cultural or religious background rather than his science. He recounts one experiment in particular that impressed upon him the inadequacy of materialism. By applying an electrode to the motor cortex of a patient's brain he could produce responses such as hand movements and vocalizations for which the patient denied any responsibility. The patient would say "You did that, not me." But Penfield reports that there was no place in the brain where electric stimulation would produce in a patient a decision or choice. With his electrode he could make a patient move his arm, but he could not make a patient decide to move his arm. This led Penfield to conclude that the self that actually makes choices is something distinct from the brain that he probed — a dualistic view born of rational inference from scientific investigation.

Toward the end of his essay, Goetz tries to sharpen the question of what (else) a dualist neuroscientist should expect to observe in the brain if the soul can cause events in the brain. Brains are very complex and only a tiny sampling of brain events has been observed directly (mostly in specialized circumstances). Moreover, there are undoubtedly random events that occur in brains. How then can we be so sure that some of those neuron firings that appear to be "random" (so not caused in a determin- istic sense) within the physical description of the brain are not actually purposeful and caused by the soul? (See also the discussion of this in the Introduction. In Chapter 5, Robin Collins will also develop this idea from the perspective of the fundamental physics.)

CHAPTER 4

Making Things Happen: Souls in Action

Stewart Goetz

THE COMMON-SENSE VIEW OF OURSELVES AS AGENTS

In a recent *New York Times* article entitled "Freedom Does More than Improve a Swing," Selena Roberts reports that Sean O'Hair, a young, twenty-three-year-old professional golfer, *chose* to free himself from domination and control by his father.[1] Roberts says that Sean's father admitted to slapping his son's face when he was too old to spank, and writes that Sean had "the power to choose," and "courageously chose to start anew. . . . Sean made the choice to accept Jackie's [his future wife's] invitation to play golf after they met on a course one day. He made the choice to let her into his life. He made the choice to shut his father out."[2]

In terms of common sense, it is indisputable that human beings make choices. It is just as indisputable that common sense includes the dualist view that human beings are combinations of souls and bodies. As William Lyons has written, the view "that humans are bodies inhabited and governed in some intimate if mysterious way by minds (souls), seemed and still seems to be nothing more than good common sense."[3] In her extremely successful Harry Potter books, J. K. Rowling makes effective use of the common-sense view of human beings by portraying the worst death a person can die as one where his soul is sucked out of his body by the kiss of a being called a dementor. And the contemporary non-dualist philosopher John Searle reports that "[w]hen I lectured on the mind-body problem in India [I] was assured by several members of my audience that my [materialist] views must be mistaken, because they personally had existed in their earlier lives as frogs or elephants, etc."[4]

In the eyes of some in the scientific and philosophical communities, however, science undermines our common-sense view of the world. As John Horgan has recently written, there is a "widespread belief that science and common sense are incompatible. . . . The result is that [w]hen I invoke common sense to defend or — more often — criticize a theory, scientists invariably roll their eyes."[5] Hence, it will come as no surprise to a person like Horgan that some scientists believe that we don't *really* make undetermined choices (have free will). According to them, while it *seems* to us that we make such choices, appearances must be and are *illusory*. For example, while Francis Crick, the co-discoverer of the molecular structure of DNA, acknowledges that we have an "undeniable feeling that our Will is free," he also embraces the view "that our Will only appears to be free."[6] In whatever sense it is true to say that we "choose," Crick believes that a "choice" must be completely determined to occur. The philosopher Daniel Dennett agrees with Crick. According to Dennett, any kind of freedom that we have must be a kind of freedom that is compatible with the truth of determinism.[7] The believed incompatibility of science and common sense extends to the existence of the soul. The philosopher Owen Flanagan claims that the soul simply has no place in what he calls the "scientific image of persons":

> There is no consensus yet about the details of the scientific image of persons. But there is broad agreement about how we must construct this detailed picture. First, we will need to demythologize persons by rooting out certain unfounded ideas from the perennial philosophy. Letting go of the belief in souls is a minimal requirement. In fact, desouling is the primary operation of the scientific image.[8]

In the next section of this chapter, I set forth and critique one of the most widely rehearsed arguments against dualist causal interactionism, which is the idea that souls exist and make undetermined choices that causally influence events in their physical bodies. Before turning to this task, however, it behooves us to have a reasonably clear and concise sketch of how souls are assumed by many to be causally related to their physical bodies on occasions when those souls make what I will assume are essentially undetermined choices (from here on, I will simply assume that choices are essentially undetermined). This picture is as follows: on certain occasions, we have reasons for performing incompatible actions. Because we cannot perform both actions, we must make a choice to do one or the other (or neither), and whichever choice we make, we make that choice for a reason or purpose, where that reason provides an ultimate and irreducible teleological explanation of that choice.

The making of a choice is a mental event that occurs in a soul and either it, or some other mental event associated with it (e.g. an intention to act) directly causally produces an effect event in that soul's physical body. In other words, there is mental-to-physical causation and its occurrence is ultimately and irreducibly explained teleologically by the reason that explains the making of the choice.

To put some flesh on the proverbial bones, consider the movements of my fingers right now on the keys of my keyboard as I work on this essay. If these movements occur because of a choice of mine to type, then these physical movements are ultimately and irreducibly explained teleologically in terms of the purpose for making my choice to write this essay, which, we can suppose, is that I make clear that there are no good scientific objections to the view that human beings are soul-body compounds and that those souls have free will (make choices). Hence, if the movements of my fingers are ultimately occurring because I made a choice to write this essay for a purpose, then a mental event involving me (a soul) must be *causing* those movements to occur as I write this essay for the purpose that I make clear that there are no good objections to the view that human beings have souls that make choices. In other words, if our common-sense view of a human being is correct, I, as a soul, cause events to occur in the physical world by making a choice to write this essay for a purpose.

From the example of my typing, it should be clear that the claim that there is causal interaction between a soul and its physical body is *not* a "God-of-the-gaps" type of argument. In discussions about God's existence, critics often argue that theists postulate God's existence in light of an inability of science to provide a complete explanation for a physical datum (or data). This lack of a complete explanation is a gap in the scientific story. By analogy, a critic might argue that I am postulating my soul's existence in light of an inability of science to provide a complete explanation for the movements of my fingers when I type this essay. But this argument would be mistaken. My claim is *not* that there are certain physical events (the movements of my fingers) for which a failure to find a complete physical causal story warrants appeal to the causal activity of a soul as their ultimate explanation. Rather, the claim is that our common-sense understanding of our purposeful activity entails that some physical events must occur whose ultimate causal explanation is not other physical events but non-physical mental events whose occurrences are explained teleologically by purposes.

THE CHALLENGE OF CAUSAL CLOSURE

What is wrong with this common-sense understanding of a human being?[9] According to many philosophers, a serious problem for the view that souls make choices that causally produce events in physical bodies arises out of the practice of science. Richard Taylor puts forth a lengthy argument, the gist of which is as follows.

> Consider some clear and simple case of what would . . . constitute the action of the mind upon the body. Suppose, for example, that I am dwelling in my thought upon high and precarious places, all the while knowing that I am really safely ensconced in my armchair. I imagine, perhaps, that I am picking my way along a precipice and visualize the destruction that awaits me far below in case I make the smallest slip. Soon, simply as the result of these thoughts and images, . . . perspiration appears on the palms of my hands. Now here is surely a case, if there is any, of something purely mental . . . and outside the realm of physical nature bringing about observable physical changes. . . . Here . . . one wants to say, the mind acts upon the body, producing perspiration.
>
> But what actually happens, alas, is not nearly so simple as this. To say that thoughts in the mind produce sweat on the hands is to simplify the situation so grossly as hardly to approximate any truth at all of what actually happens. . . . The perspiration . . . is secreted by tiny, complex glands in the skin. They are caused to secrete this substance, not by any mind acting on them, but by the contraction of little unstriated muscles. These tiny muscles are composed of numerous minute cells, wherein occur chemical reactions of the most baffling complexity. . . . These . . . connect eventually, and in the most dreadfully complicated way, with the hypothalamus, a delicate part of the brain that is centrally involved in the emotional reactions of the organism . . . [B]ut it is not seriously considered by those who do know something about it that mental events must be included in the description of its operations. The hypothalamus, in turn, is closely connected with the cortex and subcortical areas of the brain, so that physical and chemical changes within these areas produce corresponding physical effects within the hypothalamus, which in turn, by a series of physical processes whose complexity has only barely been suggested, produces such remote effects as the secretion of perspiration on the surface of the hands.
>
> Such, in the barest outline, is something of the chemistry and physics of emotional perspiration. . . . The important point, however, is that in describing it as best we can, there is no need, at any stage, to introduce mental or nonphysical substances or reactions.[10]

According to Taylor, while we are inclined to believe that certain physical events in our bodies are ultimately explained by mental events of non-physical substances, as a matter of fact there is no need at any point to step outside of the physical causal story to explain the occurrences of those physical events. Jaegwon Kim uses an example of a neuroscientist to make the same point:

> You want [or choose] to raise your arm, and your arm goes up. Presumably, nerve impulses reaching appropriate muscles in your arm made those muscles contract, and that's how the arm went up. And these nerve signals presumably originated in the activation of certain neurons in your brain. What caused those neurons to fire? We now have a quite detailed understanding of the process that leads to the firing of a neuron, in terms of complex electrochemical processes involving ions in the fluid inside and outside a neuron, differences in voltage across cell membranes, and so forth. All in all we seem to have a pretty good picture of the processes at this microlevel on the basis of the known laws of physics, chemistry, and biology. If the immaterial mind is going to cause a neuron to emit a signal (or prevent it from doing so), it must somehow intervene in these electrochemical processes. But how could that happen? At the very interface between the mental and the physical where direct and unmediated mind-body interaction takes place, the nonphysical mind must somehow influence the state of some molecules, perhaps by electrically charging them or nudging them this way or that way. Is this really conceivable? Surely the working neuroscientist does not believe that to have a complete understanding of these complex processes she needs to include in her account the workings of immaterial souls and how they influence the molecular processes involved.... Even if the idea of a soul's influencing the motion of a molecule ... were coherent, the postulation of such a causal agent would seem neither necessary nor helpful in understanding why and how our limbs move. ... Most physicalists ... accept the causal closure of the physical not only as a fundamental metaphysical doctrine but as an indispensable methodological presupposition of the physical sciences. ... If the causal closure of the physical domain is to be respected, it seems prima facie that mental causation must be ruled out ...[11]

While Kim agrees with Taylor about the lack of a need on the part of a scientist to go outside the physical explanatory story, he introduces the stronger idea that to be successful the physical sciences need to make the methodological assumption of the causal closure of the physical world. Is he right about this? To insure clarity about what is at issue, consider one more example of movements of my body that according to common sense could only be adequately explained by mental causation of a soul whose choice is teleologically explained by a purpose or reason. Right now, I am tired and feel tight in my back after typing for several minutes, so I raise my arms in order to relax. Reference to my mental activity and my purposes for acting seems not only helpful but also necessary to explain both the movements of my fingers on the typewriter while I am typing and the subsequent motions of my arms when I relax. If we assume for the sake of discussion that I, as a soul, cause my fingers and arms to move by directly causing some neural events in the motor section of my brain, then when I move my fingers and raise my arms for purposes, I must directly cause initial neural events in my brain that ultimately lead to the movements of those extremities. In other words, in order to explain adequately (teleologically) the movements of my limbs, there must be causal openness or a causal gap in my brain. While Kim believes that the common-sense view implies this causal openness, he also believes that it is because the common-sense view implies the existence of this causal gap that it must be mistaken. Because the neuro-scientist methodologically assumes causal closure of the physical world, what he discovers as the explanation for what occurs in my brain and limbs when I type and relax must not and need not include reference to the mental causal activity of my soul and the ultimate and irreduc-ible explanatory purpose for its choice to act. Given that the principle of causal closure entails the exclusion of a soul's mental causation of a physical event and the ultimate and irreducible teleological explanation of that mental event and its effects by a purpose, it is imperative that we examine the argument from causal closure to see if it provides a good reason to believe that the movements of my fingers and arms when I am typing and stretching must be *completely* explicable in terms of neurosci-ence (or any other physical science), with the result that no reference to the causal activity of my soul and its purposes for typing and raising my arms is required.

PRESERVING CAUSAL OPENNESS

Contrary to what Kim maintains, there is good reason to think that the argument from causal closure is unsound.[12] To understand where it goes wrong, let us distinguish between a neuroscientist as an *ordinary human being* and a neuroscientist as a *physical scientist*. Surely a neuroscientist as an ordinary human being who is trying to understand how and why my fingers move and arms go up while I am typing must and would refer to me and my reasons (purposes) for acting in a complete account of why my limbs move.[13] Must he, however, as a physical scientist, avoid making such a reference? Kim claims that he must avoid such a reference because as a physical scientist he must make a methodological assumption about the causal closure of the physical world. Is Kim right about this and, if he is, is such a commitment compatible with a commitment on the part of a physical scientist as an ordinary human being to causal openness? Or must a neuroscientist, who as a physical scientist assumes causal closure, also assume, if he is consistent, that as an ordinary human being his mention of choices and their teleological explanations is no more than an explanatory heuristic device that is necessary because of an epistemic gap in his knowledge concerning the physical causes of human behavior?

In order to answer these questions, it is necessary to consider what it is about physical entities that a physical scientist such as a neuroscientist is often trying to discover in his experimental work. What is the purpose of a neuroscientist's inquiry? In the case of Kim's neuroscientist, what she is trying to discover as a physical scientist are the *capacities* of particles or micro-physical entities such as neurons to be causally affected by exercised causal *powers* of other physical entities, including other neurons. For example, in his pioneering work on the brain Wilder Penfield produced movements in the limbs of patients by stimulating their cortical motor areas with an electrode.[14] As Penfield observed the neural impulses that resulted from stimulation by the electrode, he had to assume *during his experiments* that the areas of the brains of his patients on whom he was doing his scientific work were causally closed to other causal influences. Without this methodological assumption, he could not conclude both that it was the electrode (as opposed, say, to something "behind the scene" such as an empirically undetectable human soul, either that of the patient or someone else, or God) that causally affected the capacities of the neurons to conduct electrical impulses, and that it was the causal impulses of those neurons that causally affected the same capacities of other neurons further down the causal chains to produce the movements of the limbs. There is no reason, however, to think that because Penfield's investigation of the brain required the methodological assumption of causal closure of the areas of the brains he was studying during his experiments that he also had to be committed as a physical scientist to the assumption that the physical world is *universally* (in *every* context) causally closed, where universal causal closure entails that the relevant brain (neural) events can *only* be causally produced by events of other physical entities and not instead by mental events of immaterial souls alone when they indeterministically choose and intend (plan) to act for purposes. That is, there is no reason to think that because a neuroscientist like Penfield must assume causal closure of a delimited area of the brain in the context of his experimental work in order to discover how physical entities causally interact with each other that he must also be committed as a scientist to the universal explanatory exclusion of mental events of souls that on certain occasions cause the occurrence of events in the physical world. All that the neuroscientist as a physical scientist must assume is that during his experiments souls (either the patients themselves or others) are not causally producing the relevant events in the micro-physical entities in the areas of the brain that he is studying. If the neuroscientist makes the universal assumption that in *any* context events in micro-physical entities can only have other physical events as causes and can never be causally explained by mental events of souls and their purposes, then he does so not as a scientist but as a *naturalist*, where a naturalist is a person who believes that the occurrence of physical events can *only* be explained in terms of the occurrence of other physical events and without any reference to ultimate and irreducible purposes of souls.[15]

It is relevant to note in this context that Penfield himself was not a naturalist. Rather, he was a soul-body dualist.[16] One can surmise, then, that were Penfield to have been presented with the argument from causal closure, he would have found it wanting. And for good reason. In seeking to understand how events of different physical entities affect the capacities of micro-entities such as neurons, a neuroscientist such as Penfield is seeking to learn about properties of physical entities that are essentially *conditional* or *iffy* in nature. A property that is conditional in nature is a property that is specified in terms such as "If such-and-such is done to object O (e.g. a cause C is exerted on O), then so-and-so will occur to O (e.g. O will move at rate R)." As the Nobel physicist Richard Feynman says, scientific questions are "questions that you can put this way: 'if I do this, what will happen?' . . . And so the question 'If I do it what will happen?' is a typically scientific question."[17] The following description by David Chalmers of basic particles that are studied by physicists nicely captures their iffy nature.

> Basic particles . . . are largely characterized in terms of their propensity to interact with other particles. Their mass and charge is specified, to be sure, but all that a specification of mass ultimately comes to is a propensity to be accelerated in certain ways [moved at certain rates] by forces, and so on. . . . Reference to the proton is fixed as the thing that causes interactions of a certain kind that combines in certain ways with other entities, and so on . . .[18]

What Chalmers describes as a "propensity" of a particle to be accelerated is a capacity of it to be moved which is such that *if* it is actualized (triggered) by an exercised causal power of another entity (whether physical or non-physical in nature), the particle will be necessitated to behave in a certain way. There is nothing, however, in the nature of the propensity or capacity of that particle that entails that it can only be actualized by the exercised power of a physical entity. That is, there is nothing in the nature of that propensity or capacity that entails that it cannot be actualized by persons making undetermined choices for reasons. Hence, the actualization of a micro-particle's capacity to behave in a certain way by a person on an occasion when the latter makes a choice for a reason is not excluded by anything that is discovered in a scientific study of that capacity. And it is precisely on occasions like those noted by Kim, when finger and arm movements occur seemingly for purposes, that a neuroscientist will reasonably believe that the originative micro-physical movements are traceable to the causal activity of a soul that is choosing to act for a purpose. If a neuroscientist makes the presupposition that micro-physical entities can have their capacities actualized *only* by other physical entities and never by choices made by souls for purposes, then he does so as a naturalist and not as a scientist.

My response to the causal closure argument assumes Feynman's and Chalmers' iffy picture of micro-entities that, in addition to being iffy, is also deterministic in the sense that no effect will occur in any micro-entity unless some causal event determines or necessitates that effect to take place. Might there not, however, be random (non-deterministic) changes in the system of micro-entities as well as the deterministic ones? In other words, while sometimes a neuron fires because it gets deterministic causal input from the neurons with which it is connected, at other times it fires at random (without any deterministic cause), perhaps as a result of random quantum fluctuations in a chaotic system that are magnified at the neuronal level.

If we assume for the sake of discussion that neurons do sometimes fire randomly, is it possible to distinguish sharply between those firings that occur randomly and those that occur as the result of being causally determined by a mental event of a soul? After all, the two kinds of firings are alike to the extent that neither has a physically deterministic cause. I believe that it is possible to make this sharp distinction between the two kinds of firings. The way to make the distinction is in terms of contexts that are known, in the case of ourselves, through first-person experience and, in the case of others, through third-person observation. All one need do is ask how plausible it is to maintain that every time a person purposefully chooses to do something such as move his fingers to type, an initial neuron just happens to fire at random (as a result of quantum fluctuations, etc.) with the result that finger movements occur that perfectly mesh with or map onto those that are intended by that person. Because such repeated coincidences would literally be, dare I say, miraculous, the only plausible view is that the neuron must not be firing randomly but because of the causal input from a soul choosing to act for a purpose.

The discussion to this point makes clear that it is thoroughly reasonable to believe that there can be *gaps* (causal openness) in the course of events in the physical world such that there is room for the explanation of some physical events in terms of a soul's causal activity that is ultimately explained teleologically by a purpose. To further clarify the relevance of what I have called the "iffy" nature of a capacity's actualization, consider the following argument for the nonexistence of explanatory gaps (causal closure) developed by the philosopher Ted Honderich.[19] Honderich designates the mental event of a woman, Juliet, seeing her boyfriend, Toby, who is approaching her, $M3$. $M4$, which occurs a moment later, is the mental event of Juliet choosing to tell Toby that they should have a child. $N3$ is the neural event correlated with $M3$, and $N4$ is the neural event correlated with $M4$. What, asks Honderich, is the relationship between $M3$ and $N3$ and $M4$ and $N4$? In order for Juliet to have free will, $N4$ cannot be the unavoidable (determined) effect of $N3$ or anything else because its unavoidability will make its correlate $M4$ equally unavoidable. According to Honderich, however, it is nothing less than unreasonable to think that $N4$ can be anything other than unavoidable in relationship to $N3$ and the physical story that precedes $N3$. To see why it is supposedly unreasonable to think anything other than this, let $N5$ and subsequent neural events be those that lead to the movements of Juliet's lips when she tells Toby that they should have a child. Is there or is there not an unavoidable connection between $N4$ and what causally results from it, namely, $N5$ and the neural and other physical events that follow $N5$ and yield the movements of Juliet's lips?

> If there is not a very high probability that items like $N4$ will be followed by other neural events, then actions we fully and absolutely intend will on too many occasions mysteriously not happen. So the links *after* $N4$ have to be pretty tight. But then in consistency so do the neural links *before* $N4$. That is unfortunate, since the theory [of libertarian free will] needs these earlier links to be pretty

loose in order for Juliet to be held really responsible for what is tied to [correlated with] N4, her [choice] to speak up [to Toby].

Can this problem of inconsistency really be dealt with?[20]

Honderich believes that the answer to this question is "No." The correct response, however, is that there is no problem of inconsistency, and this is the case because of the iffy nature of a capacity's actualization, which in this instance is the actualization of the capacity of a neuron to fire. Honderich's own treatment of the concept of causation supports the nonexistence of the alleged inconsistency and the possible existence of explanatory gaps in the physical story. In the course of discussing the nature of causation, he asks the reader to consider the lighting of a match here and now. I quote Honderich at some length:

> When we assume that this event was the effect of the match's being struck, what are we assuming? One good reply is likely to be that it was an event that wouldn't have happened if the match hadn't been struck. On the assumption that the striking was cause and the lighting effect, what is true is that *if the striking hadn't happened, neither would the lighting.* . . . We are inclined to think . . . that something else isn't true of an ordinary striking and lighting. We are reluctant to say that *if or since the match was struck, it lit.* The explanation of our reluctance is that even if the match was struck, had it been wet, it wouldn't have lit. . . . [N]ot only the striking was required for the lighting, but also the match's being dry. That was not all that was required. There had to be oxygen present, and the surface on which the match was struck had to be of a certain kind. . . . An event which caused a certain effect is not necessarily such that all like events are followed by like effects. Not all strikings are followed by lightings. A causal circumstance for a certain effect, on the other hand, really is such that all like circumstances *are* followed by like effects. . . . [G]iven a causal circumstance, whatever else had been the case [e.g. the match's color had been different], the effect would still have occurred. A necessitated event just is one for which there was a circumstance which was such that since it occurred, whatever else had been true, the event would still have occurred.[21]

It is true, as Honderich claims, that *given* a causal circumstance, the effect — the actualization of a capacity — had to occur, and *since* the circumstance occurred, the effect was necessitated to occur. But did the circumstance — in the case of the match, the presence of oxygen, the dryness of the match, the match's being struck, etc. — have to occur? Was it unavoidable? There is no reason to think so, *unless one has presupposed the truth of determinism.* Honderich says that "the causal circumstance for an effect will typically be made up of parts which were also effects themselves. . . . This fact about effects — the fact of what you might call causal chains — is very important to determinism."[22] While for the sake of argument it can be conceded that causal circumstances for effects will typically be made up of parts that were also effects themselves, this fact about causal circumstances is not sufficient for the truth of determinism. This is because what is typical is not necessarily universal. In the case of the causal circumstance involving the match, do we think that it was unavoidable that the match be struck? Not in the least. For example, a person might strike a match in virtue of having *chosen* to have a fire in the fireplace for the purpose that he stay warm. He need not, however, have chosen to have the fire. He might have chosen to turn up the thermostat instead for the purpose that he stay warm.

What, then, about the causal circumstance that includes $N4$ and what follows from it ($N5$, subsequent neural events, and the movement of Juliet's lips)? Was that causal circumstance unavoidable? Did it have to occur? The answer to this question depends upon what one says about the relationship between $M4$ and $N4$. If one believes that $M4$ alone causes $N4$ (there is no physical cause of $N4$), then there is no reason to think that $N4$ had to occur, because there is no reason to think that $M4$ had to occur, unless one assumes the truth of determinism. Honderich (or Kim) might respond that it is reasonable to believe that there must be a neural event such as $N3$ that produces $N4$. Why, however, should one think that this is the case? After all, $N3$ could be the cause of Juliet's seeing Toby without also being the cause of $N4$. Moreover, one can concede that a neuroscientist such as Penfield might discover in his experimental work that actualizations (triggerings) of a neural capacity (e.g. individual neural events like $N4$) can be produced by stimulation with an electrode or by exercisings of neural causal powers of other neurons (e.g. individual neural events like $N3$). But why think that every actualization of a neural capacity can be produced only in these ways? Why could not an actualization of a neural capacity (e.g. $N4$) be caused by an exercising of a mental power of a soul (e.g. $M4$) alone that is made for a purpose? There is no reason to think this could not be the case, unless one begs the question at hand and assumes the truth of determinism and the causal closure of the physical world. Keith Campbell (in a discussion of what "being material" means) succinctly captures in ontological terms the main methodological point of this section when he states that "[a] material thing can, without ceasing to be a material thing, respond to forces other than physical ones. The brain, without ceasing to be material, can act under the influence of an immaterial mind."[23]

My response to the methodological argument for causal closure is premised upon acceptance of a conception of causation that Kim, Chalmers, and Honderich also assume, which is that causation is essentially a *productive* or *generative* relationship between a cause and its effect. Some have argued that this conception of causation is outdated on the ground that the fundamental laws of physics do not mention causality.[24] For example, laws of physics about properties such as mass, electrical charge, and motion are expressed in terms of mathematical relationships. In contrast, the mental properties of minds, what I have termed their mental powers and capacities, are not mathematically represented. Hence, because the fundamental concepts of physics include neither causal productivity nor nonquantifiable powers and their exercise, physics excludes or is closed to the explanatory relevance of minds and the purposes for which they act.

Like Kim, I am not a physicist, and therefore, like him, I am hesitant about engaging the present critic for fear that I might appear to be spouting off about matters beyond my intellectual purview. Nevertheless, I find Kim's own responses to this argument about the nature of causation from the perspective of contemporary physics persuasive, and I summarize two of his points in what immediately follows.[25]

First, Kim suggests that if there is no productive causation anywhere, then there is no mental causation or human agency of any kind.[26] This is not only unbelievable, but also seems self-refuting. After all, does not the proponent of the argument that causation is not a productive relation believe that he is trying to *produce* a belief in his listeners or readers that there is no productive causality?

Second, Kim points out that the fact that causality is not mentioned in the fundamental laws of physics, or that the word "cause" does not appear in the statements of these laws, does not show that the concept of productive causation is absent from physics. There are the mathematical laws and our *interpretation* or *understanding* of those laws.

> My impression is that disputes about the interpretation of quantum mechanics, for example, are replete with causal concepts and causal considerations; e.g. measurement (as in a measurement "having an outcome") . . . observation (as having a perturbational influence on the system observed [e.g. an exercise of the power of observation collapses a Schrödinger wave function]), interference, etc. . . . Entries on "force" in science dictionaries and encyclopedias typically begin like this: "In dynamics, the physical agent which causes a change of momentum" . . . A force causing a body to accelerate strikes me as an instance of productive causation par excellence.[27]

Now if we must acknowledge the productive nature of a causal relation in a science such as physics, then the fact that dualism requires that a causal relation between a soul and its physical body be a productive relation is unproblematic. Dualism just incorporates an understanding of causation that is already acknowledged in other domains.

This brief articulation of the idea that causation is essentially a productive relation also goes some way toward helping to answer the objection against dualism that soul-body causal interaction is unintelligible. For example, in addition to claiming that there is no need on the part of the physical scientist to go outside the physical explanatory story to explain any events in our physical bodies, Taylor says that "when we come to some precise instance of the alleged interaction of body and mind . . . we find that we are dealing with something that is not merely mysterious but wholly unintelligible."[28] But if causation is essentially a productive relation, then souls, like physical objects, are able to produce effects in physical objects, provided that they have the requisite causal power and exercise it to produce the relevant effects.

To be sure, there are additional concerns raised by the idea of soul-body causal interaction. For example, there is the question about the conservation of energy in a physical system. Does not causation by a soul of, say, a movement of one of its body's limbs, initially inject new energy into the motor portion of its brain and thereby violate the conservation of energy by increasing the amount of energy within the system of which that portion is a part?

Because Robin Collins addresses the issue of the conservation of energy at length in his contribution to this collection of essays, I will make only two brief comments to the objection against dualism from the conservation of energy.

First, it is important to understand that the objection assumes that no effect can be produced by a cause without the transference of energy from the cause to its effect. The idea of productivity, however, is not synonymous with the idea of transference of energy. Because this is the case, a cause might produce an effect without transferring any energy.[29]

Second, at best energy is claimed to be conserved only in a closed system and the point at issue is whether or not the brain (or some portion thereof) of a subject is a closed system. Given the common-sense picture of ourselves set forth and defended in this essay, there is reason to believe that our brains (or portions thereof) are not closed systems. To assume otherwise is simply to beg the question at issue.

As a way of bringing my response to the argument from causal closure to its own closure, it is helpful to consider what an observer would expect to see when looking at Juliet's brain when she chooses to tell Toby that they should have a child. Given the assumption that a soul, if it exists and makes choices for purposes, directly causally interacts with the brain of its physical body, it follows that there is at least one event at some level or point in Juliet's brain that does not have a deterministic or sufficient physical cause. Thus, if one were an ideal observer of the entirety of the relevant areas of Juliet's brain, one would expect to fail to discover a sufficient physical cause of some particular brain event of a certain type (for the sake of ease of discussion, I will continue to assume that this brain event is Honderich's N4) that leads to the movements of Juliet's lips and the production of the relevant words spoken to Toby.

Of course, none of us, including scientists, is an ideal observer. As a matter of fact, no one observes any events in the brains of most people and perhaps a handful of scientists (e.g. Penfield) observe a meager number of events in the brains of a few people. When a neuroscientist like Penfield conducts his experiments, he discovers that a particular physical event of a certain type can be causally produced by another physical event of a certain type. Thus, on an occasion when he observes a particular physical event and does not observe its cause, he knows on the basis of his experimental work that that particular event, because it is of a certain type, might have had a cause of a certain type. But he also knows that it is possible that it might have had a different type of cause, even a mental event of an immaterial soul. Perhaps among those particular physical events for which he fails to observe sufficient physical causes are events that are analogous to N4 in Juliet's brain and, therefore, they do not have sufficient physical causes. Perhaps this is not the case and all the observed particular events for which he fails to discover sufficient physical causes actually do have such causes. What must be the case, however, if souls exist that make choices and causally interact with their physical bodies, is that there are N4-like events in the brains of the bodies of those souls.

In light of the points made in the previous two paragraphs about the general ignorance of what goes on in people's brains, it is simply false to claim, as some do, that we have overwhelming scientific (empirical) evidence that every event in our brains (physical bodies) can be completely explained in terms of deterministic or sufficient physical causes. At most, what we have is the *metaphysical principle* that every event has an explanation, where this principle motivates and informs the experimental work of scientists like Penfield who discover that an instance of a certain type of physical cause produces (explains) an instance of a certain type of physical effect. But as I have already argued in response to the causal closure argument, such a discovery in no way supports the position that every instance of that kind of physical effect can only be produced by instances of that kind (or some other kind) of physical cause. To arrive at that position, one needs the support of an additional metaphysical principle like naturalism and its commitment to universal causal closure. Without naturalism and universal causal closure, it is perfectly reasonable to hold that a particular physical event has a causal explanation in the form of an exercising of a mental causal power that is ultimately and irreducibly made for a purpose.

Given that we have not discovered the sufficient physical causes of so many events in our brains, does this epistemic gap provide at least some empirical support for the existence of a causal gap in the physical world? Or in a similar vein, would repeated failures of neuroscientists to find sufficient physical causes of N4-like events provide strong empirical support for dualism and the freedom of the will? What is at issue here is something like the following. In answering the objection from causal closure, I assumed that the purpose (call it "Purpose 1") of a neuroscientist's inquiry is that he discover how the capacities of microphysical entities are causally affected by the exercised causal powers of other physical entities. Though this is one purpose that explains a neuroscientist's work, must it be the only one? For example, might not a non-naturalist neuroscientist on some occasions have as his purpose for inquiry (call it "Purpose 2") that he pinpoint where a causal gap is located in the physical causal story?

What would a neuroscientist whose work is explained by Purpose 2 be looking for? Perhaps something like the following: In light of Purpose 1 and the fact that he has learned through inquiry that effect events (e.g. N4-like events) involving a neural capacity can be determined to occur by causal events (e.g. N3-like events) involving a neural power, a nonnaturalist neuroscientist is seeking to discover if in *teleological contexts* (e.g. one in which Juliet chooses to tell Toby that they should have a child) N4-like events occur but are not causally determined by N3-like events (or any other physical/neural events that he has discovered produce N4-like events).

For the sake of discussion, let us assume that this non-naturalist neuroscientist observes N4-like events for which he sees no sufficient physical causes. Would this observation provide a naturalist with (strong) empirical support for dualism and the freedom of the will? Though one might be tempted to think that it does, there is reason to be skeptical. After all, naturalists like Kim and Honderich would likely maintain that the failure to find sufficient physical causes of N4-like events is no more than a gap in our knowledge of the physical world and provides no evidence for the existence of an ontological gap in that world. They would likely hold that the non-naturalist neuroscientist simply failed to be aware of the sufficient physical causes that were there. Some such response on their part would seem to be entailed by their naturalist commitment to the universal causal closure of the physical world.

At this juncture, one would like to know what a non-naturalist neuroscientist would conclude after an exhaustive search for and a failure to find any N4-like events that lack sufficient physical causes in the relevant contexts. Would the failure to locate a causal gap in the physical world provide a non-naturalist scientist with (strong) empirical evidence for the universal causal closure of the physical world and the explanatory causal impotence of souls that make choices for purposes? Not necessarily. Such a scientist might conclude that the requisite gap must be located elsewhere than with N4-like events. Or, if he has exhaustively looked at every plausible location for such a gap, he might conclude that he must have made an observational mistake at some point and saw determining causes when there were none. As Thomas Nagel has pointed out in discussing the puzzling results of experiments done on subjects whose brain hemispheres have been disconnected, it might very well turn out that we are unable to abandon our common-sense ideas about ourselves no matter what science discovers.[30]

Finally, what about the relevance of physical events to the causal status of mental events? To illustrate what is at issue here, consider an example of Penfield's work that concerns the causation of a choice itself as opposed to N4-like events, which are the effects of choices. When he did his experimentation on patients' brains, he was impressed by the fact that they were readily aware of the distinction between their doing something and something being done to them:

When I have caused a conscious patient to move his hand by applying an electrode to the motor cortex of one hemisphere, I have often asked him about it. Invariably his response was: "I didn't do that. You did." When I caused him to vocalize, he said: "I didn't make that sound. You pulled it out of me." When I caused the record of the stream of consciousness to run again and so presented to him the record of his past experience, he marveled that he should be conscious of the past as well as the present. . . . He assumed at once that, somehow, the surgeon was responsible for the phenomenon . . .[31]

Penfield goes on to say, "There is no place in the cerebral cortex where electrode stimulation will cause a patient . . . to decide [choose],"[32] where a deciding (choosing) is a doing of an agent.

Do Penfield's findings, particularly the latter about there not being a place in the cerebral cortex where stimulation with an electrode will causally produce a choice, empirically support the idea that choices are essentially causally undetermined events? One might be tempted to think so, but most likely a naturalist will respond that Penfield's failure to find the relevant stimulus area in the cerebral cortex did not warrant his conclusion that there is no such area. Perhaps future work will locate the relevant spot. Or, if Penfield is correct and there is no such area, then perhaps the causal determinants of choices are located at some physical level below the cerebral cortex. For example, consider what Dennett says in the following quote:

> Whatever else we are, we are information-processing systems, and all information-processing systems rely on amplifiers of a sort. Relatively small causes are made to yield relatively large effects. . . . Vast amounts of information arrive on the coattails of negligible amounts of energy, and then, thanks to amplification powers of systems of switches, the information begins to do some work . . . leading eventually to an action whose pedigree of efficient . . . causation is so hopelessly inscrutable as to be invisible. We see the dramatic effects leaving; we don't see the causes entering; we are tempted by the hypothesis that there are no causes.[33]

In short, Dennett and other naturalists will insist that we cannot reasonably conclude from our failure to discover physical causes of our choices that there are none. This is because the causes, if they are there, are beyond our ken and, therefore, our lack of awareness of them is to be expected and counts for nothing in support of their supposed absence. We should not be surprised, then, that neuroscientists have so far failed to locate the causal determinants of the choices that we make.

If the preceding pages present an accurate picture of the relationship between the empirical and the metaphysical, it is plausible to hold that people do not formulate their beliefs about the existence or non-existence of the soul and free will entirely, or even mainly, on the basis of empirical investigations. These beliefs are first and foremost non-empirical and metaphysical in nature and it is difficult to envision how the findings of science already obtained, or that we can reasonably expect to obtain, could decisively confirm or disconfirm any particular view.

CONCLUSION

I conclude that the causal closure argument fails. If it does, then one of the main reasons for thinking that souls do not exist and cannot make choices that causally influence events in the physical world is undermined. Of course, this conclusion does not establish that souls that make such choices do exist. The reasons one might have for thinking that such souls exist is a topic that is beyond the scope of this essay. As I suggested at the end of the last section, however, the considerations for (or against) the existence of the soul and its making essentially causally indeterministic choices are most likely not empirical (scientific) in nature. But this is a topic for another day.

By looking at the different kinds of causal events that could be happening inside brains and how basic scientific laws apply to them, Goetz has led us into a transition from the realms of psychology and brain science into the realm of fundamental physics. The next essay, by Robin Collins, completes this transition, focusing entirely on the physical issues. Whereas some have questioned whether souls and bodies can interact with one another for very general reasons that are best categorized as philosophical, others have seen a tension between the Soul Hypothesis and much more specific work-a-day principles of physics. At the head of this list is the principle of conservation of energy. Goetz mentions this specific concern in passing, but passes the baton to Collins, who has some special qualifications to take up the matter, having trained as a theoretical physicist at the graduate level for two years before turning to philosophy.

The principle of conservation of energy is familiar in some form to all students of high school physics. It is the idea that (apart from the relativistic destruction or creation of matter), the energy within a system cannot be created or destroyed, but only changes form. For example, when a rolling ball moves up an inclined plane, slowing down in the process, its kinetic energy is changed into potential energy. Then as it rolls back down, its potential energy changes back into kinetic energy again. Using the conservation of energy, it is possible to solve precise mathematical equations about exactly how high the ball will climb on the plane given how fast it was moving originally, or how fast the ball will be moving at the end given how high up it was when it started. The conservation of energy makes these calculations much easier: one simply equates the amount of energy that is lost in one form with how much is gained in another form. The picture becomes more complex when other forms of energy are taken into account, such as chemical energy or electromagnetic energy. But the overall conception can be generalized to take these other forms of energy into account, we were told.

Now the trouble that this poses for the Soul Hypothesis is supposed to be roughly the following. When a neuron fires and causes a muscle to contract in a voluntary movement, we know what kind of energy that is: it is (say) a form of chemical energy. This form of energy participates in the law of conservation of energy in familiar ways, which we can calculate. But then where did that energy come from? If it came from the soul, which dualists say willed the movement to happen, how can this be? If the soul has no physical energy, then it seems that the release of chemical energy came from nowhere, baldly violating the principle of conservation of energy. If the soul does have physical energy, then what is this energy, and how can it be measured and calculated? Moreover, if one claims that the soul has a calculable physical energy, then it has at least this property in common with normal physical objects. Maybe this means that the soul itself has physical properties of some kind, which seems to undermine the main idea of dualism (though see Collins's soul model in Chapter 9). Or maybe the energy seen in the neuron firing does not come from the soul itself, but from some other reservoir of physical energy stored up in the brain. Then there would be no problem of conservation of energy, but it would be mysterious just how the soul influences the event of the neuron firing. Wouldn't whatever energy is transformed into chemical energy as the neuron fires be a sufficient cause for the neuron firing, so that there is no need to bring a soul into the matter at all?

Whichever way one tries to answer these questions, many critics have claimed that it is at best difficult to reconcile the basic intuition of the Soul Hypothesis with the well-known principle of conservation of energy, and unlikely that one will succeed. And since basic physical facts are among the most certain things we know scientifically, it seems to be the Soul Hypothesis that needs to give way here. This is a version of the objection to dualism from the Principle of Energy Conservation that Collins's chapter takes up.

The essential point of Collins's contribution is to remind us that in fact physics has come a long way from what we were taught in high school over the course of the last century . . . and most of us have not kept up. The landscape has changed radically with the advent of relativity and quantum mechanics. While we were not looking, simple measurements of kinetic energy were replaced by sixteen component stress-energy tensors. High school textbooks notwithstanding, the conservation of energy really only existed as a universal principle of physics for a relatively short time, in the late nineteenth century. Even in its heyday, there were always certain problems and issues that surrounded it; it was a hypothesis and an organizing intuition, but not the confirmed fact that it has been taken to be. And this becomes much clearer when the advances of the twentieth century are taken into account, particularly Einstein's theory of gravity. It turns out that there simply is no coherent principle of conservation of energy when gravitational fields are in play. Collins's essay explains in some detail both why this is the case and why it is unlikely to change as research progresses further. The effort to generalize physics to other speeds, other frames of reference, and other sizes has simply proved to be incompatible with the tidy notion of the universality of conservation of energy, so that the energy of a system can no longer be defined in a suitable way for a wide class of physical systems. But if the energy of such systems cannot be defined, except under very special conditions, then we cannot meaningfully say that it is conserved. And if there is no universal principle of conservation of energy, then there can be no tension between dualism and physics on this point. For example, Collins reports that within general relativity, gravitational fields can affect how material particles behave without having any definable energy. If that is possible, then why couldn't souls also affect material particles without having any definable energy? Similarly, Collins describes how particles in quantum mechanics can influence each other instantly across a distance, without there being any physical medium that connects them. If that is possible, why can't souls influence brains without necessarily existing in a common physical medium with those brains?

In short, then, the dualist need not say that the soul must override laws of physics in order to act in the world as a kind of miracle, as many are used to thinking. Rather, physics itself has voluntarily ceded that energy conservation is not universal, for reasons of its own. And given that physical reality as we now know it is so weird and counterintuitive, how can we be sure that causal interactions between the soul and the brain violate physical principles? This is, in a nutshell, where Collins's essay takes us.

CHAPTER 5

The Energy of the Soul[1]

Robin Collins

INTRODUCTION

There has been lots of perplexity about how a nonphysical thing could influence a physical thing. This is known as the interaction problem for substance dualism, and it is addressed in Chapters 4, 6, and 9. Many philosophers have attempted to give weight to this worry by articulating it in terms of a conflict between fundamental principles of physics and the existence of an immaterial mind; specifically, they claim that the existence of an immaterial soul cannot be reconciled with the physical principle of energy conservation. This claim is often used to dismiss substance dualism with little further argument, as illustrated by the following representative quotations from leading philosophers of mind.

> [N]o physical energy or mass is associated with them [influences from immaterial mind to brain]. How, then, do they get to make a difference to what happens in the brain cells they must affect, if the mind is to have any influence over the body? A fundamental principle of physics is that any change in the trajectory of any physical entity is an acceleration requiring the expenditure of energy, and where is this energy to come from? It is this principle of the conservation of energy that accounts for the physical impossibility of "perpetual motion machines," and the same principle is apparently violated by dualism. *This confrontation between quite standard physics and dualism has been endlessly discussed since Descartes's own day, and is widely regarded as the inescapable and fatal flaw with dualism.* . . . Just as would be expected, ingenious technical exemptions based on sophisticated readings of the relevant physics have been explored and expounded, but without attracting many conversions.[2]

Similarly, according to Owen Flanagan:

> If Descartes is right that a nonphysical mind can cause the body to move, for example, when we decide to go to a concert, then physical energy must increase in and around our body, since we get up and go to the concert. In order, however, for physical energy to increase in any system, it has to have been transferred from some other physical system. But the mind, according to Descartes, is not a physical system and therefore it does not have any energy to transfer. The mind cannot account for the fact that our body ends up at the concert. . . . We could maintain that the principle of the conservation of energy holds, but that every time a mind introduces new energy into the world — thanks to some mysterious capacity it has — an equal amount of energy departs from the physical universe — thanks to some perfectly orchestrated mysterious capacity the universe has. Unfortunately, such an assumption is totally unwarranted except as a way of saving Cartesian dualism, and, therefore utterly begs the question.[3]

Finally, Jerry Fodor remarks that "The chief drawback of dualism is its failure to account adequately for mental causation. . . . How can the nonphysical give rise to the physical without violating the laws of the conservation of mass, of energy and of momentum?"[4]

The attempt of the above authors to bring objections to dualism from metaphysics into physics proper should be commended. But this also ties the objection to the details of particular theories of physics, and those can change and have changed in relevant ways. Surprisingly, those who object to dualism based on the principle of energy conservation fail to consider the role this principle actually plays in current physics. If they had, they would realize that although the conservation of energy still plays a role in how high school and college physics is taught, the formulation required by the above objection to dualism has not been a principle in our best physical theories for the last 100 years. So the appeal to the principle of energy conservation does not make the general objection based on the perplexity of how a non-physical thing could influence a physical thing more scientifically grounded; if anything, it demonstrates the difficulty of providing a scientific grounding to this more general objection.[5]

THE ENERGY CONSERVATION
OBJECTION PRECISELY STATED

To develop our critique of the energy conservation objection, we must first precisely state the objection, something the above authors fail to do (in addition to neglecting to look carefully at the physics). In attempting to do this, one will immediately notice that it is similar to the objection to interactionistic dualism based on the so-called causal closure principle, discussed by Stewart Goetz in Chapter 4. According to one version of this principle, "every physical effect has its chance fully determined by physical events alone."[6] It is difficult to see, however, how this and related versions of the principle do not simply beg the question against interactionistic dualism by assuming what this form of dualism denies, a point argued in detail by E. J. Lowe.[7]

Does the energy conservation objection beg the question in the same way by assuming that all physical interactions must conserve energy? As C. J. Ducasse has stated, conservation of energy would be an obstacle to interactionistic dualism "only if it were known to be a universal fact,"[8] something Ducasse claims scientists do not know. More precisely, the objection assumes that interactions between physical things and non-physical things (e.g. the soul) are relevantly similar to interactions between physical things. Thus, if interactions between physical things conserve energy, then it follows that interactions between non-physical things also do. No reason is ever offered, however, for the assumption that they are relevantly similar. Given the radical difference between physical things and non-physical things, however, such an assumption requires support. At best, proponents of the energy conservation objection could argue that this denial of the universality of energy conservation leads to a less simple account of the world, hence providing some reason to reject interactionistic dualism, but certainly not a fatal blow.

But even this weakened version of the objection assumes both that the principle of energy conservation applies to all known purely physical interactions and that all causal interactions (or law-like connections) between events must involve an exchange of energy. The first assumption is false for the case of general relativity, as shown in the next section; the second assumption is false for the case of quantum mechanics. Thus, based on current physics, the energy conservation objection has little, if any, merit.

GENERAL RELATIVITY

General relativity is the theory of gravity developed by Albert Einstein and is now accepted by almost all physicists. In general relativity, the energy of a body is considered a single component of a sixteen-component mathematical quantity called a *tensor*, the first component

(T^{00}) of which gives the energy density with respect to a given frame of reference. To explain this notion, it will be helpful to review some of the problems with defining the energy of a system as an intrinsic property of a system within classical mechanics. In classical mechanics, the total energy of an object is equal to the sum of the internal energy of a body and its kinetic energy, $\frac{1}{2}mv^2$. The latter quantity, however, will depend on the frame of reference from which the velocity of the object is measured. In special relativity, the frames of reference of interest are those moving at some uniform (non-accelerating) speed relative to each other. These are called *inertial* frames of reference. A train moving at a constant velocity with respect to the ground will constitute one such frame of reference, with the ground being another.[9] Now suppose we calculate the total kinetic energy of a ball at rest with respect to a moving train car — e.g. a ball that stays at the same position on the floor from the viewpoint of the passengers in the car. Observers inside the train will calculate its kinetic energy as zero. On the other hand, since for observers stationed on the ground the train and ball will be moving with some velocity, v, they will measure its kinetic energy as $\frac{1}{2}mv^2$, where m is the mass of the ball. Thus, the energy of the ball will depend on the frame of reference — the train or the ground — from which one is measuring the energy of the ball. This means that unless there is a preferred frame of reference, we cannot speak of the energy of the ball as being an intrinsic, non-relational property of it.

A central idea behind both the special theory of relativity and the general theory of relativity is that the laws of physics should be formulated in terms of quantities that are independent of one's frame of reference. Special relativity does this for the class of inertial frames, whereas general relativity does this for the class of all frames of reference, even ones that are accelerating. In the case of special relativity, the frame independent quantity that substitutes for energy is a four component entity, called the *energy-momentum vector*. When expressed in a given frame of reference, the first component of this vector is the energy of the object in question and the remaining components are the momentums in each of the respective spatial dimensions. In different frames of reference, the momentum and energy components of this vector will take on different values, and thus the values of its components will vary from frame to frame. Nonetheless, there is a well-defined mathematical sense in which this four-component quantity itself remains the same, and hence can be considered a frame-independent, intrinsic quantity characterizing the object.

In general relativity, the frame-independent quantities are what mathematicians call tensors. As mentioned above, the value of energy is the first component of a sixteen-component tensor, called the stress-energy tensor. Like the energy-momentum vector of special relativity, however, even though the components — such as the value of the energy — of this tensor vary from frame to frame, there is a well-defined mathematical sense in which the tensor remains the same. Hence, in general relativity the stress-energy tensor can be considered an intrinsic property of an object or system of particles and fields, but its energy cannot. As we will see, however, the stress-energy tensor can only be defined for non-gravitational fields, thus resulting in the energy and momentum of a gravitational field being undefined, even when one only considers a single frame of reference. This means that the law of energy conservation cannot be defined for the gravitational field, and hence for interactions involving gravity.

Before discussing why energy (or stress-energy) conservation does not hold in general relativity, we first must address the issue of exactly how to define the principle of energy conservation in physics. (For the sake of exposition, below we will often use the more familiar term "energy" instead of "stress-energy," with the understanding that the total energy is not an intrinsic quantity of a system but relative to one's frame of reference.) In practice, the most general statement of this principle is what could be called the *boundary* version of this principle. According to the boundary version, from the perspective of any given frame of reference, the rate of change of total energy in a finite region of space is equal to the total rate of energy flowing through the spatial boundary of the region. Thus, for instance, if 1,000 joules of energy per second (that is, 1,000 watts) is flowing into the region of space within an oven, and 100 joules per second is flowing out through some leaks in the oven, then the boundary version requires that the amount of energy in the region increase by 900 joules per second — that is, the difference between the heat energy coming in from the element and the amount leaking out. Finally, it should be noted that unlike more popular but less precise statements of energy conservation, the precise boundary version neither makes reference to energy as a quantity that cannot be created or destroyed, nor to the idea of a causally isolated system.

Now that we understand energy and energy conservation in modern science, we are ready to explicate the problem posed by general relativity. General relativity presents a major problem for the energy-conservation objection. The problem is that no local concept of stress-energy (and hence energy or momentum) can be defined for the gravitational field in general relativity. Consequently, the boundary version does not typically apply in general relativity since typically one can neither define the total gravitational energy in a region of space nor the rate at which gravitational energy flows in or out of the region. This implies that although gravitational fields and waves causally influence material objects in precisely quantifiable ways, their influence cannot be understood in terms of movement of energy through space. As physicist Robert Wald notes, "In general relativity there exists no meaningful local expression for gravitational stress-energy and thus there is no meaningful local energy conservation law which leads to a statement of energy conservation."[10] The reason that local energy cannot be defined for gravitational fields is that no tensor can be defined in general relativity to represent the gravitational energy in a region of space-time. As mentioned above, all physical quantities in general relativity are represented by quantities that are in a well-defined mathematical sense invariant with respect to any frame of reference, whether moving with a uniform velocity or accelerating. This is called the condition of *general covariance*, and it is central to the formulation of general relativity. Since tensors are defined in such a way as to be invariant with respect to a change of coordinates (though their expression in terms of components is not), expressing a quantity in tensoral form guarantees its invariance. The problem for gravitational energy (and gravitational momentum) is that no physically plausible tensor, nor any other frame invariant quantity, can be found for the stress-energy of a gravitational field. Further, Wald notes, given the fundamental physical principles behind general relativity, "it seems highly unlikely that a generally applicable prescription exists for obtaining a physically meaningful local expression for gravitational energy . . ."[11] The only way of obtaining a local expression for gravitational energy would be to add additional structure to space-time.[12] As Wald points out, however, "such additional structure would be completely counter to the spirit of general relativity, which views the spacetime metric as fully describing all aspects of spacetime structure and the gravitational field."[13]

The fact that there is no local expression of energy in general relativity, however, does not itself imply that in some special cases a meaningful global notion of energy cannot be defined. In fact, a meaningful expression for the gravitational stress-energy — and hence the total energy — of an isolated region of space-time can be obtained in some highly special cases (and only in these cases): namely, those in which the region of space-time is asymptotically flat (that is, flat at spatial infinity for suitably defined hypersurfaces of constant time). An example would be a star surrounded by empty space in a universe with a flat space-time.

No such systems exist *within* our universe (although many star systems can be approximately described in this way for predictive purposes). Further, as philosopher Carl Hoefer points out,[14] since our universe is not asymptotically flat, strictly speaking energy is not even conserved for our universe taken as a whole.[15]

Consequently, although in one sense the principle of energy conservation is not violated in general relativity — since this would require that the total energy be well defined — this principle typically does not apply. Consequently, in systems interacting with a gravitational wave, no conserved quantity that has the right characteristics can be defined. Gravitational fields, however, clearly have real physical effects on matter, even though from within the framework of general relativity energy cannot be said to be conserved. One specific consequence of this is that in the presence of a gravitational wave the total non-gravitational energy in an enclosed region of space could decrease or increase, without a corresponding net physically definable energy flowing across the boundary of the region. For instance, since gravitational waves exert tidal forces on matter, the waves will cause an increase in the energy content of matter. Yet technically one cannot calculate the gravitational energy transferred from gravitational waves to some object since this would require that the energy of the waves be defined. At best, in the highly special case mentioned above, one could estimate the amount of energy flowing out of a region of space that was asymptotically flat — such as the region surrounding a lone star. One is therefore often simply left with acknowledging a change in non-gravitational energy within a closed region without being able to attribute this change to a transfer of energy from another source or region of space. This leads Hoefer to suggest that for the case of gravity wave detectors, "energy gain in a gravity wave detector could be thought of as genuine gain, without having to say that the energy existed somewhere beforehand."[16,17]

This non-conservation of energy in general relativity is exploited in contemporary cosmology. For example, as the universe expands, the waves of each photon are stretched and hence the wavelengths of the photons become longer and longer, a phenomenon known as the cosmic redshift. Since the energy of a photon is inversely proportional to its wavelength, photons with longer wavelengths have less energy. Finally, since the vast majority of photons in the universe — those composing the cosmic microwave background radiation — are not significantly absorbed by matter, the total number of these photons remains almost constant except for an almost insignificant contribution from starlight. Yet each is losing energy, and the energy is neither going into matter nor anywhere else. For example, in a spatially flat universe, which ours might be, it is not going into the curvature of space. Thus, it seems as though the total energy of the universe is decreasing. As cosmologist P. J. E. Peebles states, however, "the resolution of this apparent paradox is that . . . there is not a general global energy conservation law in general relativity theory."[18]

Given the non-conservation of energy in general relativity, what should one think of the applicability of the principle of energy conservation? Should one expect that a future successor to general relativity will re-establish the universality of this principle? The answer is probably no. As Hoefer points out, the tenure of this principle as a well-established idea "was arguably fairly short (limited to part of the nineteenth and early twentieth centuries), and at all times fraught with difficulties."[19] Further, Hoefer notes, Newtonian gravitational theory had difficulties with this principle and Einstein was explicitly aware of the problems with this principle as early as 1916.[20] This contrasts sharply with the statements of most advocates of the energy conservation objection who claim that this principle is one of the most, if not the most, well-established principles in physics, as in the quotations at the beginning of this chapter. Yet, despite the evidence to the contrary, even in most texts on general relativity there is "the universal, almost desperate desire to make it *seem* as though there is such a principle at the heart of the theory."[21]

The non-conservation of energy in general relativity opens up another response a dualist could give to the energy-conservation objection. A dualist could argue that, like the gravitational field, the notion of energy simply cannot be defined for the mind, and hence one cannot even apply the principle of energy conservation to the mind/body interaction. The mind, like the gravitational field, could cause a real change in the energy of the brain without energy being conserved. Of course, this leaves open the possibility of a new physical theory being developed that replaces the basic framework of general relativity or of someone finding an ingenious definition of energy that fits within the framework of general relativity. All one can say for sure is that, within current physics, energy conservation does not apply to all systems. At the very least, this puts the burden of proof on the person offering the energy conservation objection to state why, given that in the best physical theories this principle does not apply to all physical interactions, one should think that it must apply to the mind/brain interaction. This is something they have not done.

INTERACTION WITHOUT ENERGY EXCHANGE IN PHYSICS

Underlying the energy conservation objection is the idea that causal interaction requires an exchange of energy. Even apart from the considerations based on general relativity in the last section, this idea is deeply problematic within contemporary physics for an independent reason. Specifically, quantum mechanics — the cornerstone of modern physics — provides a good case of interaction (or at least lawlike correlation) without either energy or momentum exchange.[22] In quantum mechanics, there are law-like correlations between attributes of distantly separated particles — and in many realist interpretations of quantum mechanics, causal interactions between the particles themselves — without energy exchange. Following many authors, we will use the quantum attribute of the spin of a particle to illustrate these correlations. All particles in quantum mechanics have an attribute called *spin*, which comes in values of $+1$, -1, $+\frac{1}{2}$, $-\frac{1}{2}$, and 0. Further, the spin will always be measured to have one of these values, no matter what direction it is measured in: for example, in the case of spin $\frac{1}{2}$ particles — such as protons, neutrons, electrons, and some atoms — this means that the spin will always be measured with a value of either $+\frac{1}{2}$ or $-\frac{1}{2}$.

Now consider two particles each with a spin of $\frac{1}{2}$, say two nitrogen (N) atoms, initially bound together to form a system (such as the nitrogen molecule, N_2) with a total spin of zero. Suppose we break these particles apart in a spaceship between Earth and Mars, with one of the particles going to Earth and one to Mars. Call the Earth-bound particle p_E and the Mars-bound particle p_M. Further, suppose there is an observer on each planet that will measure the spin (in some prearranged direction Z) of the particle that arrives on her planet. Quantum mechanics dictates that each observer will either measure her particle as having a spin of $+\frac{1}{2}$ or $-\frac{1}{2}$. Further, because of conservation of spin and the fact that they are measuring the spin in the same direction Z, quantum mechanics dictates that if the Earth observer measures p_E as $+\frac{1}{2}$, then the Mars observer will measure p_M as $-\frac{1}{2}$, and vice versa: that is, the measurement results are anti-correlated. Consequently, if our Earth observer measures p_E as $+\frac{1}{2}$, she knows that the Mars observer will measure p_M as $-\frac{1}{2}$.

The seemingly obvious explanation of this is that when the two particles were initially separated on the ship, the process of separation caused each of them to be in some definite state that was anti-correlated with its partner — e.g. the p_M was forced into a $+\frac{1}{2}$ state while p_E was forced into a $-\frac{1}{2}$ state. This explanation is an example of what is called *local* causation. To see why this explanation only needs to invoke local causation, first note that it explains why p_E was measured as +½ by saying that it had a certain attribute, being in a +½ state, that caused the measuring apparatus on Earth to register +½. This causation is purely local, since once p_E hits the apparatus, there is no longer any relevant spatial distance between it and the apparatus. In the same way, it explains using only local causation why the Mars observer's apparatus registered –½ when measuring the spin of p_M. Finally, only local causation is required to explain why the two particles started off in their respective spin states via the mechanism that separated the two particles: when the two particles were bound together on the ship, no relevant spatial distance separated them from the mechanism that split them apart and imparted to them their respective spins, and hence only local causation was involved.

Now for the punch line. A theorem proved by John Bell in 1966, called Bell's theorem, ruled out the above explanation and any other explanation of these quantum correlations involving only local causation. Bell showed that if certain experimental results predicted by quantum mechanics occurred, explanations based on local causes could not explain the correlations. Since 1977, these predictions have been verified numerous times. Now within all physical theories energy exchange always involves non-instantaneous and hence local causation, since the packets of energy (or stress-energy) must move through space. Consequently, Bell's theorem rules out any explanation of these correlations by means of energy exchange. Consequently, quantum mechanics requires the existence of correlations that cannot be explained by an exchange of energy.

There have been two main responses to these correlations in the literature: (i) the *causal realist* response, according to which these correlations are grounded in some instantaneous causal connection between the two particles or in some non-local and thus instantaneously acting common cause; and (ii) the *causal anti-realist* response, according to which these correlations are not grounded in any further causal facts. If the causal realist response is adopted, the burden is on the advocate of the energy-conservation objection to state why she thinks that the causal interaction between the mind and the brain should require an exchange of energy when these quantum interactions do not. If the causal anti-realist interpretation is adopted, then versions of dualism in which there are law-like connections between mental events and physical events without any corresponding causal interaction become much more plausible.

These quantum correlations, therefore, show that positing an interaction (or at least a correlation) between the mind and brain that does not involve an energy exchange, or any other mediating field, has precedent in current physics, thus severely weakening the energy-conservation objection. Further, these quantum correlations are not merely some minor "technical exemption" within physics, but are pervasive throughout the microscopic world, playing a fundamental role in the operation of nature.[23] Finally, they cast severe doubt even on the suggestion that causation requires an intermediate carrier,[24] such as gravitational waves in the case of general relativity, whether or not that carrier involves a transference of energy and momentum. Since quantum mechanics predicts that, for any given frame of reference, one can always find an experimental arrangement in which the quantum correlations are instantaneous, it follows that causal interactions (or at least law-like correlations) do not require an intermediate carrier. Further, since by hypothesis there is no spatial distance between the immaterial mind and the brain, there is no need for such a carrier.

CONCLUSION

The energy-conservation objection against interactionistic dualism fails when one considers the fact that energy conservation is not a universally applicable principle in physics and that quantum mechanics sets a precedent for interaction (or at least law-like correlation) without any sort of energy-momentum exchange, or even any intermediate carrier. Of course, the more general interaction problem for interactionistic dualism still remains, a problem that is addressed in several other chapters in this volume. Nonetheless, the fact that so many leading philosophers have trumpeted the energy conservation objection as a fatal blow to dualism, without carefully examining the relevant physics, should make us suspicious that the widespread rejection of dualism within academia is based more on the fashion of the day than on sound argument.

Collins's chapter is largely defensive in nature. It uses a more-than-layman's knowledge of modern physics to protect the Soul Hypothesis from an objection that is often made against it in the name of physical science. Along the way, he reminds us how far the current scientific understanding is from the early-modern pictures of billiard balls bouncing off each other and mechanical clockwork — the closed deterministic picture of the world that many of us still have kicking around somewhere in our minds from Newton's physics.

Hans Halvorson's chapter also concerns the issues and opportunities that arise for the Soul Hypothesis within modern physics. Like Collins, he takes us into the counterintuitive world of quantum mechanics, including particles in entangled states, where what happens to one is related to what happens to another. But Halvorson's goal is a more positive and constructive one. Not only does current physics open up room to allow souls to do causal work, it may actually give them something surprising and quite fundamental to do. Taliaferro's chapter has already mentioned that practicing the scientific method at any level involves making observations, and this involves perception, which in turn seems to point to there being a soul as well as a body. Now Halvorson draws our attention to the fact that observations play an even deeper role in physical reality as we now know it. Observations demonstrably change how particles behave in certain experimental settings, such as when photons pass through narrow slits in two-slit experiments! As Halverson discusses in detail, the pattern that shows up on the screen beyond the two slits changes dramatically depending on whether photon detectors are activated at the slits themselves or not, even if everything else in the experiment is held constant.

This surprising experimental result relates directly to a paradox — even worse, an outright contradiction — that is at the very heart of quantum mechanics. On the one hand, quantum mechanics is arguably our best-confirmed scientific theory ever, and it provides the essential basis for many powerful modern technologies. Therefore, it must be true, since it works so well. On the other hand, it simply cannot be true, because it manifestly contradicts itself. Scientists and philosophers have been *working hard for nearly a century to try to find some coherent way out of this conceptual conundrum.*

Halvorson shows that this contradiction at the heart of quantum mechanics arises only because of a tacit assumption that scientists typically leap to. This is the materialistic assumption that human observers are themselves purely physical things, and therefore are subject to all and only the same laws of quantum mechanics to which other physical objects are subject. But of course the Soul Hypothesis explicitly denies this assumption. Halvorson shows that if one changes the underlying assumption in a simple way that is inspired by dualism's basic claim that psychological states are distinct from physical brain states, then the contradiction goes away immediately. The idea is that, whereas quantum mechanics tells us that physical properties like position, momentum, spin, and charge can all be in indeterminate states called "superpositions," psychological properties like "see the indicator light on" and "see the indicator light off" cannot be indeterminate in this way. Indeed, this fits exactly with our own first-person experiences: when we are awake and alert, we see one thing or another but not both simultaneously, or some kind of indeterministic combination of the two. This difference between physical states and psychological states can be made quite precise within the mathematical axioms of the quantum mechanical theory. Once this is done, there is a principled reason why observations by sentient creatures like human beings should affect physical reality, by "collapsing the wave function." This is an effect that other attempts to provide an interpretation for quantum mechanics either miss entirely, or are forced to put in artificially, as a post hoc stipulation. Halvorson's chapter thus raises the intriguing possibility that all of contemporary physics hints at the reality of souls, if one pays due attention to its most basic assumptions.

It is worth noting the role that Halvorson gives to the Soul Hypothesis in his investigation. He does not claim to be looking for evidence in favor of dualism directly, by performing some kind of experiment that will reveal the presence of a soul. Rather, he assumes dualism from the outset, taking the existence of the soul to be a reasonable possibility given (for example) the kinds of historical, philosophical, and scientific considerations reviewed in other parts of this book. What he does do, though, is allow dualism as a basic assumption to inform and contribute to the range of hypotheses one considers, how one develops one's theories, and so on. If this way of using the Soul Hypothesis proves to be fertile, leading to interesting theories and confirmed predictions, this fertility redounds back indirectly to the credit of the Soul Hypothesis. This approach is roughly analogous to the one that Baker took in his chapter on the very different *science of linguistics. It is also in practice analogous to how other, more conventional researchers employ their beliefs and background assumptions about materialism. In general, we expect any high-level theoretical hypothesis — such as either dualism or materialism — to have a complex and indirect (although crucial) relationship to observable data. Its true test, then, is not likely to be a single decisive experiment, but rather the overall success of the comprehensive theory that includes it as one essential ingredient among others.*

We warn the reader that this chapter is the most technical in this book. The author has worked hard to make the material as accessible as he can, but average readers will still have some rather hard work to do themselves. The good news is that if they manage to get the gist of this, understanding it only in part (no one understands this material completely!), they will be rewarded with a unique glimpse of the positive role that dualism might play even in the hardest of the hard sciences.

CHAPTER 6

The Measure of All Things: Quantum Mechanics and the Soul

Hans Halvorson

INTRODUCTION

The twentieth century saw several significant developments in our understanding of the physical world. One of the most significant of these developments was the replacement of the classical physics of Newton, Maxwell, and Einstein with the quantum physics of Planck, Bohr, and Heisenberg.

Usually our understanding of the universe grows at an agonizingly slow pace. For example, a group of scientists might spend years figuring out the next digit in the decimal expansion of some seemingly insignificant numerical parameter. Of course, every now and then, there is a discovery that finds its way into the popular consciousness. For example, scientists might discover a new object (e.g. a new star) or even a new type of object (e.g. a new species). But it is only on the rarest of occasions that an actual scientific revolution occurs, when an old theory (and its accompanying world picture) is dispensed with in favor of a new theory (with a new understanding of ourselves and our place in the universe). The introduction of quantum mechanics may be the greatest scientific revolution to date in human history: the replacement of classical physics by quantum physics requires a thoroughgoing modification of our world view; or as philosophers might say, it requires a modification of our fundamental metaphysics.

That much is clear. But there is little consensus about how to build a new world view around quantum mechanics. For example, some claim that quantum mechanics proves that the universe is indeterministic, and the future is open. Others claim more radically that quantum mechanics shows that there is a multitude of parallel universes, and that each time a measurement is made, our universe branches again. Still others claim that quantum mechanics proves that there is no objective world outside of our perceptions.

The main goal of this chapter is to put forward an alternative view of the metaphysical lessons of quantum mechanics. But let me begin by staking out my methodology: I do not believe that it is feasible to approach quantum mechanics from a standpoint of "metaphysical neutrality," and expect it to tell us the nature of the universe. Rather, we always approach scientific theories in light of our background beliefs; we can then ask if this theory is consistent with these beliefs, and whether or not it suggests modifications of these beliefs.[1] For example, these background beliefs might include the belief that there is an external world, or the belief that the universe did not come into existence (along with all of our memories) one second ago, or the belief that there are conscious persons besides myself.

One of the more controversial background beliefs that I bring to this investigation is the Soul Hypothesis — namely the belief that human beings are more than just their bodies, but are also living souls. I will argue that quantum mechanics says nothing to suggest that we must abandon the Soul Hypothesis. Indeed, I will show that the Soul Hypothesis allows us to reject some of the more wild and implausible metaphysical speculations based on quantum mechanics.

The remainder of this chapter will proceed as follows. In the second section, I give an informal sketch of quantum mechanics; in particular, I isolate four central features of the theory that give rise to various paradoxes. In the third section, I discuss a much more serious paradox, the so-called "measurement problem" of quantum mechanics. The measurement problem supposedly shows that an observer (like you or me) could not ascertain facts about the physical world by making observations, and so (among many other things) could not actually test quantum mechanics. In the fourth section, I briefly pause to discuss some popular resolutions of the measurement problem before returning, in the fifth section, to discuss the bearing of the Soul Hypothesis on the measurement problem.

BASIC ASSUMPTIONS OF QUANTUM MECHANICS

"Classical physics" is a catch-all phrase for a number of different theories developed roughly between the time of Galileo Galilei (1564–1642) and James Clerk Maxwell (1831–1879). Radically abstracting from the rich detail of these theories, they are all based on two main assumptions: first, the state of each object in the world can be completely specified by assigning values to all of that object's quantitative properties (such as its position, its velocity, its mass, etc.). Second, there are laws of nature such that the state of each object at any future time is completely determined by the state of all objects at any previous time.

The classical physicists also successfully pursued a strategy of reductionism by finding a small number of "basic quantities" from which the values of all other quantities could (in principle) be determined. Famously, these basic quantities include things such as position and velocity, but exclude many quantities that figure centrally in our everyday lives, such as color and temperature.

How did these physicists know that they could not reduce the collection of basic quantities even further? For example, how did they know that velocity could not be reduced to position? They knew that velocity could not be reduced to position because these two quantities satisfy a *mix and match* principle. For example, the position and the velocity of a baseball can be mixed and matched in the sense that, in principle, the position of the baseball (e.g. over home plate) can be matched with any velocity of the baseball (e.g. traveling at 60 miles per hour). In contrast, the color of the baseball cannot be mixed and matched with the position and velocities of its constituent atoms; indeed, the color is completely determined by, or reducible to, the position and velocity of the constituent atoms.

During the late nineteenth century, physicists found ways to put classical mechanics to work even in cases where they lacked precise knowledge of the states of objects. In particular, given partial knowledge of the states of objects, the (deterministic) dynamical laws of the theory can be applied to yield partial knowledge about the future states of objects. Let's consider a highly simplified example: suppose that there is a machine that releases a certain sort of classical particles, but that we do not have full control over the outgoing direction of these particles. Suppose then that the machine is confined to a box that has an optical screen at one end, and that between the machine and the screen there is another blocking screen that has two doors (see Figure 6.1). In each case when a particle is emitted, it will go through either the left door or

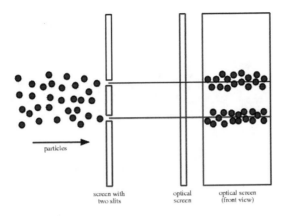

screen with   optical   optical screen
two slits   screen   (front view)

FIGURE 6.1 Particles

the right door; however, in any given case, we do not know which door will be traversed. Nonetheless, at the end of several runs of the experiment, it is overwhelmingly likely that there will be one "lump" on the optical screen behind the left door, and an equal sized lump behind the right door. In other words, after the particles pass through the doors, they follow the trajectories predicted by classical physics and so continue in a straight line to the optical screen. Extending the use of the word "state," we can say that this apparatus describes a state that is a probabilistic mixture of a state in which the particle goes through the left door and a state in which the particle goes through the right door.

Classical physics made another important advance when its domain was expanded from particles — i.e. well-localized discrete objects — to waves (as occur in media such as water and air) and fields (such as the electromagnetic field). One of the novel physical features of waves and fields is their ability to be superposed on top of each other. For example, if a certain wave machine at Waterworld produces 2-foot waves, and a certain other wave machine produces 3-foot waves, then if we set both machines in sync we would get 5-foot waves. In contrast, if we set the machines out of sync, then the peaks and troughs will interfere with each other so that we only get 1-foot waves. This special feature of waves (and fields) is called "superposability"; the wave that results from combining two other waves is called the "superposition" of those waves.

Of course, waves superpose in more than just one dimension. For example, suppose that we set up a source of monochromatic light (e.g. a laser) on one side of a box and an optical detector screen on the other side of the box. Suppose, moreover, that we place a barrier with two

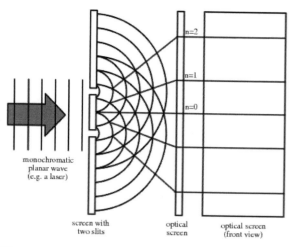

monochromatic
planar wave
(e.g. a laser)

screen with
two slits

optical
screen

optical screen
(front view)

FIGURE 6.2 Waves

open doors in the middle of the box. Then as light waves come out of
the individual doors, they will superpose with each other, reinforcing
each other at some points and canceling each other out at other points,
to form a characteristic diffraction pattern on the optical screen (see
Figure 6.2).

SUPERPOSITION

Classical physics proved itself flexible enough to accommodate uncer-
tainty (probability), and also to accommodate physical systems (such as
waves) that are not composed of discrete particles. However, at the end
of the nineteenth century, several new experiments provided data that
could not be explained by classical physics. A striking example of these
experiments is the famous two-slit experiment for electrons. In order to
show that this experiment cannot be understood within classical physics,
we must briefly recall the state of physical knowledge and of experimental technology at the end of the nineteenth century.

At the end of the nineteenth century, physicists had experimental
data indicating that atoms exist, and moreover that atoms themselves
are complex physical objects consisting of a dense nucleus with positive electric charge, and a less dense outer region with negative electric
charge. But what is the negatively charged region made of? Is it made
of small particles (viz. electrons) with empty space between them, or

is it simply a continuous, infinitely divisible field of negative charge? Fortunately, experimentalists had devised methods of dislodging pieces of this negative charge, and so made it possible to perform experiments to test whether negative charge is carried by waves or particles.

Consider then an experiment in which there is a source of negative electric charge that is directed towards a detector screen, but that between the source of electrons and the detector, there is a barrier with two doors. The first experimental finding suggests that negative charge is carried by particles: if one of the two doors is open, and the other is closed, then the detector flashes only in the small region directly behind the open door. If electric charge were carried by a continuous, wavelike medium, then we would expect the charge to spread out after it passes through the door, and then to leave a broad, diffuse mark on the detector.

Now let's apply a second test: turn the source on for an extended period of time, and attach the two doors to a coin flipping machine (which opens the right door when the coin comes up tails, and opens the left door when the coin comes up heads). If the experiment is run several times, then the resulting pattern on the screen is exactly what we would expect for particles (as in Figure 6.1): there are two lumps of equal size, one behind each door.

Now let's apply a third test: turn the source on for an extended period of time, and open both doors. If electrons were localized particles, then they must pass through one of the two doors. Thus, if the source is set up so as not to bias one of the two doors, then over many runs of this experiment, a pattern would build up on the detector screen — one lump behind the left door, and another equal-sized lump behind the right door. But, in fact, that is *not* what happens in this experiment. Rather, at the end of the experiment, the detector screen displays the diffraction pattern that we saw in the two-slit experiment for waves (see Figure 6.2).

In the early days of quantum mechanics, a thought experiment was devised to try to settle the question of whether electrons are particles or waves: put a detector over each door and see if one, both, or neither detector goes off. Only very recently have technological advances made it possible to perform this experiment, and the result is surprising: in any particular run of the experiment when the detectors are turned on, exactly one detector goes off (confirming that electrons are localized particles). But when these detectors are turned on, the interference pattern on the optical screen disappears, and instead we get the two-lump pattern on the optical screen. It is as if the electron behaves like a particle in the presence of the detectors, but like a wave when there are no detectors.

So is negative electric charge carried by particles or waves? The pioneers of quantum mechanics refused to answer this question; instead, they constructed a hybrid theory that draws on features both of the classical theory of particles and of the classical theory of waves. In particular, they invented a new concept called the "quantum superposition of two states," and they claimed that when both doors are open, then the electron is in a quantum superposition of passing through the left and the right doors. If $|left>$ is the state of the electron passing through the left door, and $|right>$ is the state of the electron passing through the right door, then the quantum superposition state is usually written $|left>+|right>$.

In some ways, a quantum superposition behaves like a classical superposition of waves; e.g. when both doors are open but no detectors are turned on, then the quantum superposition also results in a diffraction pattern on the optical screen. But in some ways it does not; e.g. when both doors are open and both detectors are turned on, a classical superposition of waves would always set off both detectors at the doors, but a quantum superposition of waves will only set off one of the detectors at a time.

The key feature of the superposition state $|left>+|right>$ is that it *cannot* be thought of merely as a state of our ignorance of which door the electron will pass through. That is, it cannot be thought of as a probabilistic mixture of the two states $|left>$ and $|right>$. If it were merely a description of our ignorance, then there would be no diffraction pattern on the optical screen! And yet, the state $|left>+|right>$ does predict what we would see if we were to look at which door the electron is passing through: we would see it go through the left door half of the time, and through the right door the other half of the time. In other words, when an electron is in state $|left>+|right>$, then it does not have any determinate position whatsoever, i.e. it is neither in the state $|left>$ nor in state $|right>$. And yet, if we measure the position of the electron, e.g. by placing detectors over the doors, then there is a 50 per cent chance that the electron will change into state $|left>$, and a 50 per cent chance that it will change into state $|right>$. Since quantum states are often called "wave functions," this remarkable change of state has been given the infamous name, "collapse of the wave function."

Before we proceed further, it is *crucially important* to undercut a possible misunderstanding — a misunderstanding into which many professional physicists and philosophers have fallen. What are we to say about the condition of the electron before the wave function is collapsed, e.g. before we look at which door the electron is passing through?

Should we say that before a measurement is made, there is no reality, that the facts about physical reality are brought into existence by the act of measurement? No: such an idea is based on a complete misunderstanding of the formalism of quantum mechanics.

To clear up this misunderstanding, we need to point out that the states of quantum mechanics are *not* like the natural numbers, i.e. the numbers 1, 2, 3 . . . The natural numbers can be divided into two classes: the composite numbers (a number that can be divided by at least one number besides 1 and itself), and the prime numbers (those that are not composite). There is then a clear sense in which some numbers are simple and others are complex; the complex numbers can always be decomposed into simples, but the simples cannot be further decomposed.

But there is no similar distinction in quantum mechanics between states that are composite (superpositions), and states which are simple (not superpositions of other states). On the contrary, quantum states are like angles on a disc, or like points on the face of an analog clock, and the superposition operation "+" on quantum states is like taking the average (i.e. the midpoint going clockwise from the first angle) between the two points on the clock. For example, the states $|left\rangle$ and $|right\rangle$ are themselves superposition of other states, namely the state

$$|moving\rangle = |left\rangle + |right\rangle,$$

in which the electron is moving, and the state

$$|stationary\rangle = |left\rangle - |right\rangle,$$

in which the electron is stationary. There is no sense whatsoever in which some quantum states are *not* superpositions. As a result, there are no "safe" quantum states in which all "elements of reality" are fully determinate: in every quantum state, some quantities fail to have a determinate value.

But if every quantum state is a superposition (of some other states) then don't we have a serious reality crisis? Didn't we say that when an electron is in a superposition of states, then it fails to have the features specified by those states? Doesn't this mean that at any given time, some features of the electron will remain in a shadow land between existence and non-existence? Yes, if quantum mechanics is true, then an electron can *never*, in any state, have determinate values for all of its quantities. At any given time, an electron will either have no position, or no velocity, or no value for some other quantity.

Perhaps you can accept with equanimity the claim that electrons are in superposition states; after all, we cannot see them. But unfortunately for our grip on reality, it is not just subatomic particles that are in superpositions. As we will see in the next section, superpositions percolate upward in the sense that anything composed out of subatomic particles also has superposition states, indeed is always in a superposition of states. But rocks, trees, and human bodies are composed out of subatomic particles; and so we are always in a superposition of states!

ENTANGLEMENT

What happens if there are *two* electrons, both of which are in a superposition of states? Suppose, for example, that two separate two-slit experiments are performed in two different laboratories. If both electrons are in the state $|left> + |right>$, then what is the state of the composite of both electrons?

We can make some progress on this question by asking what we should expect to see if we were to measure the position of both electrons simultaneously. To keep track, let's give the two electrons names: Anke and Bert. If we simultaneously measure the position of both Anke and Bert, then since Anke is in the state $|left> + |right>$, there is a 50 per cent chance that she will go through the left door, and a 50 per cent chance that she will go through the right door. Similarly, there is a 50 per cent chance that Bert will go through his left door, and a 50 per cent chance that he will go through his right door. Now, supposing that these two experiments are independent from each other, the outcomes of the two measurements should satisfy the mix-and-match principle; that is, Anke's going through the left door is compatible with Bert's going through either the left or right door, and vice versa. Thus, we should expect to see each possible combination — left-left, left-right, right-right, right-left — 25 per cent of the times we do the experiment. And, indeed, that is the result that is observed when such experiments are performed.

Let us write $|left>_A|left>_B$ for the state in which both Anke and Bert go through their respective left doors. Then we began the discussion of this section by postulating that Anke and Bert are in the state:

$$(|left>_A + |right>_A)(|left>_B + |right>_B),$$

in which both Anke and Bert are in the superposition $|left> + |right>$. Here we simply set the states side by side (with no space in between), to indicate that the state on the left belongs to Anke and the state on the right belongs to Bert. The evidence of joint measurements indicates that this state is in fact equal to a superposition of four terms,

$$|left>_A|left>_B+|left>_A|right>_B+|right>_A|left>_B+|right>_A|right>_B.$$

Notice that this superposition of four terms is what we would expect if we could distribute the superposition operation "+" over the composition of two systems. And indeed, quantum mechanics accepts the validity of distribution, for example:

$$|moving>_A(|left>_B+|right>_B) = |moving>_A|left>_B+|moving>_A|right>_B.$$

Again, this equation is completely plausible when you think about the results of measuring the velocity of Anke and the position of Bert. In particular, if Anke is definitely moving, and Bert is in a superposition of $|left>$ and $|right>$, then a joint velocity-position measurement will yield either "moving and left" or "moving and right."

Now, the composite of two electrons is still extremely small, and so certainly still within the domain of validity of quantum mechanics. In particular, the states of a pair of electrons should, theoretically speaking, be superposable. And, indeed, this theoretical prediction has been confirmed via extensive experimentation, most particularly through experimental tests of Bell's inequality.[2]

But this simple fact — that any two states of a composite system can be superposed — has utterly profound consequences. For example, since Anke and Bert can be in state $|left>_A|left>_B$ or in state $|right>_A|right>_B$, they can also be in the superposition state $|left>_A|left>_B + |right>_A|right>_B$. Let us call this superposition state $|E>$ for short. Then state $|E>$ says that if we perform a joint position-position measurement, we will always get the same result for both electrons; i.e. Anke and Bert always go through the same door.

But when the state of Anke and Bert is $|E>$, then what is Anke's state? Obviously, Anke is not in the state $|left>$, because $|E>$ says that it is possible for Anke to go through the right door. Similarly, Anke is not in the state $|right>$. So is Anke in the superposition $|left>+|right>$? No, that's not possible, because if Anke were in that state, then whatever state Bert is in, it would then be possible both that $|left>_A|state>_B$ and that $|right>_A|state>_B$. However, by replacing $|state>$ with either $|left>$, $|right>$, or a superposition thereof, you always get too many possibilities — you always get a state in which there is a chance of Anke and Bert going through opposite doors, which is inconsistent with $|E>$. Thus, the state $|E>$ rules out every possible one of Anke's states; when the composite system is in state $|E>$, then Anke is not in any state! All of Anke's quantities — position, velocity, etc. — lack determinate values. The pioneers of quantum mechanics invented a special name — "entanglement" — for situations like this where two objects are so intertwined with each other that they cease to have *any* individual characteristics.

So, quantum mechanics applies to small composite systems, such as a pair of electrons; and it predicts that such systems will have entangled states. In fact, there is nothing special about the number two; if we put together three or four electrons, we still get a system that obeys the laws of quantum mechanics. We might suppose, however, that this process of composition cannot go on indefinitely. At some point, we must reach a limit where quantum mechanics ceases to be valid. However, that supposition is false: despite many experiments, physicists have never found a cut-off point at which quantum mechanics ceases to be valid. In other words, all the evidence indicates that the composite of any two quantum-mechanical systems is another quantum mechanical system. Consequently, the laws of quantum mechanics hold for any objects, no matter how large or heavy, that are built out of other objects obeying the laws of quantum mechanics.

As a variation on a classic example, consider a cat called Tibbles. We can, in thought, build Tibbles up piece by piece from elementary particles. Beginning with two elementary particles A and B, which obey the superposition principle, we form a composite particle $A + B$, which then also obeys the superposition principle. We then add a third elementary particle, C, which of course obeys the superposition principle, and the result is a larger object $A + B + C$ that also obeys the superposition principle. Proceeding in this manner, we finally end up with Tibbles, a composite $A + B + C$ of elementary particles, who also is subject to the superposition principle. In particular, for any two states that Tibbles can be in, he can also be in the superposition of those two states.

Consider, for example, the state $|alive>$, in which Tibbles is alive, and the state, $|dead>$, in which Tibbles is dead. Then Tibbles can also be in the superposition state $|alive>+|dead>$, in which he is neither definitely alive nor definitely dead. Similarly, consider the state

$$|alive>_A|alive>_B+|dead>_A|dead>_B,$$

in which Tibbles is entangled with a mouse. Then Tibbles has no state at all, is neither alive nor dead, is not awake or asleep, etc. These consequences of quantum mechanics are not mere curiosities; they have utterly profound consequences for our understanding of physical reality.

Dynamics

The fact that cats can be in indeterminate states is hard to swallow. Believe it or not, though, there is an even more troubling consequence of quantum mechanics — namely it seems to show that when we "make observations" then we become entangled with physical objects, and so we end up having no determinate properties. This most troubling consequence of quantum mechanics is the result of combining the previous two postulates (superposition and entanglement) with the following simple fact about how quantum states change over time.

The theories of classical physics postulate the existence of deterministic dynamical laws. These laws provide a collection of conditional statements: if the state of the system at some earlier time is S, then the state of the system at some later time will be S'. Now, the situation in quantum mechanics is, in fact, the same: quantum states change in time according to the Schrödinger equation, which is completely deterministic in the sense that the current quantum state of an object determines uniquely its future quantum state. In addition, however, changes of quantum state always preserve superpositions. If the state $|S>$ were to evolve into the state $|S'>$, and if the state $|T>$ were to evolve into the state $|T'>$, then the state $|S>+|T>$ would evolve into $|S'>+|T'>$. The assumption that superpositions are preserved through time is called "linear dynamics" or "unitarity."[3]

The most profound puzzle of quantum mechanics — namely, the measurement problem — is a result of linear dynamics in combination with the facts described in previous sections. Before we present the measurement problem, let's briefly summarize the features of quantum mechanics from which it follows.

- Superposition principle: any two possible states can be superposed. In a superposition state $|left>+|right>$, an object is neither in the state $|left>$ nor in the state $|right>$; rather, its location is indeterminate.
- Entanglement: a pair of objects can be in an entangled state in which neither of the objects has any determinate properties.
- Linear dynamics: superpositions are maintained through dynamical changes.
- Size does not matter: the previous postulates apply to all physical objects, regardless of their size.

The measurement problem

Perhaps you can deal with the fact that electrons are in superposition states. Perhaps you can even accept that cats can be in entangled states in which they cease to have any properties whatsoever. After all, these are predictions of quantum mechanics, and we believe that quantum mechanics is true.

But why do we believe that quantum mechanics is true? We think it is true because it makes predictions, and these predictions are almost always correct. But how do we check these predictions? We check these predictions by making measurements — e.g. if quantum mechanics says that an electron has a 50 per cent chance of going through the left door, then we set up a detector to see how often it goes through the left door.

In order to measure whether the electron goes through the left door, we need some sort of detector. Let's suppose that there is a computer with sensors attached to both doors. If it detects an electron going through the left door, then it displays "left" on its monitor, and if it detects an electron going through the right door, then it displays "right" on its monitor. Suppose that before the computer detects anything, it displays "ready" on its monitor. Of course, the computer itself is a physical object, composed of stuff that obeys the laws of quantum mechanics. Hence, the computer must obey the laws of quantum mechanics — in particular, it must have superposition states, and it must be able to enter into entangled states with other physical objects.

Now we have just stipulated that the computer is a reliable detector of the door through which the electron travels. In other words, this means that if the initial state of the electron and computer is $|left>|$"ready">, then its final state will be $|left>|$"left">. Similarly, the initial state $|right>|$"ready"> leads to final state $|right>|$"right">.

But now let's check the prediction that quantum mechanics makes for when an electron is in the state $|left>+|right>$. (Recall that quantum mechanics predicts that in 50 per cent of the cases, the electron goes through the door on the left, and in 50 per cent of the cases it goes through the door on the right.) We begin then with state

$$(|left>+|right>)|\text{"ready"}>,$$

which (since superpositions distribute over composition) is the same as the state

$$|left>|\text{"ready"}>+|right>|\text{"ready"}>.$$

We then ask, what will the state of the detector be after it interacts with the electron? But quantum mechanics (linear dynamics) tells us that superpositions are preserved through dynamical change, thus the final state of the electron and computer will be

$$|left>|\text{``}left\text{''}> + |right>|\text{``}right\text{''}>.$$

But this is an entangled state! In this state, the computer neither displays "left" nor "right"; in fact, the computer has become so entangled with the electron that it has no properties of its own. Our attempt to check the prediction has resulted in utter failure, since the computer displays nothing at all.

We have a mental problem

At this stage, you might be tempted to say: quantum mechanics makes a false prediction when it says that the computer ends up in an entangled state. In fact, we know (from experience) that the computer ends up either in the state $|\text{``}left\text{''}>$ or in the state $|\text{``}right\text{''}>$.

But that is too fast. We do not know from experience that the computer ends up either in the state $|\text{``}left\text{''}>$ or $|\text{``}right\text{''}>$. What we know from experience is that if we look at the computer monitor, then we will see either the state $|\text{``}left\text{''}>$ or the state $|\text{``}right\text{''}>$. The fact that the computer ends up in an entangled state is consistent with our experience; in fact, it accurately predicts what our experience will be. Recall that a superposition state predicts equal probabilities for each of its components. But then if the computer and electron are in the superposition/entangled state

$$|left>|\text{``}left\text{''}> + |right>|\text{``}right\text{''}>,$$

we should expect that 50 per cent of the time $|left>|\text{``}left\text{''}>$ will obtain, and 50 per cent of the time $|right>|\text{``}right\text{''}>$ will obtain. But that prediction is accurate; that is what we do see when we perform this experiment.

If, however, we attempt to describe the observer herself in the language of quantum mechanics, then we face a serious problem. This problem is presented with force in the classical work *Quantum Mechanics and Experience*, by the philosopher David Albert. I quote his exposition at length (I use "left" and "right" in the place of Albert's "hard" and "soft," and I use a computer monitor in the place of a pointer):

Suppose, then (just as we did before), that literally every physical system in the world (and this now includes human beings; and it includes the brains of human beings) always evolves in accordance with the dynamical equations of motion . . . Being a "competent observer" is something like being a measuring device that's set up right: What it means for Martha to be a competent observer of the computer monitor is that whenever Martha looks at a monitor that displays "left", she eventually comes to *believe* that the monitor displays "left"; and that whenever Martha looks at a monitor that displays "right", she eventually comes to believe that the monitor displays "right". What it means (to put it more precisely) is that the dynamical equations of motion entail that Martha (who is a physical system, subject to the physical laws) behaves like this:

$$|ready>_o|ready>_m \rightarrow |\text{"}ready\text{"}>_o|ready>_m,$$
$$|ready>_o|\text{"}left\text{"}>_m \rightarrow |\text{"}left\text{"}>_o|\text{"}left\text{"}>_m,$$
$$|ready>_o|\text{"}right\text{"}>_m \rightarrow |\text{"}right\text{"}>_o|\text{"}right\text{"}>_m.$$

In these expressions, $|ready>_o$ is that physical state of Martha's brain in which she is alert and in which she is intent on looking at the monitor and finding out what it says; $|\text{"}ready\text{"}>_o$ is that physical state of Martha's brain in which she believes that the monitor displays the word "ready", [etc.] . . .

Let's get back to the story. The state of the electron and the computer is the strange one $|\text{"}left\text{"}>_m|left>_e + |\text{"}right\text{"}>_m|right>_e$. And now in comes Martha, and Martha is a competent observer of the computer monitor, and Martha is in her ready state, and Martha looks at the monitor. It follows from the linearity of the dynamical equations of motion (if those equations are right), and from what it means to be a competent observer of the monitor, that the state when Martha's done is with certainty going to be

$$|\text{"}left\text{"}>_o|\text{"}left\text{"}>_m|left>_e + |\text{"}right\text{"}>_o|\text{"}right\text{"}>_m|right>_e.$$

That's what the dynamics entails.

. . . That state described [in the prior paragraph] is at odds with what we know of ourselves by *direct introspection*. It's a superposition of one state in which Martha thinks that the monitor displays "left" and another state in which Martha thinks that the monitor displays "right"; *it's a state in which there is no matter of fact about whether or not Martha thinks the monitor displays anything in particular.*

And so things are turning out badly.[4]

Thus, according to Albert, quantum mechanics entails a fact — that at the end of a measurement, a person will not have any belief about the outcome — that would utterly destroy our ability to test the predictions of quantum mechanics. Therefore, quantum mechanics is incoherent.

Interpretations of quantum mechanics

Superposition states and entangled states might be puzzling, and they certainly require a stretch of our conceptual framework. But the *measurement problem* is not merely a puzzle; rather, it is an apparent proof of the incoherence of quantum mechanics. We must do something to save quantum mechanics from incoherence; otherwise, the best physical theory in history is shown to be a sham, and certainly not worth your attention as a guide to understanding the nature of reality.

An *interpretation* of quantum mechanics is an attempt to explain how it could be true. But of course, if the theory leads to a contradiction then it cannot possibly be true. Thus, an interpretation of quantum mechanics must reject or modify one of the assumptions that was used to derive the measurement problem.

Since the origin of quantum mechanics, there have been a number of responses to the measurement problem, and these responses can be classified according to which assumption they reject. First, some interpretations of quantum mechanics (so-called "hidden variable interpretations") solve the measurement problem by rejecting the superposition principle. Second, some interpretations of quantum mechanics (especially dynamical reduction theories) solve the measurement problem by rejecting the dynamical laws of quantum mechanics. Third, some interpretations of quantum mechanics (especially Everettian or *many worlds* interpretations) solve the measurement problem by denying that observation really does occur in the sense we normally suppose it does. In the remainder of this section, I will give a brief overview of each of these interpretive strategies. In the following section, we will explore the interpretation of quantum mechanics in light of a conscious presupposition that human beings are more than just hunks of physical matter.

First, the measurement problem can be blocked by denying that there are superposition states in which some quantities are indeterminate. Nobody denies that the state $|left> + |right>$ is possible. However, we are not *necessitated* into saying that it is a state in which the electron has no position. The argument that the electron lacks a position is roughly as follows: if the electron had some position (but we didn't know which), then we would not get a diffraction pattern on the screen; rather, we would get the two lumps behind the doors. But that argument is not air-tight: the conclusion only follows if we assume that the electron is a classical particle not subject to any additional forces or laws. It remains a possibility that a particle-like entity could produce a diffraction pattern if it obeyed laws of motion that were quite different from the laws discovered by Newton.

The strategy outlined above is sometimes misleadingly called giving a hidden variable interpretation of quantum mechanics, the most famous example of which is the theory developed by David Bohm, now called Bohmian mechanics.[5] While this strategy promises to solve the measurement problem while maintaining determinism (which some find desirable), it also has several difficulties. Most notably, Bohmian mechanics postulates the existence of a guiding field of somewhat questionable metaphysical credentials. In particular, the guiding field (unlike all the other physical fields we know and love) carries no energy-momentum, and so is empirically undetectable. Furthermore, the components of the guiding field are not associated with localized regions of space in the way that, say, the electromagnetic field is. Thus, the guiding field is not a field in the traditional sense, and in particular it does not play the traditional role of a field as a mediator of cause and effect relations in space and time. The mysterious nature of the guiding field was itself an insuperable obstacle for Einstein (who otherwise longed to replace quantum mechanics with a deterministic theory). On the other hand, Bohm himself proposes a new metaphysics in which the guiding field is itself a quasi-mental entity.

> These new properties suggest that the field may be regarded as containing objective and active information, and that the activity of this information is similar in certain key ways to the activity of information in our ordinary subjective experience. The analogy between mind and matter is thus fairly close. This analogy leads to the proposal of the general outlines of a new theory of mind, matter, and their relationship, in which the basic notion is participation rather than interaction.[6]

Bohm's ideas might sound intriguing, but they are far from metaphysically innocent. We might wonder: does quantum mechanics require a radically new theory of mind and matter, or is it consistent at least in general outlines with the wisdom handed down to us through the ages?

Second, some physicists blame the measurement problem on the dynamical laws of quantum mechanics, and in particular on quantum mechanics' supposition that superpositions are preserved over time.

According to these physicists, quantum mechanics is simply a *false* theory, and needs to be replaced by a different theory. Moreover, these physicists have gone on to provide concrete proposals for these alternative theories. The most famous alternative to quantum mechanics is the dynamical reduction theory proposed by Ghirardi, Rimini, and Weber.[7] According to the GRW theory, quantum mechanics is *usually* right about how things change over time. However, once in a blue moon, there is a random and spontaneous collapse of the state of an object. For example, there is an extremely small probability that an electron in state $|left> + |right>$ will spontaneously transition into state $|left>$ or $|right>$. This probability is so small that it is extremely unlikely that an individual electron's state would collapse, even over the entire history of the universe. However, in order to solve the measurement problem, GRW take advantage of the fact that collapses are contagious; i.e. if one particle is entangled with another, and if the state of the first collapses, then the state of the composite automatically collapses. But it follows, then, that for a system consisting of a very large number of particles — e.g. a measuring device — there is a non-negligible probability that one of its constituent particles will collapse, and hence that the state of the big composite object will collapse. So, GRW dynamics would explain why quantum mechanics is *almost* true for very small objects, but often false (since wave functions collapse) for large objects.

Finally, some propose to solve the measurement problem by rejecting the intuition that a measurement ends with one definite outcome to the exclusion of the other possibilities — in particular, by rejecting the claim that a reliable observer will believe either that the computer monitor shows "left" or "right." The most famous version of this strategy — alternately called the Everett interpretation or the many worlds interpretation — was introduced by Hugh Everett.[8] According to Everett, when a person makes an observation or measurement she becomes entangled with the measuring device and with the object under study. Thus, at the end of the measurement, the person is not in the state "I believe that the monitor displays 'left'" and she is also not in the state "I believe that the monitor displays 'right'."

But why then do we mistakenly believe that we often have definite perceptual beliefs? Proposed answers to this question are, by necessity, sophisticated and involve serious grappling with the metaphysics of the mind-body relation. (To follow some recent developments, one might look at the work of the physicist Don Page of the University of Alberta, or of the philosophers Hilary Greaves, Simon Saunders and David Wallace of Oxford University.) In short, the Everett interpretation proposes that when a person makes a measurement, then the universe itself splits into several branches, and the person making the measurement is split into several copies of herself.

Now, the idea of a branching universe is not, in and of itself, so metaphysically absurd that it counts decisively against the Everett interpretation. Indeed, a branching universe would be a natural way to cash out the idea that the future is open and not determined by the past. If that was the only metaphysical revision required, then I might be tempted to recommend the Everett interpretation to you. In fact, there are versions of the Everett interpretation that are explicitly consistent with mind-body dualism, namely the single mind and many minds interpretations of David Albert and Barry Loewer.[9]

But, unfortunately, the naive *many worlds* version of Everett's interpretation, as well as the single and many minds interpretations, are vulnerable to a number of objections that have been cataloged over the past thirty years. For example, in the many worlds interpretation, the universe is supposed to split into many parts when a measurement occurs. But how can a measurement in one place cause a change in the entire universe, including very distant regions, without violating the laws of special relativity? Furthermore, if all the possible measurement outcomes are actualized (in some universe, or relative to some mind), then what sense does it make to say that certain outcomes are more likely than others?[10]

I will not claim that these problems with the Everett interpretation cannot be solved. Indeed, an extremely clever and philosophically cogent version of the Everett interpretation has been developed recently by the Oxford University philosophy of physics group. But this recent work makes it clear that the Everett interpretation is no friend of mind-body dualism. Indeed, the Everett interpretation is most plausibly and compellingly developed in the context of a form of "functionalist physicalism."[11] Thus, while a physicalist may have good reasons to look to the Everett interpretation as a key to understanding physical reality, a dualist has just as good a reason to look elsewhere.

Each of these interpretations of quantum mechanics agrees that there is a problem that needs to be solved. The first two interpretations solve the problem by rejecting an assumption of quantum mechanics — in one case the assumption that superpositions entail indeterminacy, and in the other case the assumption that superpositions are preserved through time. The third interpretation solves the measurement problem by revising our intuitive idea about what happens when we make observations or measurements. Each strategy has its virtues and its drawbacks. However, none of the strategies takes seriously the idea that "observation" involves a non-physical thing (e.g. a mind or a soul). Some might claim that it is a virtue of these interpretations that they need not assume the existence of non-physical things. But if you already and independently believe in the existence of non-physical things, then there is no good reason to forget this fact when interpreting quantum mechanics.

Quantum mechanics on the Soul Hypothesis

I claim that a dualist should be wary of the textbook derivation of the measurement problem (as, for example, in Albert's book), because this derivation relies on a tacit assumption of reductionist physicalism. In particular, Albert tacitly assumes physicalism when he says that "|"*left*"> is that physical state of Martha's brain in which she believes that the computer monitor displays the word 'left'." (Note how the first part of the sentence is about a physical feature of Martha's brain and the second part of the sentence is about Martha's mental state.) According to dualism, there are two states in play here: there is the state of Martha's brain, and there is her mental state. So, Albert is using one name for what the dualist claims are two different things; in other words, he is tacitly equating mental states with physical states. But if we distinguish the two sorts of states, then it is not obvious that the argument for the measurement problem will go through.

In the remainder of this chapter, I reexamine the measurement problem in light of the fact that human observers are not just chunks of physical matter. First, I argue that mental states, unlike physical states, cannot be superposed, and therefore cannot become entangled with physical states. This point itself would be sufficient to block the derivation of one half of the measurement paradox — the claim that an observer fails either to see "left" or to see "right." But I will go further; in order to demonstrate, beyond a doubt, the coherence of quantum mechanics and the Soul Hypothesis, I suggest a model of the interaction of physical states and mental states relative to which mental states reliably track states of the physical world.

The two state space hypothesis

The Soul Hypothesis is, of course, a pre-theoretical idea in the sense that the statement "human beings are more than just their bodies" is not yet precise enough to bring to bear directly on the question of how we should describe a person's mental states when she is performing measurements on objects like electrons. So, if we are to say something concrete about the interaction of physical and mental states, then we must — with all due humility! — try to translate the Soul Hypothesis into something like a precise metaphysical thesis.

Many philosophers throughout history have proposed and defended precise versions of the Soul Hypothesis. I will not, in this chapter, try to survey the various proposals, or elaborate on my choice of a proposal. Suffice to say that the Logical Independence Hypothesis, a precisification of the Soul Hypothesis, has been defended by several notable dualists.[12] It holds that mental states are *logically* independent from physical states. That is, for any possible mental state, and any possible physical state, it is possible that the two states could obtain at the same time.

Of course, there are stable correlations in our world between physical states and mental states, and so there are probably laws of nature connecting the two. But the point of the logical independence hypothesis is that the two sorts of states are *conceptually* distinct — a physical state is a different sort of thing than a mental state, and physical states do not *logically* or *conceptually* necessitate mental states, and vice versa.

The sort of independence that the dualist postulates between mental states and physical states is just like the mix and match principle that holds between distinct physical quantities (e.g. position and velocity in classical physics), or between quantities of distinct physical objects (e.g. the position of Jupiter and the position of Mars). Thus, if $|M>$ is a mental state, and $|P>$ is a physical state, then we can borrow from quantum mechanics the notation $|M>|P>$ to denote the conjunctive state whose possibility is asserted by the independence thesis. But this notational adjustment is far from trivial: if we have distinct names for physical states and mental states, then obviously conclusions about physical states (e.g. they can be superposed) cannot be *automatically* transferred to mental states.

The non-superposability of mental states
Quantum mechanics entails that Martha's brain can be in a superposition of states. But if Martha's mental states are not identical to her brain states, then it does not immediately follow that she can be in a superposition of mental states. In fact, I claim that mental states cannot be superposed. I will back this claim up both by pointing out a lack of evidence for their superposability, and by providing positive arguments against the superposability of mental states.[13]

Why do we think that physical states can be superposed? The answer is *not* that we *see* that one state is a superposition of two other states

— indeed, we have no idea what that would look like. Rather, superposition is an unobservable, theoretical relation between states; and this relation was postulated because it explains phenomena (e.g. the two-slit experiment). The postulation of unobservable structure, behind the phenomena, is a common strategy of theoretical science; its justification comes from the fact that it explains empirical facts that would otherwise be puzzling. For example, Einstein's theory of relativity postulates that space and time have hidden geometrical structure; this postulate is justified by the fact that it explains the motions of planets and stars. But are there phenomena for which we would have an explanation if we posited the existence of an unobservable relation of superposition between mental states?

If we can trust the scientific experts (namely, psychologists), then the answer is no: psychologists have not postulated the existence of superpositions of mental states, and indeed they have found no use for this concept. But we can make the argument even stronger. What makes the concept of superposition as found in quantum mechanics scientifically acceptable is the fact that quantum mechanics provides the means to identify which states are superpositions of which other states (e.g. superpositions of spin-x states are spin-y states); and moreover it describes the empirical manifestations of superposition states (e.g. the superposition of $|left>$ and $|right>$ manifests a diffraction pattern). In other words, superposition is not an empty concept, but a concept with testable empirical content. But now let's apply this sort of rigorous standard to mental states. Consider the state of your mind when you see "left" on the computer monitor, and the state of your mind when you see "right" on the computer monitor. Now, if someone claims that these two states can be superposed, then he should be able to back this claim up by identifying the resulting state, and describing that state's empirical manifestations. Otherwise, his claim that such a state exists is empty, and does no explanatory work. But nobody has the first clue how to identify superpositions of mental states; indeed, no serious scientist has even ventured a speculative theory of the superposition of mental states. So, the claim that there are superpositions of mental states cannot be taken to be a serious scientific claim.

What, in contrast, might somebody say to argue for the existence of superpositions of mental states? The only possible argument I can imagine would be an argument by analogy: all physical states can be superposed, therefore (in absence of further evidence) we should suppose that mental states can be superposed. But why should we think that what's true of *physical* states should also be true of *mental* states

— unless of course, we have already decided that mental states are nothing but physical states in disguise? Perhaps the defender of mental superpositions will claim that if mental states are to be correlated with physical states, then these mental states will themselves need to be superposable. But that supposition is provably wrong: in what follows, I will show that physical states and mental states can be strictly correlated, even though the latter cannot be superposed.

The non-existence of mental superpositions has profound consequences for the states of a composite mental-physical system. In particular, according to quantum mechanics, composite physical objects can enter into entangled states in which neither individual object has any determinate properties — and this is precisely what was shown to happen in a measurement. But entanglement requires superposition: if states cannot enter into superpositions, then they also cannot become entangled.

INTERACTIONIST DYNAMICS

To this point I have argued — based on the assumption that mental states are distinct from physical states — that mental states are not superposable, and that mental states cannot become entangled with physical states. These points are enough to block the derivation of the measurement problem: they block the derivation of the claim that Martha fails, at the end of a measurement, to be in a state of seeing that something is so.

To defend the coherence of quantum mechanics against the measurement problem (in particular, to show that it does not entail a contradiction), it is fully sufficient to uncover an error (or tacit, but false, assumption) in the proof of one of the contradictory claims. But Albert's derivation of the measurement problem tacitly assumes physicalism, in contradiction with the starting point of this chapter and of this book as a whole. So, we would be fully justified in concluding this chapter at this point, having noted that the most severe problem for quantum mechanics emerges from an overly simplistic view of the mind-body relation.

But we always want to know more, in particular how mental and physical states might interact in such a way that we (conscious observers) are able reliably to gain information about the external world. Accordingly, I will proceed to sketch some ideas that might lead to a coherent understanding of how mental and physical states interact when we make observations, and in particular observations of quantum mechanical objects.

Consider again the computer monitor with its two states $|left>$ and $|right>$. Let $|"left">$ be Martha's mental state in which she believes that the computer screen displays "left," and let $|"right">$ be Martha's mental state in which she believes that the computer screen displays "right." If Martha is a reliable observer, then an initial state $|ready>|left>$ should lead to the final state $|"left">|left>$, and an initial state $|ready>|right>$ should lead to the final state $|"right">|right>$. But now suppose that the initial state is:

$$|ready>(|left>+|right>) = |ready>|left>+|ready>|right>.$$

If Martha's mental states could become entangled, then we would expect the final state to be an entangled state — that would follow from the assumption of linear dynamics (i.e. that superpositions are preserved through changes). But the resulting entangled state is *not possible*. We cannot apply the requirement of linear dynamics if it would lead to an impossible state.

In fact, it is impossible to fill out the story of what happens to Martha and the computer using deterministic dynamical laws. That is, if the computer starts out in state $|left>+|right>$, then the future state of Martha and computer is not determined: sometimes it will be $|"left">|left>$, and sometimes it will be $|"right">|right>$. Indeed, if we were to measure the initial state of Martha and the computer, then in 50 per cent of cases it would yield $|ready>|left>$, and in 50 per cent of cases it would yield $|ready>|right>$. Furthermore, we stipulated that $|ready>|right>$ would lead to $|"right">|right>$, and similarly $|ready>|left>$ would lead to $|"left">|left>$. Thus, applying the principle (as in common sense and classical physics) that probability is preserved through time, the final state should predict $|"right">|right>$ in half of the cases, and $|"left">|left>$ in the other half of the cases. However, because Martha's mental states cannot become entangled with the computer, there is *no* state that makes this prediction. Therefore, the future state of Martha and the computer cannot be determined by its initial state.

Could there then be indeterministic, or probabilistic dynamical laws that govern both aspects of the universe — physical and mental — and their interaction? From a purely mathematical point of view, there certainly could be. Indeed, the difficulty at this point is that we have *too many* options, and not enough evidence to choose between them.

First, we already have a dualist-friendly interpretation of quantum mechanics in the work of Henry Stapp.[14] But since Stapp has already written extensively and accessibly on his approach to quantum mechanics, I leave it to the diligent reader to explore these ideas on his or her own. Thus, I conclude this chapter by mentioning a few more of the possible options a dualist has for interpreting quantum theory.

First, one could take the equations of motion of Bohmian mechanics and reinterpret the terms referring to determinate particle configurations as referring to determinate mental states, in which objects are observed to be in determinate locations in space. (The resulting theory might be similar to Albert and Loewer's single mind theory.[15]) However, the resulting theory might not be the most natural for traditional interactionist dualism, because the theory would seem to endow perceptual states with their own autonomous dynamics rather than making them responsive to the states of the external world.

Second, and more promisingly, the Ghirardi-Rimini-Weber (GRW) collapse theory solves the measurement problem by introducing indeterministic dynamical laws. But one problem with GRW is that it seems to lack independent motivation: the collapse dynamics seems to be ad hoc, and put in by hand to solve the measurement problem. But here the dualist may have an advantage. In particular, we live in a universe with two types of things (physical and mental) with different natures; in particular, the physical things have superposition states, but the mental things do not. Now, suppose that the "natural" dynamics of physical things are the laws of quantum mechanics. However, we have seen that if a physical thing (e.g. a brain) is joined to a non-physical thing (e.g. a mind) in such a way that their states are correlated in a law-like way, then the physical thing *cannot* exactly and without exception obey the laws of quantum mechanics. (The non-existence of superpositions of mental states entails that the joint physical-mental object cannot obey the laws of quantum mechanics.) But what then is the next best thing? If the physical part in isolation would follow the rules of quantum mechanics but is constrained by the nature of its mental counterpart, then the GRW laws would provide a highly natural and harmonious way for these two sorts of objects to interact with each other and with other physical objects. Thus, a dualist could happily follow (or contribute to) the development of the GRW theory, but could underwrite it with independent motivation coming from his or her background metaphysical framework.

In conclusion, the sciences rightly take a central place in our efforts to develop an accurate system of beliefs. After all, the sciences are nothing more than a systematic effort to submit our beliefs to the tribunal of the external world. But the example of the measurement problem shows poignantly that it is naive or disingenuous to claim to approach the data from a standpoint of metaphysical neutrality, and to expect the data to provide its own interpretation. Rather, we always see the world through the lens of our background metaphysical assumptions; and if we put bad metaphysics into our scientific theories, then we can expect to get bad metaphysics out of them. (And, tragically, people of common sense sometimes throw out the baby with the bath water: they blame the scientific theories themselves rather than the interpretative supplements to these theories.) In the case of quantum mechanics, if one presupposes physicalism, then one quickly lands in the measurement problem; and one may then say crazy things about a new metaphysics of unfolding conscious wavefunctions, or minds being nothing but functional patterns in a universal wavefunction, or there being no objective reality outside of our perceptions. In contrast, if one begins with a common sense assumption of dualism, then one finds no reason in quantum mechanics to reject this assumption; quite to the contrary, quantum mechanics proves to be surprisingly in harmony with the accumulated wisdom of our metaphysical and scientific forebears.[16]

As we move on to our next essay, we point out that the two-slit experiments that Halvorson describes show that people's observations — the perceptions made by their souls — influence the outcomes of experiments in the laboratory. If that is true, is it really any more incredible that the decisions of their souls influence the outcomes of neurons firing in their brains, as assumed for example in Goetz's essay? We now know experimentally that more incredible things than this are happening all around us.

Halvorson has led us back from the physical to the psychological by way of the measurement problem — the role that people's observations play in current physics. With Dean Zimmerman's essay, we return entirely to the psychological level of our more everyday experience, considering again in more detail the implications of the (we believe) undeniable fact that people have perceptual experiences.

Like Halvorson, Zimmerman adopts the assumption that a psychological property of me like "I am seeing a patch of red over there" is (at least) logically distinct from any physical property that I have, such as my various brain states. Indeed, Zimmerman fills in briefly some of the reasons why many contemporary philosophers make this assumption, which Halvorson simply assumes. For example, it seems logically possible that there could be creatures that behave just like we do, but have no inner life, no first-person experience of qualia at all — what philosophers refer to as "zombies." Or it seems possible that there could be creatures just like us who have perceptual experiences, but whose experiences are systematically different from ours: for example, maybe when they see something that gives me the quale that I call red, they actually have a quale that I would call green, whereas what I experience as green they experience as red. If such differences are possible, then it seems that psychological states are partially independent of physical states. This leads to a view that is known among the professionals as "property dualism"—the idea that there are fundamentally different kinds of properties that something like a person might have. Much as a single object like a ball can have two different physical properties at once (say, being red and being hard), so I might have two different kinds of properties at once: the physical property of having a certain kind of cone fire on the retina of my eye, and the psychological property of experiencing red.

But instead of considering the implications of the distinction between physical and mental properties for quantum physics, Zimmerman considers its implications for the Soul Hypothesis more directly. Many people in the current intellectual scene are open to the idea of property dualism (that there are two distinct kinds of properties, physical properties and psychological ones) who are not open to traditional substance dualism — the idea that there are two distinct kinds of things, physical things like bodies and non-physical things like souls. Mere property dualism no doubt seems like a safer, more conservative hypothesis to them. But Zimmerman presents a philosophical line of argument that it is harder to take this easy way out than it might appear at first.

Zimmerman's argument centers on the issue of vagueness. This is the undeniable fact that all middle-sized objects that we are familiar with have imprecise boundaries in both time and space. It is not perfectly clear just where they start or stop, or exactly when they first begin to exist or stop existing. As I hiked from the level valley up to the peak of the mountain, at what point did I first set foot on the mountain itself? As an acorn in my yard germinated and sprouted and grew large and strong, at what instant did it first become a tree? We do not expect precise, non-arbitrary answers to questions like this. But our simplest and most fundamental experiences are not vague and fuzzy in the same way that these physical objects are. How then can a vague and imprecise physical object, like my brain or my nervous system or my whole body, directly produce the discrete and unique experiences that I have? Zimmerman suggests that careful thinking about this should free us from the notion that property dualism is really simpler and more conservative than substance dualism. On the contrary, he suggests that it is much more plausible that new kinds of properties like "seeing red" exist because new kinds of things exist that have those properties — namely souls.

In essence, Zimmerman's argument is as follows. The vague objects that are the standard candidates for what a person fundamentally is according to materialism are a brain, or a nervous system, or a human body, or the like. These are the obvious candidates because (i) they can be identified as distinguishable units by (say) an anatomist, and (ii) the direct causes of mental events seem to be located inside them. But it turns out that vague objects like brains and bodies are not suitable candidates for having mental properties because the laws of nature that presumably link physical properties and mental properties in systematic ways must be precise. After all, the fundamental physical laws that we know of refer to precise things like electrons and photons, not to imprecise composite things like mountains and trees, and crucially so. It follows, then, that the subject of basic mental properties must also be precise in nature, and human brains and bodies do not fit the bill. (Or, even if the mental properties are not entirely precise, there is no reason to think that any vagueness they might have corresponds directly to the familiar kind of vagueness that bodies and brains have.) One prevalent way to think about vague objects like mountains and trees is to say that there is a veritable host of objects in the vicinity that could be the precise mountain or the precise tree that we refer to in a particular situation. If we said the same thing about human brains and bodies, then there would also be a veritable host of objects (e.g. slightly different collections of cells or molecules or atoms) in the vicinity that could be the precise brain or body that is the subject of mental properties. But none of these arbitrarily chosen but precise objects presents itself as the better candidate for being the precise subject of mental properties. In the face of this quandary, then, Zimmerman bids us remember that substance dualism provides a natural alternative: that we are in essence souls, and not some imprecise physical thing. Since souls are (by hypothesis) not physical things, they are not a composite of cells, molecules, and atoms. Therefore, their boundaries in space and time need not be vague in the ways that medium scale physical objects necessarily are. They could then be precisely the right things to have the psychological properties that we know we have.

CHAPTER 7

From Experience to Experiencer

Dean Zimmerman

VARIETIES OF DUALISM AND MATERIALISM

Throughout history and pre-history, the majority view of humankind seems always to have been that there is more to a person than the body, and that an "afterlife" is possible because this "something more" — the soul or spirit — does not pass away with the death of the body. Many philosophers have agreed, developing various forms of mind-body dualism. Philosophical dualists such as Plato, Aquinas, and Descartes — and, more recently, Karl Popper, Richard Swinburne, and William Hasker — disagree about many details. But they have this much in common: they believe that, for every person who thinks or has experiences, there is a thing — a soul or spiritual substance — that lacks many or most of the physical properties characteristic of non-thinking material objects like rocks and trees; and that this soul is essential to the person, and in one way or another responsible for the person's mental life.

Nowadays, this view is often called "substance dualism," and contrasted with various forms of "property dualism." Property dualism is the idea that the mental properties of persons are significantly independent of, or in some other way distinct from, the physical properties of persons. The distinction between the two kinds of dualism allows for an intermediate view, the combination of property dualism with substance materialism. On this conception of what it is to be a human person, each of us is a material object — something that, ultimately, is made up entirely of parts that can be found in non-thinking things — but a material object with a special kind of properties — mental properties

or states, varieties of feelings and thoughts — that are at least somewhat independent of our purely physical aspects. This combination of
property dualism with substance materialism is sometimes called "the
dual-aspect theory."

The dual-aspect theory, so understood, is a version of substance
materialism. As Robin Collins points out in Chapter 9 of this book,
there is a version of substance dualism (or "entity dualism," as he calls
it) that also attributes two aspects to persons: a subjective or experiential
aspect, and non-subjective aspects that help explain how the soul and
brain work together to generate a rich conscious life. Nothing in my
chapter turns upon whether the substance dualist should follow Collins
in positing a complex, non-subjective aspect to persons. Perhaps *his* sort
of dual-aspect theory is correct. What I shall be criticizing, however, are
dual aspect versions of substance materialism.

One might worry whether it is even possible for the materialist to
formulate a stable kind of dual aspect view. Many substance dualists
have claimed that thinking is impossible for mere matter. But this claim
surely needs some serious argument; on the face of it, the combination
of property dualism and substance materialism seems to be a consistent position. In general, the fact that one class of properties can vary
independently of another does not rule out the possibility that some
things have both kinds of properties. Substance materialists who are
property dualists can point to the example of colors and shapes. Color
properties and shape properties seem to be independent of one another.
Yet a single object, such as a red ball, can have both; it does not have
a part that is red but shapeless and another part that is spherical but
colorless. Philosophers who deny substance dualism while advocating
a robust form of property dualism are claiming that mental and physical
properties are independent in something like the way color and shape
are, while affirming that they are attributes of a single object, consisting
entirely of ordinary matter.

In this chapter, "dualism" shall usually carry its more traditional
meaning: substance dualism. But I will defend property dualism as
well, and argue that property dualism makes trouble for the more
plausible forms of substance materialism. And this leaves the more
plausible versions of substance dualism looking better than one might
have thought.

The paper begins with a meditation on the question, "What am I?,"
to which dualism and materialism are competing answers. The most
plausible versions of materialism and dualism are then described —
"garden variety materialism" and "emergent dualism." Property dualism

is then defended, in its own right. It turns out that, if property dualism is true, objections to dualistic interaction become less pressing. Finally, garden variety materialism is criticized for the vagueness of the material objects it offers as candidates to be me. Their temporal vagueness makes it hard to know what "I" could refer to. And their spatial vagueness leads to more severe problems: given the nature of vague objects, it is hard to see how one of them could be the subject of the fundamental phenomenal states required by property dualism. The upshot: only very weird versions of materialism are left standing, and emergent dualism starts to look like a better alternative. Given the truth of property dualism, it should not be too surprising to discover that substance dualism is true as well.

FINDING ONESELF

Substance dualism and substance materialism are competing answers, at a high level of generality, to the question each of us may ask with the words: "What am I?" (spoken in a metaphysical tone of voice, with emphasis on the word "am"). Answering the question with any specificity turns out to be harder than one might think. These days, many people will take it to be just obvious that we are mere material objects. But there are at once too many candidates, and not enough sufficiently distinguished candidates, for the role of *the* material object with which I am supposed to be identical.

The problem can be approached by way of the unity of consciousness. Each of us knows that whatever is asking the question "What am I?" must be a single thing capable of exemplifying a plurality of psychological properties. Its unitary nature consists in the impossibility of its exhibiting a certain sort of "division of psychological labor." If a single thinker can recognize the difference between sounds and colors, this thinker does not enjoy the ability to compare the two simply by having one part that does its seeing and another that does its hearing, even if these parts are tightly bound together. As Brentano put it, this "would be like saying that, of course, neither a blind man nor a deaf man could compare colors with sounds, but if one sees and the other hears, the two together can recognize the relationship."[1]

The unity of consciousness poses a difficult question: what is this single thing that has auditory and olfactory and visual and tactual and gustatory sensations? I know that I am whatever thing it is that has all of the sensations I am now having; how could I fail to be? But can I know what kind of thing this is; that is, can I know what *other* characteristics I have?

We can't tell, merely by thinking about the meaning of the word "I," what the word refers to in our mouths — nothing about the function of the word "I" will tell us much about the intrinsic nature of persons. If dualism is false, it's what philosophers call an *a posteriori* falsehood (i.e. something we could only discover to be false by learning things about the world). Likewise, if materialism is true, it's an *a posteriori* truth. In other words, I need to learn about what kinds of things the world contains, and which ones are most closely connected to my conscious states, before I should reach any conclusions about the kind of thing I am.

My exploration of the contents of the world, in search of myself, may begin with mere introspection — "looking into my mind" and seeing what it contains — but it cannot end there. Introspection reveals "bodily sensations," but the phenomenon of phantom limbs should convince us that such sensations do not require that one actually *have* the bodily parts one *seems* to feel. Perhaps a version of materialism is true according to which my leg is a part of me; but the mere fact that I have bodily sensations *as of a leg* does not mean that I have a leg as a part. Conversely, if I have taken certain drugs or undergone a "near death" episode, introspection may reveal what feels like an "out-of-body experience"; but again, the experience may be an illusion. Drugs, brain trauma, and psychological illness may cause all sorts of delusional but utterly convincing experiences. The thesis that George Graham calls "weak ontic ignorance" seems very plausible: the intrinsic nature of the self is simply not given in introspection.[2]

Recent work in the philosophy of language can help explain why the self proves so elusive — how it is that our own intrinsic nature can be opaque to us. Our self-conception "leaves a blank" to be filled in by how things happen actually to be. The function of the word "I," and of the concept of *myself*, is to pick out the thinker of these thoughts, no matter what that thing is like intrinsically (whether material or immaterial or something else), and no matter what I may believe about my own nature. And that is why I cannot figure it out, *a priori*, just by reflecting on the meaning of "I."

A person, like me, who thinks he's an immaterial soul uses "I" in roughly the same way as a person who thinks that he's a brain, or a body, or even (like some "madmen" Descartes mentions) that he is made out of glass. Changing your views about your intrinsic nature doesn't change the general rules in virtue of which "I" picks out its referent.

And such changes may well fail to shift the referent of the word "I" in your mouth.[3]

This is merely the application, to first-person pronouns, of what has come to be the orthodox view about how natural kind terms and indexicals function. (Indexicals include terms like "I," "now," "here," and "that" or "this" when these latter two words are used by a person pointing to things.) Here is Thomas Nagel's comparison of "I" to the natural kind term "gold":

> The essence of what a term refers to depends on what the world is actually like, and not just on what we have to know in order to use and understand the term. I may understand and be able to apply the term "gold" without knowing what gold really is — what physical and chemical conditions anything must meet to be gold. My prescientific idea of gold, including my knowledge of the perceptible features by which I identify samples of it, includes a blank space to be filled in by empirical discoveries about its intrinsic nature. Similarly I may understand and be able to apply the term "I" to myself without knowing what I really am. In Kripke's phrase, what I use to *fix the reference* of the term does not tell me everything about the nature of the referent. . . . Various accounts of my real nature, and therefore various conditions of my identity over time, are compatible with my concept of myself as a self, for that concept leaves open the real nature of what it refers to.[4]

To sum up, then: materialism isn't shown to be true just by reflection, or by *a priori* reasoning; it's an hypothesis about the referent of "I" — perhaps the most plausible hypothesis, at least on first blush, but not something revealed to us by armchair reflection. It is not obvious to me that substance dualism is in a better position, given just *a priori* evidence. At least, I shall not try to show that dualism can be conclusively supported by *mere* reflection upon my experience; nor will I try to argue, *a priori*, that no thinking thing could be made out of the kinds of particles that constitute my body. It is time to get out of the armchair and look more closely at the contents of the physical world, in order to see whether there is a place for ourselves.

THE VARIETIES OF "GARDEN VARIETY MATERIALISM"

Some versions of materialism give quite implausible answers to the question, "Which physical thing am I?" Descartes mentions some insane materialists who believe "that their heads are made of earthenware, or that they are pumpkins, or made of glass."[5] A couple of otherwise sane contemporary philosophers have taken seriously the thesis that we are tiny physical particles lodged somewhere in our brains.[6] But more popular by far (and rightly so) are versions of materialism that pick more familiar physical objects to be me — what I'll call "garden variety material objects," the kinds of things we bump into every day, and for which we already have names. Tables and chairs, and many of their detachable parts (for example, chair and table legs, table-tops, seats, cushions, nuts and bolts) are garden variety material objects; as are trees, and many of their parts (such as their seeds, leaves, bark, limbs, and roots). But the best candidates for being a human person, among garden variety material objects, are human organisms and their familiar, naturally demarcated parts — most especially, our brains.

Here is what I mean by calling a part of a living body a "natural part": its spatial boundaries are reasonably sharply defined, and, assuming that it is made out of parts itself, these further parts work together to perform some function. Examples include: a single atom within a strand of DNA, the heart, the kidneys, the spine, an individual blood cell, the respiratory system, the entire nervous system, the brain, the cerebrum, a single cerebral hemisphere, and the complete organism (the "biggest part"). Basically, if it is worth listing in a book about human physiology or biochemistry, it will count as a natural part, for my purposes. Now that we have had plenty of experience examining the insides of mammalian bodies, including human bodies, all these organs have become "garden variety material objects" to us — just as examination of a flower reveals petals, stamen, pollen, and so on. Among the natural parts of a human body, some are better candidates than others for being the person associated with that body. For one thing, if there is a physical "organ of thought" — a smallest natural part that includes all the parts upon which my ability to think most immediately depends — then I surely ought to have that organ as a part. The parts that fit these criteria are primarily: the complete organism I refer to as "my body," the entire nervous system within it, the brain, the cerebrum, and perhaps one or the other single hemisphere of that cerebrum. These are garden variety objects, in the sense that they are the physical objects with naturally demarcated boundaries that we find when we stroll through the "garden" of the human body; and I will sometimes call them "the standard candidates" for being me. Garden variety materialism, then, will be the thesis that each human person has the size and shape of one of these naturally demarcated, garden variety parts.

I am only interested in one fact about the standard candidates: all of them, being garden variety objects, are vague in their spatial and temporal boundaries. I shall argue that this vagueness raises insuperable difficulties for standard materialism, leaving dualism looking better off — for it will then only be competing with versions of materialism that pick unfamiliar physical objects to be me, and so far, the pickings are slim. In these circumstances, materialists must adopt a more speculative form of materialism; and, so far, there has emerged no such version of materialism that would compare favorably with the better versions of substance dualism — to which I now turn.

AN ALTERNATIVE TO STANDARD MATERIALISM: EMERGENT DUALISM

I now describe the version of dualism I find most appealing, the one I believe to have the best chance at competing with substance material- ism, namely, the kind of "emergent dualism" defended elsewhere in this volume (Chapter 8) by William Hasker. Although something like it has been widely accepted by ordinary folk all over the world and through the millennia, it may strike many scientifically educated people as ridiculous, an exploded myth. What I hope to show is that, when all is said and done, it is at least no crazier — no more improbable, on first blush, as an answer to the question "What am I?" — than the more speculative versions of materialism to which I shall attempt to drive the dual aspect theorists.

The empirical facts strongly suggest that human minds are depen- dent, both for their existence and many of their characteristics, upon brains. Some dualists have denied this. Descartes thought that: (i) no mere brain could produce conscious states without interacting with a soul, (ii) brains are not themselves capable of generating souls naturally, and (iii) God does not care to work the miracle necessary to bring a brain into interaction with a soul in the case of non-human animals. And so Descartes was led to deny that any non-human animal has conscious experiences. But surely at least the higher mammals *are* conscious; so at least one of these three theses is false. Do all sentient creatures have souls, then? If (i) is true, and brains alone cannot produce consciousness, then they must. But, according to (ii), brains do not natu- rally produce souls, and so each animal soul would have to be specially created by God, just like human souls. Some dualists have accepted this result, rejecting (iii): God does intervene in nature, distributing animal souls wherever and whenever they are needed. Assigning God this role would be a relatively minor departure from fully fledged Cartesianism. But would there really have to be so much divine tinkering, simply in order to insure that each organism with a sufficiently complex nervous system is able to be conscious? Couldn't God have designed creatures in which consciousness arises *naturally*? Many dualists have thought it would be sloppy for God to create a world requiring nearly constant miraculous intervention. And, despite a close association between dualism and theism, many dualists have not believed in a personal God who could intervene, or in any sort of God at all. One needn't be a Christian, like Descartes, in order to be a dualist. And of course atheistic or deistic dualists cannot follow Descartes in supposing that divine intervention is needed to introduce souls into the natural order.

Many dualists, then, will not want to reject (iii). They must, then, reject either (i) or (ii) — and, with it, some other part of the Cartesian picture. One could, I suppose, reject (i), holding instead that, in nonhuman animals, there are conscious states but no souls. On this view, a mere organism, or a brain, or some other physical part of the animal can have experiences; no soul is needed. But here is an argument that (i) should be retained, and that it is rather (ii) that must go: If the events in the brain of a chimp were causally sufficient to confer conscious states upon its body or brain, then the very similar events in my skull ought to do the same for *my* body or brain.[7] But dualists want to deny this — it is, in human persons at least, the *soul* that has the conscious states. Consequently, the dualist should reject (ii): brains like ours, and also those that are less complex but still quite similar, are naturally capable of causing souls to exist.

Some contemporary dualists, like William Hasker[8] and Richard Swinburne,[9] accept this conclusion, advocating a view sometimes called "emergent dualism", whereby organisms having nervous systems complex enough to generate conscious states automatically *also* generate nonphysical subjects for those states. Though brains and souls share no parts in common, each soul remains radically dependent upon one brain for its continued existence and for many, if not all, of its powers and dispositions. Since Hasker and Swinburne believe in an afterlife, they affirm that God could (and does) miraculously prevent the dissolution of the soul that would (or at least might) naturally occur when the nervous system upon which it is dependent ceases to function.[10] Hasker also supposes that each nonphysical subject is located somewhere within the nervous system that generates it.

Some will say emergent dualism is not *real* dualism, reserving the name for nothing but Cartesianism. But why should Descartes's version of dualism be the only game in town? In order to count as a genuine dualism of substances, a theory must say that persons, unlike plants and the bodies of animals, are not made of the same kinds of stuff as ordinary inanimate objects. Where dualists disagree is over just how radically different from ordinary matter these new substances, or souls, must be. A soul posited by a particular version of dualism will seem less physical the fewer the number of properties that are said to characterize both substances capable of thought (and their parts, if any) and substances utterly incapable of thought. As a matter of fact, dualists have disagreed about how much souls have in common with ordinary matter; they have meant different things by calling souls "nonphysical." The result is a spectrum of dualisms, with Cartesian dualism near one end and emergent dualism closer to the other end.

The maximal difference a dualist might posit between soul and body would be to identify souls with necessarily existing abstract objects, outside of space and time, like numbers or Plato's Forms. This sort of dualism goes even further than Descartes'; it makes souls out to be even more radically unlike material objects. But almost no one would want to accept a dualism so radical as that.[11] Almost all dualists will agree that souls have this much in common with ordinary material things: they are concrete entities, existing in time, and capable of change.

Descartes allowed at least *that* much similarity between souls and ordinary matter, but little more. Cartesian souls have no position in space. Descartes also claimed that souls are "simple," or without parts. Since he believed that everything in space was infinitely divisible, this was another way in which souls were unlike anything made of ordinary matter. Dualists who deny these aspects of Descartes's particular form of dualism are merely staking their claim at a different location along the spectrum of possible dualisms about persons.

Emergent dualism is much less extreme than Cartesian dualism. Emergent dualists make souls a part of the natural order, generated by any brain sufficiently complex to support conscious experience. If souls are in space, some of the worst problems of interaction are easily solved. Although I shall not try to defend the claim here, I am convinced that the better arguments for dualism do not require that the soul have all the features Descartes attributed to it, or that it lack all those he withheld from it. Less radical dualisms are, in fact, safer — they posit no more differences between souls and material objects than are required by the reasons for rejecting materialism.

PROPERTY DUALISM

I have claimed that emergent dualism is less implausible than other forms of dualism, and that substance materialism is not conclusively established simply by reflecting upon the nature of my experience — for example, from the fact that I can "feel my limbs" it does not immediately follow that I am identical with the body that has those limbs among its parts. One may, however, grant all of this while nevertheless insisting that, *obviously*, we are mere material objects. Materialism will seem to many to be the default view about our nature. We know that human brains and bodies exist, and that they are entirely and unproblematically physical; we know that our ability to think and feel and act is radically dependent upon their proper function. Why go out on a limb, positing the existence of some extra, nonphysical thing? In the absence of a compelling argument for immaterial souls, the only sensible conclusion is that we are entirely physical in nature. At least, that's how many materialists will see the matter.

Are there positive reasons to posit immaterial substances in addition to the material substances that constitute our bodies? Many philosophers have given arguments for the conclusion that human persons are immaterial souls; some are more impressive than others.[12] The line of thought I shall pursue here is to argue, first, for property dualism. The considerations I raise are familiar ones, and they have convinced many philosophers that, even if we are made entirely of physical particles — just like rocks and trees — we nevertheless must have a "side" to us that is independent of our physical nature. Our conscious experience presents us with an "aspect" or set of properties that is not fully determined, in any very strong sense, by the properties we share with unconscious physical objects. In subsequent sections I will argue that, given property dualism, garden variety materialism cannot be maintained, and more speculative forms of materialism turn out to be even less plausible than emergent dualism.

The case for a dualism of mental and physical properties is most compelling when it focuses on conscious experience, especially the distinctive "way that it feels" to have experiences of different kinds — what philosophers sometimes call the "phenomenal aspects" of conscious experience. Some mental events have no distinctive phenomenal aspects; there is, for example, no single, characteristic way that it feels to believe the Pythagorean theorem. Experiences, however, do include phenomenal aspects (or, in philosophers' jargon, qualia). Most people who look at a stop sign experience phenomenal redness — the quality (or quale) that fills an octagonal part of one's visual field when looking at the sign, and which also turns up in red after-images or the hallucination of a bloody dagger. Similar things can be said about the phenomenal aspects of tastes, smells, sounds, pains, tickles, and so on.

Qualia make trouble for materialists. Today's materialists have learned to live with little agreement among themselves about the nature of mental states; and they would not presume to guess what physics will finally say about the nature of matter. In the absence of a positive consensus, they have rallied their forces around the following more general doctrines, under the banner "physicalism": the universe consists entirely of atoms in the void, or particles and fields, or hyper-dimensional superstrings, or whatever physics ultimately settles upon as the terms of the most fundamental causal transactions. These basic physical entities, physicalists suppose, do not include minds or anything else with the tincture of mentality about it. And everything that happens in the universe boils down to nothing but mindless, physical interactions among these basic entities.

There is controversy about what "boiling down" requires, but most who accept the label "physicalist" seem to agree upon two components. (i) "Higher level" phenomena — biological, psychological, sociological, and so on — are determined by what goes on at the basic physical level. A universe that exactly duplicates our distribution of matter throughout space-time must include organisms, thoughts, and political movements exactly like ours. (ii) "Higher level" phenomena must be ultimately explicable in basic physical terms. It may not be very useful, given our usual purposes, to describe a case of cirrhosis of the liver, or a red sensation, or a revolution, in terms of the activity of subatomic particles, and the laws governing such phenomena may not be reducible in any tidy way to laws of physics. But, physicalists will insist, there must in principle be a story that could be told that would show how all the facts about human beings — including facts about diseases, sensations, and wars — are necessitated by the physical facts discussed by physics.

To some philosophers, this version of physicalism seems almost to be part of "enlightened common sense." A vocal minority disagrees, offering several arguments against physicalist orthodoxy. Here, I shall focus exclusively upon two such arguments, based upon famous thought experiments. One can tell stories about creatures who behave like humans, but lack all phenomenal experiences ("zombies"), and one can tell stories in which a subject's phenomenal experiences change in systematic ways, but leave the physical states of the brain unchanged (inverted spectrum arguments), and although these stories may sound bizarre and improbable, they do not strike us as outright incoherent and impossible. And if these stories really do describe some possible creatures, however "far out" and unlikely they might be, then physicalism is false.

In the philosophy of mind, as in the cinema, zombies are everywhere. But the philosophers' zombies do not gibber and drool and eat brains. A philosophical zombie is a creature that is outwardly and behaviorally exactly like a normal human being, and is even perhaps identical in its internal physical makeup, but is somehow completely devoid of conscious experience. Philosophers tell stories about these imaginary creatures, hoping to shed light on the relationship between mind and matter. When pricked, a philosophical zombie bleeds, and says "ouch!" But it has no feeling of pain. Its eyes respond to light just as ours do; it says "Bananas are yellow," and it won't eat green bananas. But it never experiences yellow qualia, never has a yellowish patch of color in its visual field — in fact, it has no visual field. The zombie experiences none of the qualia we know through taste, smell, hearing, touch, and other forms of sensation (philosophical zombies are more like the angels in the German film *Wings of Desire* than the "living dead").

Are zombies *really* possible? Consider a body somewhat like ours, but controlled remotely by radio communication with a giant computer. Ordinary human beings may be extremely complex, but it is plausible to suppose that our complexity could, at least in principle, be replicated by a monumentally complex computer. Putting these two thoughts together, there could, in principle, be creatures behaviorally indistinguishable from us but with computers for "brains." Would they be conscious? Would they feel pain, experience our spectrum of colors, and so on? The natural reaction is: Who knows? How could we tell whether exactly duplicating the human brain's functional capacities in different "hardware" would generate qualia? It is an open question, one that we human beings might never be able to answer, were we actually confronted with such creatures. A growing number of philosophers of mind believe that this natural reaction is the right reaction to have — it represents a positive insight into the nature of qualia, the presence or absence of qualia within a given computer-brain is a merely *contingent* matter. It is possible — one wants to say, "God could make" — computer-brains with qualia, and ones without. But then it should be a merely contingent matter whether *other* complex objects generate qualia — including objects that look, from the outside, just like our brains. Of course *we* know that *our* brains do — we know this "from the inside." But if it is a contingent matter whether non-organic beings have conscious experience, it must be a contingent matter whether organisms more closely resembling us have conscious experience. So zombies are possible.

If creatures completely devoid of experience seem too outrageous, there are less extreme scenarios that work just as well, for the property dualist's purposes. One needn't be a philosopher to wonder whether one's own experiences of color might not be the same as others'. The colorblind miss shades that the rest of us see, and some kinds of animals can see wavelengths of light that make no impression on us. How do the colors they see compare to those present to one's own consciousness? The natural reaction is: there must be an answer, but there is no telling what it is.

The possibility of more radical shifts in visual qualia can turn this reaction into an argument for property dualism. Suppose goggles were constructed that would systematically shift one's experiences of shades of color. Whenever one would normally have an experience as of something red, the goggles cause an experience as of something violet; whenever one would normally experience orange, the goggles cause an experience of indigo; and so on, inverting the entire spectrum of experienced colors (except for one lone shade of green, in the middle, which the goggles leave alone). Someone fitted with the goggles from birth would learn to use color words in the same circumstances as the rest of us, and would discriminate shades just as finely as the rest of us, but her experiences would be radically different, phenomenally, from ours — as she would discover, when the goggles were finally removed. If goggles can invert the spectrum of experienced colors, so could the right sort of interference with the workings of the eyes, or the optic nerves. Presumably, the trick could be pulled off by fiddling with processes still deeper in the brain, where our color experiences are "constructed" (the final character of the visual field is based rather loosely on the information provided by the rods and cones in the eye).

These possibilities show that no amount of attention to the color discriminations a person is able to make, or even the way her eyes respond to light, will rule out the possibility that her experience, when she says something "looks red," is phenomenally like our experience when something looks violet to us. Still, it would seem safe to conclude that, if two humans have equally good color vision, and similar eyes and optic nerves, then the way their visual cortexes work is probably similar, and that similarity at that level should be reliably correlated with similar experiences — so one could reasonably assume that most humans have the same qualia when they say something "looks red." But suppose we encounter a species of intelligent alien that registers visual information using binocular eyes much like ours, and describes experience using words that seem to correspond to "red," "green," and so on; however, in these aliens, the brain is made of quite different stuff. We can no longer infer similarity of their qualia with ours on the basis of similarity in the mechanism by which color experience is ultimately generated within the brain. Two genuinely different possibilities present themselves: colored objects may look to them as they do to us now, or objects may look to them as they would look to us were we wearing the spectrum-inverting goggles. (No doubt there are other possibilities as well.)

There will be a physical story to be told about the generation of color experience in alien brains by wavelengths toward the red end of the spectrum; and whatever it is, the question will remain: Is an experience similar to ours, when things appear red, hooked up with this physical process? Or is it an experience of phenomenal violet, instead? (Or does the experience have some quale from a range of phenomenal colors with which we are unfamiliar?) Whatever the answer, it *feels* as though it should be a contingent one. These particular wavelengths of light were associated, in the aliens, with the range of color experiences enjoyed by normal folks, say; but they *could* have been associated with the kinds of experiences enjoyed by the goggle-wearer. And if that is the right thing to say about the aliens, one should also say it about us. As a matter of fact, God (or Nature or whatever) built us in one of these ways; but creatures could have been designed along physically similar lines, but with inverted phenomenal experiences arising from the workings of their otherwise identical brains.

Once you accept the bare possibility of *either* zombies *or* creatures just like us but with inverted spectra, you have rejected physicalism in favor of a dualism of mental and physical properties. Take all the facts about the world that can be stated within a "final physics" that mentions no mentality. If zombies are possible, it would remain an open question whether the world contains phenomenal experience at all. If it is possible for there to be physically similar creatures with systematically shifted color experiences, it would remain an open question which individuals had *which* qualia. To settle the matter, one would need to know about some extra laws of nature, linking brain states and qualia.

The conclusion supported by appeal to the possibility of zombies, inverted spectra, and the like is, I take it, a thesis about which kinds of similarity and difference "carve nature at the joints." Plato's metaphorical talk of "joints" in nature is a way of expressing the idea that some properties are more "natural" than others, some kinds of similarity are deeper than others. The truly natural properties are the ones responsible for the most fundamental kinds of objective resemblance among things. Naturalness comes in degrees because resemblance comes in degrees; and property dualism is a claim about where phenomenal similarities and dissimilarities lie on the spectrum from more to less natural. Some phenomenal properties or conditions are less than perfectly natural (for example, highly gerrymandered or disjunctive ones, like seeing-red-or-feeling-an-itch; and very general ones, like hearing some sound or other). But, like other families of properties, the phenomenal ones come in more and less precise forms — some are highly determinate or specific, while others are determinable or more general. Examples include: having some mass or other, being roughly one kilogram in mass, and being precisely one kilogram in mass; and having some shape or other, being quadrilateral, and being square. Similarly, the phenomenal aspects of experience come in more and less determinate forms. If someone describes an experience as being "as of something colored," "as of something red," and "as of something scarlet," the property dualist will suppose there is a corresponding series of properties ascribable to qualia: phenomenal color, phenomenal redness, and phenomenal scarlet. In such families of properties, the more general ones are exemplified because the most precise ones are; and the most precise ones are the most natural ones, the real joints in nature. The arguments for property dualism support the conclusion that similarities and differences among experiences, due ultimately to these precise qualia properties, are independent of the similarities and differences determined by physical properties of things.

How natural are these properties? If they are not determined by the physical properties of things, nor by any other family of properties that does not include them, they must simply be another basic respect in which things can resemble one another. When we ask ourselves whether there could be creatures physically like us, but with inverted spectra, we are not, most of us, imagining, in vivid detail, the true neurophysiological side of color experience — since *we* don't know its details. We are simply imagining creatures just like us with respect to *whatever* other properties our brains may have, besides the qualia with which we are familiar in experience. There is little prospect of finding some other family of properties — neither those mentioned in physics, nor those discovered in experience — that could be more basic than our qualia, somehow grounding phenomenal similarity and difference in another realm, beyond the reach of physics or our experience.

The property dualist is, then, committed to the idea that our experiences resemble one another in virtue of some family of most basic phenomenal properties — the most precise qualia, whatever they are and whatever has them — and that these qualia represent perfectly natural "joints in nature" — as natural as the most natural properties that would be mentioned in an idealized "final physics."

With qualia fundamental, yet obviously caused by the workings of brains, the property dualist will have to suppose that the catalogue of fundamental properties and fundamental laws includes more than just the kinds one finds in physics as it currently stands. Paul Churchland considers the hypothesis that "mental properties are *fundamental* properties of reality . . . on a par with length, mass, electric charge, and other fundamental properties." Churchland notes that a property dualist might cite, as historical precedent, other cases in which a property was thought to be reducible but turned out to be fundamental — e.g. "electromagnetic phenomena (such as electric charge and magnetic attraction)" which were once thought to be "just an unusually subtle manifestation of purely *mechanical* phenomena" but ultimately had to be added to "the existing list of fundamental properties."

> Perhaps mental properties enjoy a status like that of electromagnetic properties: irreducible, but not emergent. Such a view may be called *elemental-property dualism*. . . . Unfortunately, the parallel with electromagnetic phenomena has one very obvious failure. Unlike electromagnetic properties, which are displayed at all levels of reality from the subatomic level on up, mental properties are displayed only in large physical systems that have evolved a very complex internal organization. . . . They do not appear to be basic or elemental at all.[13]

Churchland's objection is not a trivial one, and property dualists need to do more than they have so far done to answer it. I will not address it seriously here, beyond a couple of remarks. For one thing, I disagree with Churchland if he is implying that the qualitative properties that characterize my experience — e.g. the particular color qualia exemplified in the parts of my visual field — do not *seem* basic or elemental. They certainly seem so to me (though the complicated patterns in which they occur do not). A second point is relevant to the prospects for substance dualism. Churchland seems to be presupposing that mental properties are exemplified by "large physical systems" that display "complex internal organization"; but, even though property dualists who accept some version of garden variety materialism must accept this, the emergent dualist, at least, need not.

I shall take property dualism to be true, a thesis supported by cogent philosophical arguments having nothing to do with substance dualism and souls. And I will argue that accepting it makes substance dualism look much better than it otherwise would. Property dualism requires that we posit fundamental laws governing fundamental phenomenal properties. Ultimately, this will raise serious problems for any form of garden variety materialism.

THE STRUCTURE OF PHENOMENAL STATES

Stories about inverted spectra and zombies are supposed to show that, had the laws relating brains and conscious states been different, the objects we see would have appeared differently to us, despite precise similarity in the light waves hitting our retinas and the patterns of neural firing in our brains. Stop signs now appear red, but in the inverted world, they appear violet. Somewhere, qualia have been switched — but what is it that switched properties, what kind of thing has the most fundamental phenomenal properties?

The property dualist has a choice: she can either suppose that qualia are exemplified by some range of things to which the subject is related in experience; or she can regard them as properties had by conscious subjects themselves. Philosophers (and psychologists, when the discipline was younger) have engaged in considerable armchair speculation about the amount and kind of complexity to be found in phenomenal states; and each of the two choices for the subjects of qualia has had its defenders. The most popular versions of the two approaches have been called the "act-object theory" and the "adverbial theory."

Take the kind of experience I have when I see a stop sign in front of me, or I hallucinate a bright red object before me, or am in some other situation that would lead me to say that something red is in the center of my visual field. To some, it has seemed obvious that *appearing red* is something that can only be done by an object or entity of some kind, distinct from the experiencing subject; to have an experience "as of something red" is to engage in an "act" of sensing which acquires its reddish character from the nature of its "object." To be an "act-object theorist" about a certain kind of phenomenal experience is to attribute a relational structure to the experience. According to an act-object theory, the distinctive qualia of this type of experience belong to something other than the subject of the experience; and differences among similar types of phenomenal state are construed as differences in the properties had by the entities to which the subject is related. G. E. Moore and other sense data theorists took all phenomenal states to have such an act-object structure.[14] Sensing is relational; there is no sensing without sensibilia.

Some philosophers reject the analysis of sensory experience in terms of a relation between a thing that is appeared to in a certain way (the subject of the experience) and an appearance (the object). To be sure, in the case of visual experience, it is natural to give an act-object analysis. Even in complete visual hallucination, it seems as though one is related to *some* sort of object — a two-dimensional colored surface, albeit one that turns out not to be part of the surface of any physical object or even to be located in physical space. But it is less obvious that, when experiencing a dull headache, for instance, there is a meaningful distinction to be made between an act of experiencing and a sensible object — a thing that appears to the subject in a dull, painful way. The main alternative to act-object theories of the phenomenal is *adverbialism*: the thesis that all talk about the appearances of things (including visual appearances) should be understood as descriptions of "ways of being appeared to," so as to avoid commitment to the existence of a special class of phenomenal objects (i.e. the sense-data of Russell and Moore) that can appear even when no physical object is appearing.

When it looks to a person as though there is something red in front of him or her, the person is experiencing "in a reddish way" — "sensing redly," as Roderick Chisholm put it. The phenomenal quality peculiar to experiences "as of something red" is not borne by a thing to which the experiencing subject is related. "Red," as a term used to describe types of phenomenal experience, is better construed as an adverb modifying the type of feeling or sensing undergone by an experiencing subject. So such accounts of the structure of experience have been dubbed "adverbial theories of appearing."[15]

Frank Jackson sums up the differences between these two approaches by saying that act-object theorists take an experience to be a "relational state," involving a person and a sensed particular; while adverbialists take an experience to be a "unitary state," "a state of that person not essentially involving anything over and above that person."[16]

C. D. Broad considered the relative merits of act-object and adverbial theories under the heading "Are Sensations Analysable into Act of Sensing and Sensum?" Broad discerns a kind of continuum of sensation types:

> If we consider the various experiences called "sensations," we seem to be able to arrange them in an order, starting with those of sight, passing through those of taste and smell, and ending with bodily sensations, like headache. Now, as regards the top members of the series, the analysis into act of sensing and object

sensed seems pretty clear. A sensation of red seems clearly to mean a state of mind with a red object, and not to mean a red state of mind.

If we now pass to the other end of the series the opposite seems true. It is by no means obvious that a sensation of headache involves an act of sensing and a "headachy" object; on the contrary, it seems on the whole more plausible to describe the whole experience as a "headachy" state of mind. In fact the distinction of act and object seems here to have vanished; and, as there is clearly *something* mental in feeling a headache, just as there is in sensing a red patch, it seems plausible to hold that a sensation of headache is an unanalysable mental fact, within which no distinction of act and object can be found.

Now this contrast between the top and the bottom members of the series would not greatly matter, were it not for the fact that the two kinds of sensation seem to melt insensibly into each other at the middle of the series. It is about equally plausible to analyse a sensation of a sweet taste into an act of sensing and a sweet sensum, or to treat it as an unanalysable mental fact, having no object, but possessing the property of sweetness.[17]

The continuum naturally tempts systematizing philosophers to develop a theory of sensation based on examples from one end or the other, and then to force the whole spectrum of sensory states to fit into a single (possibly Procrustean) bed. Broad resists the unifying impulse; the states we call "sensations" are so called because of their similar causes (each is "the immediate response to the stimulation of a nerve"), but they may be quite different in their intrinsic structure.

I shall set aside the act-object account of the phenomenal, and assume that adverbialism is correct. There are two reasons it is safe to do so. For one thing, I believe the act-object property dualist can hardly avoid attributing qualia to entities like the sense-data of Russell and Moore — things that have size and shape but are very hard to fit into the three-dimensional space inhabited by physical objects. Sense data, so conceived, are not to be found in unconscious material objects, and they are responsible for the fact that we have conscious lives. So the act-object theory leads, if not exactly to a dualism of thinkers and physical objects, at least to a dualism of parts of our experiences and physical objects.[18] Another reason to ignore act-object theories is that adverbialism about even *one* fundamental phenomenal state that humans experience would be sufficient for the argument based on vagueness that comes next. Headaches, smells, tastes . . . these seem to submit most naturally to an adverbial analysis. Smelling a skunky smell is like waltzing a waltz, not like kicking a tire. When you kick a tire, there is you, your act of kicking, and the tire you kick. When you waltz a waltz, there is you, and there is the act of dancing, but there is not a third thing, something that you do the dance *to*. "The waltz" is a name for the kind of dancing activity in which you are engaged. Likewise in the case of the skunky smell that you smell; "the smell," in this context, is a name for the kind of activity in which you are engaged — the olfactory experience you are undergoing.

From now on, I shall assume that the property dualist who would reject substance dualism must also reject the act-object theory in favor of adverbialism: the subject of phenomenal experience is the very thing that bears the qualia.

THE VAGUENESS OF HUMAN BODIES AND BRAINS

Garden variety materialism identifies me with a garden variety object, a thing that already has a place in our commonsense conception of the world. Such an object will have relatively natural boundaries, such as those of an organism, or a brain, or even a single hemisphere of a brain. But animals and their organs belong on a spectrum that includes bushes, branches, clouds, mountains, rivers, tidal waves, and all manner of fuzzy entities. These familiar denizens of the physical world exhibit vagueness or indeterminacy in their spatial (and, for that matter, temporal) boundaries. And the strategies typically implemented to resolve the puzzles posed by vague objects do not seem so satisfactory when applied to *oneself*.

All the sensible material candidates for being the referent of someone's use of the word "I" appear surprisingly like clouds upon close inspection: it is not clear where they begin and end, in space or time. Many particles are in the process of being assimilated or cast off; they are neither clearly "in," nor clearly "out." The boundaries of animals and organs are infected with vagueness. Where does the brain end and the brainstem begin? When I hit my fingernail with a hammer, and it slowly blackens and eventually falls off, when exactly did it cease to be a part of my body? If its cells are dead, and it is barely attached, shouldn't we say it is no longer a part of me? But at what minute or second, prior to falling off, did it cease to be mine?

One might hope to find answers to such questions from biochemistry. Our bodies and brains are made of cells – perhaps biochemistry can fill in the missing pieces, locating a precise parcel of matter that stands out from the rest of the physical world as uniquely my own. If the boundaries of an organism or organ are to be perfectly precise, the boundaries of the cells that make it up must be perfectly precise. So, what are those boundaries like? The membranes of cells allow liquids and gases to pass through them. Are these substances always, or only sometimes, parts of the cells through which they pass? Does an H_2O molecule, for example, count as part of a cell, no matter how briefly it falls within its borders? What about larger molecules that are selected for transport into the cell by proteins in the cell's membrane? When *precisely* does such a molecule become part of a cell, as a transport protein binds with it, and causes it to pass, as a whole or in parts, through the membrane and into the cell? And when *precisely* does a useless molecule cease to be part of a cell? As soon as it no longer serves a function? Or only after it passes through the cell's outer membrane?

What makes such questions seem hopelessly hard to answer, or simply misguided, is the fact that the binding of proteins and the breaking of molecular bonds include the movements of parts of the molecules in question, and motion seems always to be a continuous process — that is to say, one can take the period during which a motion happens, and divide it up as finely as you like, and for each part of the period there will be a stage of the motion, slightly different from those that came before and after. The chemical reactions involved in one of these changes will be measured in nanoseconds; nevertheless, as a continuous process, the passage of a particular molecule into or out of a cell can be broken down, at least in principle, into an indefinite number of smaller movements and changes in the relationships among the parts of the molecule and other parts of the cell. The withdrawal of the glaciers was a slow, continuous motion; the metabolic processes within a cell are astonishingly fast, but they may be continuous for all that, in which case they pose the same problem, when one considers sufficiently brief periods of time. Choosing the picosecond, say, at which a molecule truly becomes part of a cell is like dating the end of the last ice age to within 1,000 years.[19]

If an object is perfectly precise — if it in no way resembles a cloud — there must be an answer, at each instant of the object's existence, to the question: Which other objects (including cells, molecules, and atoms) are to be counted among its parts at that time? When the question is asked about garden variety objects like organs, and organisms, it simply does not admit of a precise answer. To be a part of one of these things is to be caught up in its metabolic processes, and whether a thing is caught up in the metabolism of a cell, say, is often a vague matter.

When dealing with a vague object, it is tempting, when issues about boundaries become important, to simply *stipulate* answers to questions about precisely which things are or are not among its parts. And why not? When there is no sharp boundary in nature, but we need to draw one for legal or other purposes, we can choose, more or less arbitrarily, among the many equally eligible ways to do it. Where does Mount Everest end, and its foothills begin? We are free to lay down conventions in various ways to settle such questions, when they need to be settled. Similarly, one could lay it down that a certain kind of molecule does not truly become part of a cell until it is entirely within the cell membrane, but one could just as well have chosen the beginning of the process, when it is first bound to a transport protein.

The existence of many, equally good, ways of stipulating a boundary for a vague object provides a key that unlocks the nature of the phenomenon of vagueness. The indeterminacy of the borders of garden variety objects — including mountains, clouds, plants, and organisms — is due to an embarrassment of riches. Wherever we say there is "one" mountain, cloud, tree, or animal, there is really a plethora of what are, in some sense, equally good candidates for being the object in question. I confine my discussion to what I take to be the most popular, and most plausible, approach to the vagueness of mountains, clouds, living bodies, and organs: that it is an essentially linguistic phenomenon, due to "semantic indecision." We have, by means of the conventions governing our languages, decided to use "mountain" to refer to mountains (rather than to lakes), "cloud" to refer to clouds (and not, say, trees), and so on. But, in doing so, we have failed to specify very precisely what the boundaries are of these things we call "mountains" and "clouds"; there are many different chunks of the earth's crust, each of which is a good candidate to be "the" mountain to which we refer on some occasion, and many different masses of water vapor that could be selected as "the" cloud to which someone points. Instead of trying (hopelessly) to select just one of them, we gesture indeterminately at them all. We could, if we like, specify somewhat more precise meanings, thereby cutting down on the number of these potential referents of "mountain" and "cloud"; but, given our limitations, there will always be some vagueness about exactly where we want to place the boundaries for objects belonging to these garden variety kinds. Given the vagueness of human bodies and brains, they deserve similar treatment. As with clouds and mountains, the vagueness of bodies and brains is to be accounted for by pointing out that there are many equally eligible candidates for being "the body" and "the brain," and we have failed to do enough to determine which one we are talking about. We speak of a human body or brain as though there were just one physical object in the vicinity, when in fact there are many largely overlapping, perfectly precise things.[20]

If our terms and names for garden variety physical objects refer only indeterminately— if our uses of these words are really vague "gestures" in the direction of a host of objects — how do we ever manage to say anything *true* about these things? The vagueness of our ordinary terms is, generally speaking, harmless, because much of what we say about a garden variety object will be true of *every one* of the precise candidates for being that object. They will all have nearly the same mass, size, shape, color, and so on. When we use a sentence with vague terms, and all the things we could mean by it are true, the sentence itself should count as true. We manage to say true things about vague objects because we are usually not interested in the tiny differences in the properties they have. But suppose some feature — say, *being entirely in Switzerland* — is *not* had by all the good candidates for being "that mountain"; there are places that could reasonably be judged to be parts of the mountain — for example, some piece of ground where the foothills meet the slopes — that are in Italy; though the bulk of the mountain's mass falls squarely within Switzerland. Then it would be problematic to say: "the mountain is entirely in Switzerland." Suppose only a few of the good candidates for being "that mountain" stick out into Italy. If I said these words — "The mountain is entirely in Switzerland" — I would *almost* speak the truth. If, however, almost all the good candidates for being "that mountain" overlap Italy, the sentence would be more problematic; it would be *almost* flat-out false.

Applying the theory of vagueness to bodies and brains, one reaches the following conclusion. If I am a garden variety body or brain, there are many human-shaped or brain-shaped physical objects, each an equally good candidate to be what I refer to when I use the word "I." And, when I say "I have such-and-such feature," I speak truly only if all the candidates have the feature. Otherwise, what I say is false, or at best *kind of* true. In the next section, I argue that it is very difficult to accept this account of the vagueness of our boundaries, while affirming property dualism and adverbialism about qualia.

ADVERBIAL QUALIA AND VAGUE SPATIAL BOUNDARIES

Given what we know about the close connections between brain activity and phenomenal experience in our own case, laws of qualia generation dictate that, *very* roughly, whenever some neurons are organized and behaving like *so* — e.g. like the ones in my brain right now — something-or-other will be caused to have such-and-such fundamental phenomenal property. (The fundamental laws might not be about neurons, per se; they might relate qualia to some more general feature of the brain's activity — e.g. to changes in some kind of "pattern,"[21] or in information-state.[22]) Given adverbialism, whatever has this phenomenal property will be a conscious subject — one that feels a very precise pain, senses a very precise smell, etc. But what is the something-or-other that is caused to have the property in question? According to garden variety materialism, it is a familiar object such as a brain or a complete human organism.

If "brain" or "human organism" are terms for garden variety, vague material objects, and I am such a thing, then there must be many equally eligible candidates for being this brain or this organism. There is no problem, in principle, with vague macroscopic objects exemplifying fundamental, perfectly precise properties. All that is necessary is that each of the eligible candidates has the fundamental property. But, since the candidates differ from one another in tiny ways, and these tiny differences are fully determined by differences at more fundamental levels, it should be very surprising if it ever happens. It is easy for a vague object such as a table to weigh *about* 20 kilograms, because every eligible candidate for being the table has a mass very close to 20 kilograms — some a little more, some a little less. It is much harder for a table to weigh precisely 20 kilograms; some table candidates will, but very many will be ever so slightly heavier or lighter, rendering it less than completely accurate to say that the table has *exactly* that mass.

Adverbialism about some fundamental phenomenal properties requires that there be a family of perfectly natural properties which can be had only by conscious beings. If I am conscious in one of these precise ways, and I am an ordinary vague object, the laws governing the generation of qualia must insure that every eligible candidate for being me has this perfectly precise property. How likely is it that the fundamental laws select all and only the eligible candidates?

I suppose a property dualist should grant that it is *possible* that the natural process of qualia generation is *prodigal* in the production and distribution of fundamental phenomenal properties; that the brain generates very many instances of each phenomenal type, one for each of very many distinct but overlapping physical objects. But the defender of garden variety materialism must hope for more than that. The firing of neurons that causes something to have adverbial qualia must somehow target *all and only* the precise objects that are eligible candidates for being what we mean by "organism" or "brain." The fundamental physical laws governing qualia generation, even if they are prodigal in the number of instances produced, should not be expected to choose precise objects in exactly the same way that our everyday terms for brains and bodies choose many objects – that would be to attribute to nature itself a touching deference to our linguistic practices and to our rough-and-ready concepts.

If fundamental laws of adverbial-qualia-generation select fewer than every single one of the eligible candidates for being this organism or brain, the organism or brain will be at best *sort of* conscious. Whatever else I know about myself right now, I know that I am *definitely* conscious; so if a smaller thing or things *definitely* have the adverbial qualia, I am not the thing that is only indefinitely conscious, I am that smaller thing, or I am one of those things, or perhaps I am indefinitely identical with each of them — "I" might be a vague term, indeterminate in reference among many of the things that truly have the qualia generated by my brain. On the hypothesis that one or a few candidates are truly conscious, my boundaries are not those of an ordinary, garden variety, macroscopic object; they are determined not by our ordinary, rough-and-ready standards for being part of an organism or organ (which advert to vague notions like cohesion and functional role). Instead, my boundaries are set by a special, sharp "halo," a boundary drawn by possession of the precise qualia. The property dualist should admit that this *might* be so. And the resulting view is materialism, fair enough, but it is a kind of *speculative* materialism, not the kind of materialism that finds a thinking person to be just another garden variety physical object of the sort we clothe, or remove surgically, or push around. The precise material object I am becomes a matter of theoretical speculation, determined by laws linking brain activity with a particular physical object or objects, presumably somewhere in the vicinity of my brain.

Suppose the laws select *more* than all of the eligible candidates — including, among the many objects that share my adverbial phenomenal states, some objects with parts that fall just outside all of the garden variety candidates for being this brain or body. In that case, there are larger objects of which this brain or body is a part, and it is just as true of them that they are conscious as it is true of me. Any object that largely overlaps an eligible candidate for being me, and that shares my conscious experience, ought to be a good candidate for being me, so, unless these slightly larger things differ drastically from the slightly smaller things, garden variety materialism is once again false — a halo surrounds a different collection of precise objects from the eligible candidates for being this brain or body. Although words like "brain" and "body" are not vague terms used to refer to such a thing, we could easily invent some terms, indeed, given the platitude that *I* am the subject of my conscious states, perhaps "I" in my mouth is already a term indeterminate in reference among *these* material objects.

Even if the laws are prodigal, causing many physical objects to be conscious, there remains a kind of magic halo surrounding me (or, rather, around the sum of all the candidates for being me), so long as the perfectly natural qualia are either exemplified, or not, by an object — and this is something one does not find in ordinary, vague, macroscopic objects. The halo remains even in the wildly lucky case of laws that select *just* the eligible candidates for being this brain or body. In a garden variety object, there are not just bits of matter that are neither definitely part of, nor definitely not part of, the object — there are not just things one might call "borderline parts." There is also no sharp cut-off between the bits of matter that are, and are not, borderline parts. Notoriously, this requires higher-order vagueness; but higher-order vagueness would be obliterated by precise facts about which physical objects have adverbial qualia.

Prodigal laws of qualia production are needed by the adverbialist property dualist, if conscious persons are to have a *chance* of being garden variety bodies or brains. But even then, the chance is slim; it is much more likely that I am a physical object of a different size and shape — one determined by the sizes and shapes of whatever things are caused to have my qualia. A host of overlapping conscious subjects could make "I" a vague term, so that it would be true to say that I am a vague object. Still, my vagueness would be unlike that of garden variety objects, and the resulting metaphysics of persons should count as a form of speculative materialism.

If phenomenal properties are genuinely new and genuinely fundamental, there is little reason — other than our affection for certain familiar, macroscopic, vague objects — to suppose they are produced in abundance and exemplified willy-nilly by a host of subjects that overlap the neurons that are their source. Non-prodigal laws force the materialist to adopt a speculative frame of mind. Brains generate adverbial qualia, which are not exemplified many times over, but rather by just one or perhaps a handful of physical objects. The thesis would not be so bad, were there a heretofore unnoticed kind of physical thing, distinct from the familiar examples of macroscopic objects, suitable to be the true bearer of qualia and the true subject of consciousness. But when one looks around for precisely demarcated physical entities to receive the adverbialist's phenomenal states, no natural candidates present themselves. No cell or molecule or atom in the brain is distinguished in a way that would suggest that it is a better candidate than any of its rivals for being conscious; there seems no precise physical entity in the vicinity that fundamental laws could pick out in virtue of some special physical status, either intrinsic (for example, a special type of particle, atom, or molecule) or extrinsic (for example, a special place in my brain where only one particle, atom, or molecule could be located). Of course, it might be that the precise subjects of phenomenal states are one or many tiny particles selected randomly — in virtue of indeterministic laws, say — from among those in my brain, or that the subjects are randomly chosen larger portions of the matter in my head. Perhaps different regions of my brain are chosen at different times, depending upon the location of the brain activity causing the experience. Speculative materialisms could take many forms; many different algorithms could be proposed to link neural activity with some specific material object or objects, or perhaps with some portion of a field, or even with points of space-time. But, given all the precise objects in the vicinity, there is a "pairing problem": what natural feature (intrinsic or extrinsic) of a physical entity in the vicinity of my brain could figure in fundamental laws selecting one or several such entities to be the bearer of the newly generated phenomenal property? There is no obvious candidate, so far as I know. Perhaps the special part of the brain has yet to be discovered; therein lies a research program! Perhaps the laws about qualia generation choose physical objects to be experiencers in some indeterministic way, or the laws are strange ones, linking particular neural events with particular physical things but not in virtue of any natural relation that can be seen to hold between the neural events and those particular things.

In any case, property dualism and adverbialism lead the materialist into dark speculations about the true location and physical nature of persons. I do not say that such speculation would be unjustified, or scientifically unfruitful. But I do claim that those willing to engage in it are not in a position to scoff at the speculations of the emergent dualists.

EMERGENT DUALISM: BACK ON THE TABLE FOR THE ADVERBIALIST

Either the fundamental laws of adverbial qualia generation are prodigal, or not. If prodigal, there are many physical objects caused to have each of "my" experiences; in which case, I could believe that I am one of them or, better, that "I" is ambiguous or indeterminate in its reference to many of them — but I should *not* suppose that the ambiguity lines up with the ambiguity or indeterminacy in our use of words for garden variety objects belonging to biological kinds. If the laws are less prodigal, and more choosey — so that neural activity causes only one instance, or only a few instances, of each quale — the materialist can hardly pretend to know the size and shape of a conscious person; as a matter of empirical fact, there are no promising candidates for being the unique, conscious physical object in the vicinity of a human brain or body.

The emergent dualist is bound to point out that another possibility remains: the possibility that, as in other circumstances in which a new fundamental property is exemplified, the phenomenal states come with a new subject. And of course this is exactly what the dualist believes to be the case. Once there is neural activity sufficient to generate consciousness, a subject for that consciousness is also generated. Given the perfect naturalness of the properties that are newly instantiated, one should suppose that any subject of such properties is itself as natural in kind as a fundamental particle.

The details of the mechanism by which brains generate souls remain, admittedly, as speculative as the search for a special conscious particle or a precisely demarcated conscious chunk of brain matter. Perhaps there is some minimal level of neural activity that could be identified as *the* sustaining cause of the soul. Perhaps, for every brain-and-soul pair at every time, there is a single pattern of neural firing that is responsible for the soul's overall phenomenal state, then and there. I suppose that the following hypothesis is more likely: that many overlapping sets of events occur in the brain, none of which is the minimal cause of the soul's ongoing existence, nor the single cause of its overall phenomenal state. With many overlapping patterns of neural firing, each lawfully sufficient for the existence of a soul with the same phenomenal states, there could still be just one soul, its existence and phenomenal state simply *overdetermined*. There need be no vagueness about which activities in the brain generate the subject of consciousness — in fact, on this supposition, *many* precise (and largely overlapping) events are equally responsible — nor about how many subjects there are.

Emergent dualism is clearly not the only coherent way to combine property dualism with adverbialism about the most natural phenomenal states. But, given the unlikelihood that the laws of qualia-generation choose just the macroscopic candidates that have captured *our* attention, garden variety materialism is extremely unlikely to be true. And more speculative forms of materialism become quite bizarre, so long as no precise, physically special parts of the brain (or special fields or special sets of space-time points inside the brain) present themselves. The substance dualist alternative is to suppose that phenomenal states come with their own natural kind of subject, like new fundamental particles. Property dualists ought to accept this as a genuine possibility — a speculative hypothesis worth taking seriously, especially if there are no promising leads in the search for a physical alternative.[23]

An important point that Zimmerman discusses in the course of his article is that there can be a range of different notions about the soul, and so a range of different dualisms. (We also mentioned this in the Introduction.) Different views can be arranged on a kind of scale in terms of how many properties souls have in common with physical objects, ranging from none at all, or almost none, to some, or even many. When most people think of dualism they think of Cartesian dualism, a particular and relatively radical kind of Soul Hypothesis. For Descartes, souls shared very few properties in common with bodies. For example, Descartes seems to have held that while bodies are located in space, souls are non-spatial: they have no parts, no definable size, and no location in space whatsoever. In the minds of many, positing radical differences of this kind between souls and bodies makes it harder to understand the causal interaction that must be going on between a body and a soul. Against this background, Zimmerman suggests that we should consider other, "milder" forms of the Soul Hypothesis as well. In this connection, he mentions favorably William Hasker's notion of emergent dualism.

In our next chapter, Hasker himself presents the essentials of emergent dualism. In order to introduce this notion, he bids us keep in mind not only human beings but also animals from the viewpoint of the Soul Hypothesis. Some of the reasons why we think people have souls as well as bodies include the distinctive qualia that are associated with our perceptual experiences, our ability to reason, and our ability to act freely and purposefully. But as we interact with our pets and other higher animals, we find good reason to suppose that they are not so different from us in these respects. They too seem to have perceptual experiences (although we have only a third-person perspective on this), and they too seem able to act freely and rationally so as to accomplish their purposes (although these purposes may be simpler than ours). If our experiences and abilities depend on our having a soul, and animals have similar experiences and abilities, then it seems that animals must have souls too. And indeed this is a traditional conclusion that has been reached by many thinkers throughout history, at least from Aristotle onward (although not by Descartes himself).

Although it is a fairly traditional view, Hasker warns us that it is easy to lose sight of the fact that animals also have souls, and the relevance of this for developing the Soul Hypothesis. He claims that the similarities that animals bear to humans pose severe challenges for both ordinary materialism and classical/pure/extreme versions of dualism, such as Cartesian dualism. On the one hand, pure materialism cannot account for rationality, meaning, and the unity of consciousness that we experience as humans and which we share to some degree with higher animals. In rehearsing these points, Hasker presents his version of concerns similar to those raised in other forms by other authors in this volume. But on the other hand, Hasker also calls attention to one aspect of materialism that is conceptually very attractive: the fact that it can account for a continuous progression from nonliving things, to very simple creatures, to lower animals, to higher animals, to human beings. Our abilities to perceive, reason, and act purposefully seem to be continuous with those of higher animals, which are in turn not so different from those of lower animals, and so on. This makes sense if mental complexity is the same thing as physical complexity, and grows automatically as bodies and brains become more complex moving up the evolutionary scale — just as a materialist who denies the separate existence of a soul would expect. So some considerations seem to point clearly toward dualism, whereas others seem to point toward materialism. Given this tension, Hasker encourages us to "think outside the boxes," and consider options other than pure materialism and one kind of rigid (Cartesian) dualism.

More specifically, Hasker suggests that perhaps the brain generates a soul (a "consciousness field"), which is a distinct thing from the brain, but depends on the brain for its existence. One analogy that he uses to motivate this is that a collection of neurons properly arranged into a brain generates a soul in something like the way that the atoms of a bar of iron lined up correctly generate a magnetic field. The magnetic field is a different thing from the magnetized iron bar, and has its own power to cause things to happen, by electromagnetic attraction rather than by physical contact. This is true even though it is created automatically by a certain arrangement of material things, in accordance with physical laws. In the same way, souls might be different things from collections of interacting neurons, with their own distinctive power to cause things to happen, while still being created automatically by a certain arrangement of those neurons. Hasker shows that such a view has promise for making sense of the conflicting evidence for materialism and dualism. On the one hand, since the soul is a new kind of thing, generated by the brain but not identical to it, it could very well be the thing that is involved in conscious subjective experience and conscious voluntary action — those aspects of mental life that are hard to attribute to a physical object. On the other hand, since the soul is directly dependent on the brain for its existence, it makes sense that the animal brains that are most like ours will also generate souls that have similar powers to ours, whereas simpler animal brains will generate simpler souls with fewer of these powers, the simplest neural systems perhaps generating no soul at all. (This would be analogous to the fact that not every metal bar is the right kind to generate a significant magnetic field.)

This then, is a brief overview of the story that Hasker tells. And he begins the story by introducing us to an unlikely source of wisdom, the lowly polyp . . .

CHAPTER 8

Souls Beastly and Human

William Hasker

A SENSATIONAL DISCOVERY

In 1740 Abraham Trembley, a young Swiss naturalist who was teaching in Holland, made a remarkable discovery.[1] It concerned a polyp, a small gelatinous creature found in stagnant ponds. The polyp had previously been classified as a plant, but Trembley's observations of its powers of movement and its method of feeding[2] led him to regard it instead as an animal — an "insect," in the classification scheme of the day. This reclassification was determined to be correct, but it led to considerable perplexity, because the creature's similarity to plants threatened to break down the rigid separation of animal from vegetable which was axiomatic for the science of the time. An even more striking observation, however, concerned the creature's ability — unknown in any animal until then — to regenerate itself when cut into pieces. Divide it into pieces, and each piece will grow into a complete organism. These observations may strike us as merely interesting, but in their own time they were sensational. Consider the excitement expressed in the first (and, to be sure, somewhat flowery) announcement of the discovery: "The story of the Phoenix who is reborn from his ashes, as fabulous as it might be, offers nothing more marvelous. . . . From each portion of an animal cut in 2, 3, 4, 10, 20, 30, 40 parts and, so to speak, chopped up, just as many complete animals are reborn, similar to the first. Each of these is ready to undergo the same division . . . without it being known yet at what point this astonishing multiplication will cease."[3] This creature was subsequently given the name *hydra* in virtue of its similarity to the mythological serpent with nine heads; the monster would grow back two new heads for each one that was cut off.

Trembley's discovery has been called "the most fascinating single curiosity of natural history in the 1740s,"[4] and it captivated the attention of both scientists and the scientifically informed public. (Compare the sensation created in the 1960s by Watson and Crick's discovery of DNA.) R. A. Réaumur, one of the leading biologists of Europe, performed this experiment repeatedly, and was mightily perplexed by the results. He wrote, "when I saw for the first time two polyps form gradually from one that I had cut in two, I found it hard to believe my eyes: and this is a fact that I cannot accustom myself to seeing, after having seen and re-seen it hundreds of times."[5] Martin Folkes, president of the English Royal Society, wrote in a letter that "we wish here passionately for some explanation of so extraordinary a fact."[6] The phenomenon gained and held the attention of many of the notables of the day, including Rousseau and Voltaire.

But why such a stir over a discovery concerning a tiny and, on the whole, insignificant creature? Over and above the curiosity value of the discovery, it was recognized by many that it had a bearing on a topic of philosophical and, indeed, theological significance: the nature of the soul. The prevailing view of the day was that animals as well as human beings possessed souls; the soul was the "principle of life," the organizing and energizing factor in the living organism. Furthermore, souls were held to be immaterial, and as such incapable of being divided by a physical process.[7] But Trembley's observations threatened this: the soul, if present at all, seemed to be divisible along with the body, and to be multiplied by the physical act of cutting the polyp in pieces. This seemed to show that, rather than the organism depending on the soul for its life and ability to function, the dependence went the other way around. And from this it was but a short step to the conclusion that the soul, as a separate substantial entity, did not exist at all.

A MATERIALIST INTERPRETATION

The first thinker to draw explicitly radical conclusions from the discovery was the physician and philosopher Julien Offray de La Mettrie. In *L'Homme machine* (The Man Machine), published in 1748, La Mettrie rejected entirely the notion of an immaterial soul. But how, then, explain the development of organisms with their marvelous complexity? His answer is revealing.

> We do not understand Nature: causes concealed within herself could have brought about everything. See . . . Trembley's polyp! Does it not contain within

itself the causes which produce its regeneration? What absurdity would there be, consequently, in thinking that there are certain physical causes endowed with all that is necessary to them, and to which the whole chain of this vast universe is so necessarily bound and subjected that anything that occurs could not have not occurred?[8]

At one stroke, then, La Mettrie disposes not merely of the animal soul but also of God; he goes on to say that "to destroy Chance is not equivalent to proving the existence of a Supreme Being, since there could be something else that is neither Chance nor God: I mean Nature."[9] A further important contribution is made by the way in which (as noted earlier) the polyp seemed to break down the rigid separation between plants and animals. (Among other differences, it had been thought that animals reproduce exclusively through sexual union, but the polyp, when not being chopped up by naturalists, reproduces by sending off shoots.) This led the naturalist Bonnet to conclude that, rather than rigidly separated plant and animal kingdoms, there was a single "scale of nature" embracing all created beings.[10] This opened the way for an evolutionary interpretation; Bonnet himself never accepted evolution, but the possibility was there and La Mettrie availed himself of it. So a century before Darwin, we have in La Mettrie an explicitly materialistic (though not yet well developed) theory of evolution. And we owe this development, to a considerable extent, to Abraham Trembley and his polyp.[11]

PROBLEMS FOR A MATERIALIST INTERPRETATION

Was La Mettrie right in his materialist interpretation? Consider again his invocation of "certain physical causes endowed with all that is necessary to them . . . to which the whole chain of this vast universe is . . . necessarily bound." Has he really given us an explanation of anything? Isn't he just bundling up all of the problems and pushing them out of sight, with his vague talk of "certain physical causes?" If explanations of this sort are what we want, they are easy enough to produce, but just what has been *explained* in the process?

Contemporary materialists have gone much farther than La Mettrie and his contemporaries in working out the details of their position. But the results have been mixed at best, as is shown, among other things, by the profusion of different and conflicting materialist views on offer. Jaegwon Kim has taken some criticism for the title of his book,

Physicalism, Or Something Near Enough.[12] But I think he is to be commended for admitting forthrightly that a fully physicalist view is not viable. Why isn't it viable? Though we know little or nothing about the minds of polyps (supposing that they have minds at all), we do know something about our own minds, and some of what we know about them poses serious problems for materialism. For present purposes, it will suffice to state briefly just two of these problems; interested readers can find additional details elsewhere.[13]

The first of these problems is pointed out by what is sometimes called the "argument from reason"; it deals with the unique role reasoning plays in our mental lives, and the inability of materialist views to give a proper account of this role. All standard varieties of materialism subscribe to what is termed "the causal closure of the physical domain."[14] What this means, stated simply, is that every physical event has physical causes that are sufficient to produce it — that when we are seeking to explain some physical event, we never need to appeal to anything other than physical causes, operating according to the ordinary physical laws which govern the operations of physical bodies, particles, etc. (The physical laws may, to be sure, include some that are yet to be discovered; there is no assumption that present-day physics is complete.) It follows from this that in order to explain something done by a person — the words that she says, or the actions she performs — there is in principle no need to refer to any events and processes involving her subjective consciousness; her behavior can be explained completely without reference to her conscious experience of thoughts, plans, intentions, or desires.[15] This is really an astonishing claim, and it seems to imply what is called *epiphenomenalism*, the view that while conscious mental experiences do exist and accompany many of our activities, they have no effect whatsoever on what physically goes on in the world. Materialists recognize that this is extremely implausible; a standard reply is that these mental experiences are identical with physical events in the brain, and as such they do have effects on behavior.[16] But this evades the real point. True, if the mental event is identical with a physical event, then this event may be a cause which affects a person's behavior. But what has this effect is the *physical structure* of the event, which affects other physical events as prescribed by the laws of physics — laws which make no reference to desires, intentions, or to the rational connections between ideas (such as, for instance, the logical connection between premises and conclusion in a valid argument). The consciously experienced psychological and conceptual content of an experience cannot be a physical cause. And because this is so, the mental content is *irrelevant* to behavior; it is not the explanation for anything a person says or does. But when applied to the process of reasoning this has a startling result, namely that we never accept the conclusion of an argument because we see that it is supported by sound reasons. The chain of physical cause and effect, which alone determines what our response shall be, is *completely unaffected* by the psychological content of an experience — such as, in this case, the fact that the experience involves the affirming of certain propositions we believe to be true. Rather, we accept the conclusions of arguments, when we do so, because and only because that acceptance is the result of the "dance of the molecules" in our brains, interacting with one another according to the laws of physics. But this is wholly inadequate as an account of the way reasoning actually occurs: when we are reasoning correctly, we accept the conclusion of an argument because, and only because, we see that it is supported by good reasons. If materialism is incompatible with this truth about the way we reason, then materialism is in serious trouble.

The closure of the physical domain has another, rather surprising, consequence, namely that materialism has great difficulty in accounting for the process of evolution — in particular the evolution of conscious cognitive states. Materialism's explanation for this is typically given in terms of "evolutionary epistemology," which states that an organism's conscious states confer a benefit in the struggle to survive and reproduce. Such responses as discomfort in the presence of a chemical irritant, or the awareness of light or warmth or food, enhance the organism's ability to respond in optimal fashion. For more complex animals there is the awareness of the presence of predator or of prey, and the ability to devise simple strategies so as to increase the chances of successful predation or of escape therefrom. As the organisms and their brains become more complex, we see the emergence of systems of beliefs and of strategies for acquiring beliefs. Natural selection guarantees a high level of fitness, including cognitive fitness.

This evolutionary epistemology seems to give a fairly plausible account of the development of cognitive states, at least in cases where those states have some fairly direct relationship to survival and biological success. However, when it is combined with the materialist doctrine of the closure of the physical domain, a startling result emerges: no explanation whatsoever has been given, or indeed can be given, for the fact that our states of conscious awareness correspond even approximately to the actual situation in the world in which we are living. The reason for this is found in the point, noted just above, that "the consciously experienced psychological and conceptual content of an experience cannot be a physical cause. And because this is so, the mental content is *irrelevant* to behavior; it is not the explanation for anything a person says or does." Couple this with the fact that natural selection can operate only on physical states and physical behavior, and it becomes clear that, instead of our conscious mental states being shaped in the right direction by natural selection, those states are *entirely invisible* to natural selection, and cannot be molded by it so as to make them an accurate representation of the objective environment. To be sure, the mental state, *as a physical brain-state*, does affect behavior and can be molded by natural selection. What remains completely unaccounted for, however, is the fact that the subjective experience involved in the mental state corresponds at least approximately to the actual state of affairs in the world.[17] Natural selection, then, could account for the fact that our ancestors were inclined to take flight when being threatened by a saber-toothed tiger. What it cannot account for, however, is the fact that their subjective experience was one of "let's get out of here before that saber-toothed tiger arrives," rather than one of "isn't this a delicious meal of baboon meat." Since the experienced psychological content of the experience has no effect on behavior, natural selection is *completely indifferent* as to which of these is the case. But the correspondence between our subjective experience and the actual state of the world (a correspondence in which all of us, and not least materialists, implicitly believe), is an enormously important fact. A theory of mind that has no explanation for this fact is in deep trouble.

The other argument I want to mention is the "unity-of-consciousness argument." To appreciate this argument, you need to keep in mind two things about the materialist view. First, the thing that has experiences, according to materialism, is a physical object, namely the brain. And second, the brain is itself a collection of physical parts. For present purposes, we can think of these parts as individual neurons (of which the brain includes tens of billions), though of course each neuron is itself a very complex object. The operation of the brain is understood by materialists to consist in the coordinated activity of huge numbers of neurons, switching one another "on" and "off" in much the way that computers function by opening and closing innumerable electrical connections. (Thus the ubiquitous computer models of the brain.)

Now, keeping these two ideas in mind, think for a moment about the nature of conscious experience. Normally at any given moment you are consciously aware of a considerable amount and variety of data; think, for instance, of your awareness at this moment, as you read this page. You are aware of the shapes of the letters, and of the thoughts they communicate to you; you are also aware of the visual appearance of other objects in the immediate vicinity, and probably there are sounds in the background of which you are at least dimly aware. There may be various bodily sensations as well, but there is no need to go on; clearly, your awareness at this moment is quite complex and rich in experiential data. Now, ask yourself this question: What physical thing is aware of all of this information? The natural answer for a materialist would be, "my brain is aware of it." But remember: one's brain consists entirely of all of those individual neurons (and some other tissues that are not relevant here), all interacting with each other. No individual neuron can possibly experience all of this data; everyone would agree with that. But here is the crucial point. A complex experience cannot exist divided up among a number of different objects, such as neurons. For we are aware of our "experiential field," at any given moment, as a *unitary fact*, and this unitary awareness simply cannot be understood as the sum of a number of separate awarenesses existing in different parts of the brain. (That would be like saying that because every member of a class knows the answer to one question on an examination, the entire class knows the material perfectly and deserves an "A" on the exam!) So again we have the question: What is it that is aware, all at once, of the contents of a complex experience? That there is such an awareness can't be denied; it is an incontrovertible fact of our lives. But for the reasons given above, that which has this awareness can't be a neuron, or a group of neurons, such as the brain — nor, it seems, can it be any material object whatsoever. It begins to look as though we need to suppose that there is something *non-physical* — call it a "mind" or a "soul" — which has these experiences. And that, of course, is just what dualists have always said.[18]

These arguments have been stated here very briefly; interested readers are urged to pursue them in greater depth elsewhere.[19] It's also true, to be sure, that the arguments as we have stated them are formulated as applying to human beings. But if human beings have non-material minds this will assuredly be true of animals as well, at least of those animals concerning which we are confident that the animals do have complex experiences and that those experiences affect their behavior. (And how can you possibly doubt this, when your dog greets you as you return home after a busy day?) So the arguments are highly relevant to the topic of the souls of animals.

PROBLEMS FOR A DUALIST INTERPRETATION

But while La Mettrie's materialist interpretation of the polyp is uncon-vincing, it remains true that the polyp presents problems for traditional dualism, problems that may not yet have been adequately addressed. Note first of all that no one has proposed a way in which immaterial souls, as traditionally understood, could be divided or multiplied by the physical act of cutting an organism into parts. Indeed, the notion that this could be done seems absurd; an entity that is inherently both simple and non-spatial (as Descartes said of the soul, and as many dualists still say) cannot possibly be divided. The standard view con-cerning the origin of such souls is that they are individually created by God — but it is unappealing, to say the least, to suppose that God is standing by, ready with a fresh supply of souls, each time Réaumur does his polyp-chopping! Early on, the mathematician Cramer argued that "the polyp's manner of reproduction was a severe blow to those who defended the theory of the animal-soul against the Cartesian defini-tion of beasts as pure machines."[20] And it is quite true that Descartes, as well as some of his followers, viewed animals merely as machines; they limited the possession of souls to human beings. But this had the unpalatable consequence that animals are sheer automata, incapable of thought, emotion, or even sensation. An animal's physical reactions mis-lead us into supposing that it is experiencing joy or pain, but in reality nothing of the sort is occurring! As I have sometimes told my students, if you can believe that you can believe anything! But the belief had serious consequences for some of the animals, because the Cartesians performed painful experiments on them, secure in the confidence than no actual pain was being felt by the beasts!

A somewhat less objectionable strategy is to assign souls to animals as well as to human beings, but to limit them to the "higher" animals, those for which we have convincing behavioral evidence that they do experi-ence sensation if not actual thought. On this assumption the hydra and similar creatures would have no souls, and no mental or psychic lives, and yet our convictions about the life-experiences of dogs, monkeys, and zebras could be retained. This is certainly more plausible than Descartes's own view: most of us have rather little empathy for the inner life of a termite, supposing that it has one at all. One question raised by this proposal is, where should we draw the line? This problem is amusingly illustrated by an experience at a meeting where the topic was being discussed. One well-known philosopher thought it obvious that we should not suppose that fish possess souls, while another was far more liberal, being willing to attribute souls to all manner of bugs and worms!

But why, might one ask, is the need to draw the line especially a problem for dualism? Any view whatsoever will presumably have to draw the line somewhere — that is, will have to admit that (a) there is a difference between those living creatures that have some kind of psychic "inner life," however rudimentary, and those that do not; and (b) we lack sufficient evidence to determine with confidence where the line is to be drawn. That much is certainly true, but the problem threatens to be an embarrassment for traditional dualism in a way that it is not for other views. If the cut-off point is placed "high" on the scale — for instance, to exclude fish — this has every appearance of arbitrariness; we shall be excluding creatures that, while unable to tell us of their pains and pleasures, give every indication of having both. But if we are more liberal, we are confronted with the truly uninviting picture of God's creating individual souls for slugs, mosquitoes, and intestinal parasites. Perhaps this objection is largely aesthetic; nevertheless some of us will find it pretty compelling.

This is not the only serious problem encountered by traditional versions of dualism. Another major difficulty concerns the pervasive and fine-grained dependence of mental phenomena on the state of the physical brain, a dependence which is hard to explain for a view that attributes the power of thought and consciousness entirely to an immaterial soul. La Mettrie laid a great deal of emphasis on this dependence, but the evidence available for it today goes far beyond anything he knew about, as is seen in recent discoveries in neuroscience. It turns out that very specific forms of mental "data processing" — for instance, the recognition of familiar faces — depend on the integrity and functioning of specific, identifiable regions in the brain; this is quite unexpected, and difficult to explain, on the basis of traditional mind-body dualism. Still another problem arises from the compelling evidence for biological evolution. Just how do divinely created souls fit into the evolutionary narrative? "Higher," more evolved animals will require more complex souls, with a more extensive array of powers; so at least one would think. Does God wait until a more advanced organism has evolved through natural selection, and only then create a higher-grade soul to take advantage of the superior neural circuitry of the more advanced creature? But then where is the advantage of the more advanced circuitry before the high-grade soul has been created — an advantage which it must possess in order to be retained by natural selection? Or does the more powerful soul come first, and assist in the evolutionary development? Or should we, in the interest of preserving dualism, reject the evidence for common ancestry and insist on the special divine creation of at least the major types of living creatures? It does not speak well for a theory of mind if it requires us to reject such an impressive body of empirical evidence.

By this time the reader may well be experiencing some surprise: why, in a volume devoted to the defense and advocacy of dualism, do we find such an array of anti-dualist arguments? Little is to be gained, however, by ignoring the kinds of reasons that make materialism seem plausible, and dualism unattractive, to many of our contemporaries. Instead, my proposal is that we should take these objections into account, and develop a version of dualism that is not subject to them.

A THIRD PATH? MIND AS EMERGENT

Consider briefly where we've come up until now. We have been introduced to Trembley's polyp, and have seen the materialist interpretation given by La Mettrie. We have also considered the formidable problems for such a materialist interpretation, problems which apply also to contemporary versions of materialism. We have looked at some difficulties for mind-body dualism (particularly the version developed by Descartes), all revolving around the relation between divinely created souls and the facts about animal and human embodiment. It may well be that by this time the reader is experiencing a degree of frustration. Every account we consider, you may be saying to yourself, is subject to apparently insuperable objections, so how will we ever find our way out of this quagmire? If that is what you are thinking, you are to be congratulated: you are beginning to grasp the fact that the mind-body problem is *really hard*; it is a problem that does not readily yield a solution. All of the obvious, plausible answers that occur to one turn out to be flawed; in order to find a viable solution, we may need to "think outside the box" — to investigate ways of understanding the situation that are beyond our usual habits of thought. That is not a reason to give up, however; where would the physical sciences be today if physicists had been unwilling to consider strange and radical ideas? (Perhaps the most important thing to understand about quantum mechanics, according to some of its leading theorists, is that *nobody really understands* why nature works the way it does!) So let's see whether we can make some progress.

Here is an initial proposal: a viable solution needs to consider the mental lives of human beings and animals together, rather than separately. The reason for this can be seen in some of the views we've already considered. To those who begin by thinking just about the minds/souls of humans, especially when the topic is viewed in a religious context, the very idea of "soul" tends to have some rather lofty, "spiritual" connotations. When we turn from that exalted idea of the soul to consider the "lower animals," there is a disconnect. Descartes's view may be the best philosophical illustration of this, but it is not by any means the only one. And for a good many people, the very word "soul" has religious associations that make it very difficult for them to attribute souls to animals. On the other hand, thinkers more inclined to naturalistic or materialistic views tend to start with animals and reduce the psychic life of human beings to what can be explained in the same terms they apply to animals. Either approach is bound to result in distortions, so we need a view that takes seriously the commonalities between humans and other animals and is also able to recognize the differences between them. This much at least seems reasonably clear: animals experience sensation and have desires; some of them have emotions and engage in at least rudimentary rational thought. In view of this, the basic metaphysical account of the nature of conscious experience needs to be the same for humans and for non-human animals. It just will not do to say that human beings have souls and animals don't; the differences between humans and other animals (and those differences are real and massive) need to be accounted for in some other way.

Now, there is a way of approaching such topics, not considered in this chapter until now, that goes under the name of "emergence."[21] The general idea of emergence is that when one brings together elements of a certain sort, and arranges them in the proper way, something genuinely new appears, something that did not exist in the elements prior to their combination. The new thing isn't just a rearrangement of what was there before, but neither is it something dropped in to the situation from the outside. It "emerges," comes into being, through the operation of the constituent elements, yet the new thing is something different and often surprising; we wouldn't have expected it before it appeared. Take a mathematical equation of a certain sort, plot it onto a set of coordinates, and a fractal pattern appears — complex, unexpected, and sometimes stunningly beautiful. Dissolve some chemicals in water, let the solution stand for a while under the right conditions, and regular, highly organized crystals are formed. When the right numbers and kinds of chemical molecules are arranged in a particular complex structure, we have something new — a living cell. And given a sufficient number of the right kinds of cells, properly organized, there is the wonder of awareness, involving sensation, emotion, and rational thought. In each case, what "emerges" is something qualitatively new – a fractal pattern, a crystalline structure, life, consciousness. But if you view these phenomena in the light of emergence, you will not think of this new element as something "added from the outside," but as arising somehow out of the original constituents of the situation.

That this is so is evident in the first two cases: the beautiful and surprising pattern is simply the result of tracing the values assigned by the mathematical equation onto the coordinate grid, and the crystal structure is a straightforward consequence of the way in which the constituent atoms align themselves as a result of chemical bonding. The other two cases, however, have been more controversial. Some have supposed that in order for there to be life there is needed, over and above the physical structure of the cell, an additional component, sometimes called "vital energy" or "life force", or, in the story we recalled from the eighteenth century, "animal soul." This view is now thoroughly discredited among biologists, but it was taken seriously by some of them as recently as the early twentieth century. And in the final example, the view that the human soul is something "added to" the body by a special act of divine creation is seriously advocated today by a number of philosophers. But as we have already seen, it is subject to serious (though possibly not fatal) objections. The theory of emergence offers a different way to approach the situation.

The four examples also serve to highlight the fact that there are different *varieties* of emergence — or, if you prefer, different senses in which a phenomenon may be said to be emergent. The fractal pattern is what may be termed a *logical emergent*; for all its complexity and beauty, it is simply a logical consequence of the elements that make up the situation — the mathematical formula, the coordinate system, and the convention for matching values of the variables in the formula with positions in the coordinate system. The crystalline structure, on the other hand, is a *causal emergent*; it is a consequence of the causal powers of the constituent atoms, as ascertained by the science of physics, that this new and interesting structure appears. The existence of instances of emergence of these two kinds is uncontroversial, though not everyone uses the language of emergence in describing them.

But now consider the following possibility: an animal or human brain consists of ordinary atoms and molecules, which are subject to the ordinary laws of physics and chemistry. But suppose that, given the particular arrangements of these atoms and molecules of the brain, new laws, new systems of interaction between the atoms, etc., come into play. These new laws, furthermore, play an essential role in such characteristic mental activities as rational thought and decision-making. The new laws, however, are not detectable in any simpler configuration; in such configurations the behavior of the atoms and molecules is adequately explained by the ordinary laws of physics and chemistry. These, then, are *emergent laws*, and the powers that the brain has in virtue of the emergent laws may be termed *emergent causal powers*. Given this much, it is clear that to postulate the existence of emergent causal powers is to make a dramatic, and in fact extremely controversial, metaphysical claim. Many philosophers and scientists strongly resist such a claim, pointing to the immense explanatory success of standard physico-chemical explanations in accounting for a broad range of natural phenomena. What has worked so well so often before, they say, should not be abandoned just because at the moment we seem to find ourselves stymied in explaining a particular range of phenomena. Nevertheless, a number of philosophers have felt compelled to assert the existence of emergent causal powers; they hold that crucially important facts about our mental lives cannot be explained in any other way.[22]

Suppose, finally, that as a result of the structure and functioning of the brain, there appear not merely new *modes of behavior* of the fundamental constituents (as in the case of emergent causal powers), but also a *new entity*, the *mind*, which does *not consist* of atoms and molecules, or of any other physical constituents.[23] If this were the case, we would have an *emergent individual*, an individual that *comes into existence* as the result of a certain configuration of the brain and nervous system, but which is *not composed of* the matter which makes up that physical system. This, clearly enough, represents yet a further stage of emergence, one that is resisted even by some of those philosophers who acknowledge emergent causal powers. Such an emergence theory would be, in fact, a variety of dualism, in that the emergent mind is an entity not composed of physical stuff. But it would be an *emergent* dualism, unlike traditional dualisms which postulate a special divine act of creation as the origin of the soul. This is the theory I am advocating in this chapter.[24]

Having set the stage by this account of emergence, it is time to present the resulting view of the person. The fundamental idea is actually rather simple. As a consequence of a certain configuration and function of the brain and nervous system, a new entity comes into being — namely, the mind or soul. This new thing is not merely a "configurational state" of the cells of the brain (as, for example, a crystal is a configurational state of the molecules that make it up). The mind, in this view, is a "thing in itself"; it is what some philosophers call a "substance." It isn't made of the chemical stuff of which the brain is composed, though it crucially *depends* on that chemical stuff for both its origin and its continuance. It is this mind — the conscious self — that thinks, and reasons, and feels emotions, and makes decisions; it is the central core of what we mean by a "person."

An analogy I've sometimes used in this connection can be stated as follows. As a magnet generates its magnetic field, so an organism generates its conscious field. Arrange an assemblage of iron molecules in the right way, and something new appears: a magnetic field. Arrange an assemblage of neurons in the right way, and another new thing appears: consciousness, a mind. This analogy can, I believe, be helpful in enabling us to grasp the way in which the mind is produced, but it shouldn't be pushed beyond its limits. It's not the case, for instance, that a magnetic field is conscious, in spite of all we've learned from Commander Data in *Star Trek*. Nor are the magnetic field, the gravitational field, and the other fields of physics emergent in the strong sense that applies to the conscious mind. The field analogy can be helpful, but we should not try to get from it more than it contains;[25] it is not by any means presented as a proof of the theory's truth.

It is not difficult to see how emergent dualism solves the problem of Trembley's polyp. If we assume that the polyp does possess some sort of conscious awareness (and I think it is fairly plausible to assume this, though proof is impossible), then the "field of consciousness" which is thus aware is produced by the physical structure of the polyp. And when that physical structure is duplicated as a result of the polyp's being chopped in two, so is the field of consciousness. So also for Dolly the sheep, and other instances of cloning. The theory also resolves the other difficulties for dualism noted in our earlier discussion. Since the field of consciousness is generated by the brain and nervous system, it is very much to be expected that it will be dependent on the condition and functioning of that brain and nervous system. That brain damage should cause cognitive impairment is an expected consequence (though in many cases a tragic one) of the mind-body relationship as viewed in emergent dualism. Emergent dualism also harmonizes remarkably well with the theory of organic evolution. The emergent consciousness of living creatures has its effect in guiding their behavior and therefore their survival. More complex, highly evolved brains make possible more complex states of consciousness. The consciousness in turn aids survival by making possible more sophisticated, better-adapted behavior. The result is that mind and body *co-evolve* in the history of life on earth. This in my opinion is one of the more important ways in which emergent dualism is superior both to traditional, creationist versions of dualism and also to materialistic views which affirm the causal closure of the physical domain.

Emergent dualism also solves the problems posed above for materialism. The existence of emergent laws, and emergent causal powers, means that we do not have to explain human behavior, and human thinking, purely in terms of the impersonal laws of physics and chemistry. And the emergent mind/soul answers the question posed by the unity-of-consciousness argument — the question about what it is that is aware of complex states of consciousness. The answer is, that it is the mind that is aware, a mind that is indeed generated by the brain and nervous system, but whose functioning is not merely physical and is not explainable purely in physical terms.

But finally, what of "the resurrection of the dead, and the life of the world to come?" At first glance, it might seem the implications of emergent dualism do not favor the possibility of a future life. If the mind/soul depends on the brain and nervous system for its continued existence, it would seem that destroying the brain would destroy the mind as well. And the analogy of the magnetic field seems to support this conclusion: destroy a magnet (or, in the case of an electromagnet, turn off the electric current), and the field disappears. But this is far from conclusive. The key point is that, on this theory, the conscious mind is an *ontologically distinct entity* from the physical brain. Under normal circumstances, the mind depends for its continued existence on support from the body. But to quote the neuroscientist Wilder Penfield, "whether energy can come to the mind of man from an outside source after his death is for each individual to decide for himself. Science has no such answers."[26] Penfield here alludes to the possibility that the mind, while normally dependent on the brain and body for its continuance, might be sustained directly by divine power in the absence of such support. Emergent dualism accepts this, affirming that the continued existence of the person that has died is a miracle of divine power, not a consequence of the soul's "natural immortality."

Upon closer examination, the field analogy also supports this possibility. Physical theory has been shown to imply that a sufficiently intense magnetic field can hold itself together by gravity even if its generating magnet has been removed.[27] A similar point can be made about the "black holes" that are so prominent in cosmology: according to Roger Penrose, once a black hole has formed it becomes "a self-sustaining gravitational field in its own right," and "has no further use for the body which originally built it."[28] To be sure, it may be problematic to take these ideas as a model for understanding the fate of the emergent mind. To do this might suggest that certain "high-powered" minds could become self-sustaining, whereas other, less powerful minds (perhaps those of infants and small children?) simply dissipate at death. But the models do underscore the fact that the emergent mind is ontologically distinct from the organism which generated it, and it is thus a logically coherent possibility for the mind to survive the death of the body. On the other hand, it is not necessary or inevitable that an emergent soul survives the death of the organism. It may be plausible to hold that in the case of most animals, the soul perishes along with the physical organism.

If the emergent mind can survive the death of its body, it can also be resurrected in a new or restored body. To be sure, not just any body would do. Dualists have sometimes supposed that souls could freely exchange bodies, as in Locke's story of the prince who traded bodies with a cobbler. But a new body for an emergent soul would have to be precisely tailored to fit the soul in question, otherwise, the activity of the body in sustaining the soul would clash with the already-established character of the latter. (This is just one more illustration of the way in which emergent dualism recognizes the complex dependence of mind on body, whereas traditional dualism tends to minimize this dependence.)[29]

For many readers of this essay, the very words "soul" and "animal" will make an awkward pairing. But if we humans need souls in order to think, and feel emotion, and experience sensations, then so do our friends the beasts. And we should not forget the animals; if we do, we shall be in danger of forgetting that we ourselves are animals. From that no good can come, either in philosophy or in life.

Hasker's chapter demonstrates clearly that there is more than one kind of dualism to consider. There is not just a single Soul Hypothesis, but a family of them. These hypotheses share certain features, but they also differ from one another in various ways. As a result, a range of dualistic theories can be compared, debated, refined, and ultimately tested empirically, just as in other areas of intellectual endeavor. And indeed it is very possible that some versions we had not thought of before might turn out to have very attractive properties.

In the final chapter of this volume, Robin Collins argues that contrary to the incessant claims of its critics, the Soul Hypothesis has a potential of being more in tune with the scientific approach to reality than its contenders. He does this by noting that the scientific approach to reality prefers theories that take into account the observational data (which the earlier chapters by Taileferro and Robinson claimed reductive materialism failed to do), while at the same time preferring simple and elegant laws over messy and complex laws. Further, science prefers testable and fruitful theories. He then argues that a certain version of the Soul Hypothesis — what he calls the dual aspect soul theory — potentially can fulfill these preferences over its contenders. Much of the chapter is dedicated to carefully articulating this hypothesis, and why it is potentially better than those views that deny the existence of the soul.

Collins's version of the Soul Hypothesis seems to be a bit more Cartesian than Hasker's, in that Collins does not claim that the soul is created by the brain; rather he seems to be open to the idea that the soul has a truly independent existence. But neither is Collins's version fully Cartesian, because his soul does exist in space, in the vicinity of the brain it is associated with. More than that, what is really special about Collins's idea of the soul is that it has a rich set of physical properties as well as the mental/psychological properties that motivate asserting the existence a soul in the first place. As such, Collins's proposal uses a form of property dualism (see Chapter 7), because souls have two quite different sets of properties, but nonetheless counts as a type of substance dualism, because it is a novel kind of object (the soul) that has both sets of properties, and not just a familiar physical object like the body or the brain.

One big advantage that Collins claims for his dual-aspect theory is that it can give a better account of the so-called linking laws that associate particular brain states with particular mental states. Neuroscience suggests that when one set of neurons fires in a particular way in our brain, we feel pain; when another set fires, we see a patch of red; when a third set fires we experience a salty flavor. For those (like us) who cannot believe that the neuron firings simply are the experiences in question, there must be some laws of nature that pair up the brain states and the various experiences that they go with, presumably in systematic ways. Now the brain is a very complex and many-faceted organ, which can be in an enormous number of different physical states. At the same time, our perceptual experience can also be rich and complex, filled with a very wide variety of sights, sounds, smells, tastes, and feelings, many of which can be present simultaneously or which can combine in a nearly infinite variety of ways. So brain states are complex, perceptual experiences can be complex, and the complexities of the one do not seem analogous to the complexities of the other in any obvious way. Therefore, it seems that the linking laws that relate the two must be very, very complex. And that seems problematic, since we expect the fundamental laws of nature to be relatively simple, like $f=ma$, and $e=mc^2$. (For further discussion of aspects of this problem, see also Zimmerman's chapter.)

Collins's dual-aspect theory helps to address this problem by building an analogy between the soul and a much simpler kind of physical object, namely a guitar string. A guitar string is a relatively simple object, but it can be in a wide variety of physical states simultaneously: the various vibrational states of the string as it vibrates with different energies at different frequencies. On the one hand, the vibrations of a string can be separated out into a series of discrete factors; on the other hand, they can be added up mathematically into a vast range of specific vibration patterns. And if this is true for the familiar one-dimensional guitar string vibrating in three dimensions, it should be even truer for more exotic (but still physical) objects like the superstrings or branes of recent physics.

Collins thus imagines mind-brain interactions in the following way. Vibrations of the brain can induce sympathetic vibrations in the physical aspect of the soul in more or less the same way that the sound of a musical instrument can cause a tuning fork to vibrate. Then the various vibrational modes of the soul can relate to the various psychological properties of the soul in some relatively simple and direct way, taking advantage of the fact that the soul has much simpler physical properties than the brain as a whole does, while still being able to be in an indefinitely large number of distinguishable states. The linking laws can be simpler, because one of the things being linked (the physical aspect of the soul) is simpler, and its various states are arguably already more similar in their logical structure to the structure of psychological states, even though they are not themselves psychological states. Moreover, although Collins does not discuss this much, the same model should be able to work the other way as well, with psychological decisions of the soul causing physical vibrations of the soul, which in turn cause sympathetic vibrations in the motor cortex of the brain, leading to voluntary action. In short, if one gives souls physical properties as well as psychological ones, it becomes less mysterious how souls and bodies can interact and influence one another, as we know they can. Collins even makes some preliminary proposals about how his idea might be open to new empirical testing as a bona fide scientific hypothesis.

Collins's way of looking at the mind-body problem can also address the problem of unity of consciousness, which asks what one thing is able to simultaneously see an object fall and hear the sound that it makes. It cannot be the brain, or any part of it, because very different regions of the brain process information about sight and information about sound. But it could be the soul, which Collins conceives of as a simple object with no parts, but one that can simultaneously undergo both sight-type vibrations and sound-type vibrations.

The reader will notice that Collins's chapter cites many of the other chapters in this volume, incorporating some of their insights and building on those insights. It has truly been the product of the authors' interactions with one another as a kind of research community during the course of developing this book. As such, it serves as a kind of capstone to the volume as a whole, and a sign that one can make progress by treating the existence of the soul as a hypothesis, worthy of elaboration, debate, refinement, testing, and discussion. Of course, this does not prove that the Soul Hypothesis has made a complete comeback yet, but it shows that it can make progress, and that it is a legitimate enterprise.

CHAPTER 9

A Scientific Case for the Soul

Robin Collins

INTRODUCTION

Substance dualism, which I will hereafter call *entity dualism*, is the view that the seat of consciousness is an immaterial entity, often referred to as a soul. Perhaps the most common objection to entity dualism is that it is inherently antiscientific.[1] The locus of this objection is the so-called interaction problem — the problem of explaining how an immaterial soul could interact with the brain. This is illustrated by the prominence of the "causal closure objection" and the "energy conservation objection," both of which claim that the interaction between mind and body cannot be reconciled with science (see Chapters 4 and 5 for direct responses to these objections). In this chapter, I reverse the tables on the objection that entity dualism is inherently antiscientific. After carefully examining the purported interaction problem, I argue that the right version of entity dualism has the potential of fitting the fundamental values of science much better than its contenders. In the process I develop an explicit model of how the immaterial soul could interact with the brain.

The heart of the scientific approach to reality arguably involves three criteria. Stated as preferences, these are: (i) a preference for views of reality that fit observational data over those based on prior philosophical commitments; (ii) a preference for simple and elegant laws over complex and messy laws; and (iii) a preference for potentially testable and fruitful hypotheses. Focusing on contents of conscious experience and their correlation with brain states, I first argue that *reductive materialism* — which states that conscious experiences are merely complex physical and chemical processes in the brain/body — fails to account for the data, the first criterion of good science. Then I consider the leading contender to reductive materialism, that of non-reductive materialism, a view which denies the existence of an immaterial soul but at the same time contends that conscious experience cannot be reduced to brain states. I argue that standard versions of this view have major difficulties with the second criterion — specifically with regard to providing a relatively simple set of laws connecting brain states with states of conscious experience. Finally, I show how the right sort of entity dualism has the potential of fulfilling all three criteria better than its contenders.

THE OBSERVATIONAL DATA

Although reductive materialism is the simplest view of the relation of the mind to the brain (since it postulates no entities in addition to those given by the physical sciences), many philosophers claim it fails to account for human experience and other facets of our world (see Chapters 1 and 2). In this section, I summarize the problem it has with consciousness and its contents, particularly what philosophers call *phenomenal qualia*, or *qualia* for short (with *quale* the singular form).[2] Philosopher Michael Tye introduces the notion of phenomenal qualia as follows.

> Consider your visual experience as you stare at a bright turquoise color patch in a paint store. There is something it is like for you subjectively to undergo that experience. What it is like to undergo the experience is very different from what it is like for you to experience a dull brown color patch. This difference is a difference in what is often called "phenomenal character." The phenomenal character of an experience is what it is like subjectively to undergo the experience. If you are told to focus your attention upon the phenomenal character of your experience, you will find that in doing so you are aware of certain qualities. These qualities — ones that are accessible to you introspectively and that together make up the phenomenal character of the experience —are standardly called "qualia".[3]

To understand the problem that qualia present for reductive materialism, consider a person I will call Abaz. Suppose you simultaneously peered into his brain and his mind using both a "brain scope" and a "soul scope," the former completely mapping the pattern of physical interactions in the brain and the latter allowing one to map all of Abaz's experiences and thoughts. Further suppose Abaz looks at a green backdrop and you notice a certain pattern of the firing of neurons that always take place when Abaz sees green. One puzzle is why this pattern of firing causes the particular phenomenal quale it does (which I will call the "green quale") instead of any other quale — such as that corresponding to the color red, the taste of chocolate, and the like — or no experience at all. No matter how much you physically analyze the brain, you will only detect material fields and particles causally interacting with one another, not the corresponding green quale. Of course, by asking Abaz and other subjects what they experience when a certain set of neurons are activated, you could draw a correlation between the experienced qualia and the pattern of neuronal firings, but this is not the same thing as being able to describe the qualia in purely physical terms.

To put the argument another way, suppose scientists had a perfected physics and neuroscience that provided a complete map of all the material interactions in Abaz's brain, along with a complete neurological account of the function of every system of Abaz's brain. It seems clear, at least to many who have pondered the issue, that a purely physical description of his brain will not include what it is like for him to have a particular experience, such as tasting chocolate. Further, it seems that his experiences cannot be deduced solely from such a description without knowing beforehand how brain states correlate with qualia. This is why, even after such a complete map of Abaz's and someone else's brain, it would make sense to wonder if the subjective quality of Abaz's experience is the same as the other person's. Moreover, as philosopher David Chalmers points out, these problems with reductive materialism will not go away with further developments in cognitive science and neurology. The reason is that these sciences can only explain the physical abilities and functions of systems in the brain; the problem that consciousness and qualia pose, however, is the problem of why there is an inner experience at all in systems with certain physical abilities, functions, and physical structure. This problem — what he calls the *hard problem* — remains even after all physical abilities, functions, and structures have been explained, and therefore is beyond the explanatory scope of cognitive science and neurology.[4]

Given that qualia cannot be reduced to states of the brain/body described by physics and chemistry (states that hereafter I simply refer to as "brain states"), reductive materialism fails on the most fundamental test of any theory, that of being compatible with the observational data. Two key consequences follow from this failure. First, one must hypothesize laws that link brain states with qualia, otherwise one cannot account for the observed correlation between neurological activity in certain regions of the brain and the occurrence of certain types of qualia. I will call these *linking laws*, though later I will use the term more generally to designate laws linking any set of non-subjective states with a set of subjective states. Since philosophers typically assume that laws imply or are undergirded by some sort of causal relation, I generally assume that where there is a linking law there is some corresponding causal relation. For example, if there is a linking law that correlates a material state with a quale, the material state either causally produces the quale or there is some common cause of both of them. This assumption, however, is not essential to my account.

Second, it seems to be a conceptual truth that an experience can only exist if there is an *experiencer*. For example, it seems that there cannot be an experience of pain without *something* experiencing the pain, whatever metaphysical category that "something" might fall under (such as a substance, a process, or an event).[5] In any case, even if this is logically possible, human experiences inseparably involve an experiencer: for example, it is not just that there is an experience of the sofa's being red, but that some particular person — such as Abaz — experiences the sofa as being red. It should be noted, though, that while I believe there is only one experiencer per human body, my argument does not depend on that assumption.

What is the nature of the experiencer? Leaving aside the question of the number of experiencers associated with a given human brain/body, the views on what an experiencer is can be divided into two camps: those who claim the experiencer is composed of other entities, and those who deny this. Those who advocate the composition view virtually always identify the experiencer of a given quale with the brain, some region of or set of processes in the brain, or some combination of the brain and the rest of the body. This view is commonly called *non-reductive material-ism*, because while its proponents believe that the entity that experiences the qualia is a material thing or process, they also maintain that qualia themselves cannot be reduced to any features or states of the brain that can be described by the physical sciences. (Nonetheless, many non-reductive materialists consider qualia [and even being an experiencer] material properties; they just do not consider them properties that are reducible to those in physics, but rather as being so-called emergent properties. This issue will not affect my overall argument, however.) I now argue that standard versions of non-reductive materialism seem to need enormously complex linking laws, and hence are likely to fail badly on the second scientific criteria mentioned previously: that of providing an account that invokes relatively simple laws.[6]

THE ENORMOUS COMPLEXITY CHALLENGE

The problem of the enormous complexity of the laws linking qualia with brain states has been recognized by many other philosophers. For example, this problem has led Thomas Nagel, one of the most influential critics of reductive materialism, to question his prior advocacy of reductive materialism.[7] To understand the complexity problem faced by non-reductive materialism, it is helpful to introduce some terminology, beginning with some terms concerning qualia. Qualia are distinguished by what it is like to experience them: if two purportedly distinct qualia are experienced as identical, then they are identical. Now, qualia can be classified under very broad natural categories — e.g. as visual, auditory, tactile, and gustatory qualia. Some of these categories might have further natural subtypes, such as various types of visual qualia: e.g. the qualia associated with the subjective experience of seeing red. Presumably, at some point, there will be no further natural subcategories, with the qualia only differing by mathematically quantifiable features, such as their intensity, or in the case of visual qualia, their intensity and position within the visual field. Following biological classification schemes, I call the lowest category of qualia *species*, with the category up one level a quale's *genus*, the next level the quale's *family*, and so forth. Thus, presumably the quale involved in experiencing pure redness (of a certain hue, saturation, etc.) is a species of quale containing many different individual qualia of various intensities, whereas the class of color qualia is a genus since particular species of color qualia fall under it. These groupings are to be determined by the inherent experienced nature of the qualia. The correct scheme of classification, however, is not important to my argument. Further, for the sake of exposition, in the rest of the paper I only consider species of qualia and the various qualia they contain.

Presumably, there are laws that specify for each brain state whether or not it gives rise to qualia, and if so, what qualia it gives rise to. I call these laws *linking laws*. In specifying the qualia a brain state gives rise to, the law will have to specify both the species of qualia and their respective intensities, and in the case of visual and certain other types of qualia, their apparent spatial location. Finally, since there cannot be qualia without an experiencer, non-reductive materialists must postulate a law or metaphysical principle that specifies which material systems constitute experiencers; this law constitutes a special linking law that will become relevant at the end of the section entitled "The dual aspect soul model," when I consider possible non-standard forms of non-reductive materialism.

Laws of nature have two sorts of variables. One type of variable is called a *dependent* variable, which can be thought of as a quantity whose value the law specifies. The other set of variables are called the *independent* variables; these are the factors which determine the value of the dependent variable. For instance, Newton's law of gravity says that the force of gravity between any two masses is proportional to the product of their respective masses divided by the square of the distance between them.[8] In this case, the dependent variable is the force of gravity (since it is the quantity that the law determines) and the independent variables are the values of the two masses and the distance between them (since these are what determine the force).[9]

In the case of the qualia linking laws, there are two dependent variables: the species of the qualia and its intensity. (For simplicity of exposition, I neglect the apparent spatial location of many types of qualia until near the end of the section "The dual aspect soul model.") The independent variables will be the relevant features of the brain or other material systems that determine these aspects of the qualia. Now, in general, the more variables a law invokes, the more complex the law is. Specifically, the more independent variables a law invokes that cannot be combined into a single variable, the more complex the law is. This is nicely illustrated by laws enacted by human beings, though the same analysis applies to the laws of nature. Consider, for instance, sales taxes that many states have adopted in the US. A maximally simple sales tax would apply the same tax rate — say 6 per cent — to all items that are sold. Many states do not have maximally simple laws, but rather charge different rates for different items. For example, California charges an 8.5 per cent sales tax on all items except unprepared food items. One could imagine even more complex tax laws, ones that charged different tax rates for paper products, dairy products, crackers, honey, cereal, and so forth. Each of these items would constitute a different variable that could not be lumped together under a single variable, but would have to be considered independently. Clearly, the more such variables there are, the more complex the law. At some point, one could only imagine the difficulty a store clerk would have in calculating the sales tax without the use of a computer! An ideal of science is for the fundamental laws to invoke relatively few independent variables, an ideal which is largely fulfilled by the basic laws in the physical sciences. For instance, Newton's law of gravity only contains three independent variables — the values of the two masses and the distance between them.

THE CHALLENGE EXPLAINED

The challenge for non-reductive materialism is that the qualia linking laws appear to need a vast number of independent variables, making them enormously complex. The most general case of the laws linking material states with qualia will be a law that specifies which material states give rise to consciousness itself, since this is required for any qualia to exist. For simplicity of exposition, I focus on this law, showing why it seems that it must be enormously complex, though the same sort of analysis applies to the specific laws linking brain states with specific qualia.

To begin, imagine that one could see — using my fictitious "experience scope" — whether or not a material system gives rise to conscious experience. Some systems, such as those associated with brains, give rise to consciousness, and others do not. As one performed more and more experiments with different types of material systems, one could construct a list of those material configurations that are correlated with consciousness and those that are not. Eventually, one would have a vast listing of such conditions, far larger than any telephone book.

Now suppose one made each condition a law — for example, a law might state that when the condition given by the nth listing is met consciousness arises, whereas when the one given by the kth listing is met, there is no consciousness. Clearly, this would result in an enormously — in fact, infinitely — complicated set of laws. A challenge for non-reductive materialists is to indicate how this enormous listing of correlations could be derived from a few simple laws.

To be simple, such laws must only invoke a few basic physical variables, upon which the existence of consciousness depends. This is where the difficulty lies. The existence of consciousness, let alone specific qualia, seems to depend on the right sort of complexity in the arrangement of the parts of a physical system, along with the interactions between the parts. That is what appears to separate brains from other material systems, such as a rock in my garden, that presumably are unconscious. Further, there does not appear to be any set of basic physical variables (such as energy or the vibrational frequency of some material field) that can be used as part of a simple law to separate those material systems that give rise to consciousness from those that do not. This suggests that any law that directly connects material configurations with consciousness will itself have to invoke that complexity.

An analogy can help illustrate this last point. Suppose that the members of a primitive tribe were trained to identify basic elements and chemical compounds, but were not given the concept of an electron or that of an electromagnetic wave, such as a radio wave. (For example, they would be able to identify iron, but would not know that atoms of iron contained electrons.) Further, suppose that they were given the means of analyzing the arrangements of elements and compounds of various types of radios along with that of the radio station. Finally, suppose they were given the means of manipulating the material structure of the radios.

The tribe could then go about recording those material configurations which resulted in functioning radios (that is, ones that emitted the same sounds as produced in the studio) and those that did not. This too would involve an enormous listing of conditions. Without invoking electrons and radio waves (or some functional equivalent of these), it is unlikely that there would be any way of deriving this listing from a few simple laws containing a few independent variables. Specifically, they could not distinguish functioning radios from non-functioning radios via simple laws that invoked the basic physical parameters available to them, such as color, density, energy, or the like. The problem is that the kind of complexity that makes a radio function is not reducible to a simple set of laws invoking these factors. However, once electrons and radio waves are postulated, along with the relatively simple fundamental laws governing them, the reasons for these correlations between material configurations and functioning radios would become clear; the tribe would no longer be stuck with simply postulating a law for each correlation (see Figure 9.1).

The lesson here is that by invoking a few new entities that cannot be directly observed with a few new variables describing these entities (e.g. electric charge and the value of the electric and magnetic field), one can derive a highly complex set of correlations via a few simple laws. In fact, historically this is exactly what happened with the introduction of atoms. During the nineteenth century, more and more laws connecting observable features of physical systems — what philosophers call *phenomenological laws* — were discovered. For example, scientists discovered the ideal gas law (which states that if one heats a particular type of gas in a box, its pressure increases in proportion to its temperature), along with a host of laws that stated the results of combining chemical compounds in various proportions. As the nineteenth century progressed, more and more such laws were discovered; the number of such laws mushroomed, and without the introduction of some new entities (specifically, atoms), no one could find a way of deriving them from a few simple laws. As one instance of this, the relation between volume, pressure, and temperature of many gases deviated slightly

FIGURE 9.1 A photograph of the inside of a modern-day radio. Just as the postulate of electrons and radio waves (with their own fundamental laws) allows us to understand why certain material configurations result in a functioning radio, it is argued in the next section that the postulate of the right kind of soul with the right sort of linking laws could help us understand how brain states are connected with conscious experiences.

from the ideal gas law, but there was no simple way of accounting for the deviations.

One way of thinking about the situation is that phenomenological laws governing the observed features of a physical system — which could be thought of as its dependent variables — required that one take into account more and more independent variables (the particular type of gas, the particular chemicals being combined, and so forth) without being able to derive these laws from some small set of laws with a few independent variables. The hypothesis of invisible (and at the time undetectable) atoms allowed one to predict the mushrooming number of phenomenological regularities using the much simpler set of laws postulated to govern atoms. Essentially, this hypothesis introduced new fundamental entities and corresponding fundamental variables describing those entities (such as atomic weight and atomic number). The introduction of these new entities and fundamental variables allowed physicists to eliminate the enormous number of independent variables that the phenomenological laws had to invoke.

The above examples show that postulating new entities with their own fundamental properties can result in a great reduction of complexity of fundamental laws that more than compensates for the increase in ontological complexity entailed by the hypothesis of the new entities. In fact, this is the motivation for postulating new particles and other entities in physics, and so is standard practice in science. On the other hand, it is almost universally assumed that the introduction of the immaterial soul can only increase the complexity of one's theory; thus, it is almost universally assumed that the scientific way of thinking is in conflict with entity dualism. The above examples indicate that the reverse might be the case. In fact, in the next section I sketch how such a reduction in complexity of the laws linking subjective states with material states can be achieved by introducing a new metaphysical entity, the soul, with the right fundamental properties. This will constitute the core of my case for the scientific merits of the right sort of entity dualism.

I have no proof that non-reductive materialists cannot achieve such a reduction in complexity without invoking new entities and variables, but I do think that there is good reason to believe that they are in the same situation as the aforementioned tribe, and as scientists in the nineteenth century who belonged to the so-called "energist school," who attempted to provide a simple account of the various known phenomenological laws without appealing to atoms. The reason is that no simple relationship between the variables recognized by the physical sciences — such as energy, temperature, mass, and the like — seems to capture what differentiates those material systems that are conscious from those that are not. Rather, it is something about the complex configuration of components — as occurs in animal brains — that makes the difference.

This last point is brought home by considering a simple thought experiment, that of taking a group of neurons that constitute an experiencing brain and slowly changing the chemical and other interactions among those neurons, along with the shape, composition, and structural features of the neurons themselves. With enough such changes, the brain will go from being conscious to being unconscious. Now, there are an enormous number of seemingly independent ways of making these changes — for example, one corresponding to a change in the strength of a particular type of chemical reaction between some pair of neurons, along with all the possible combinations thereof. For every one of those seemingly different types of changes, the linking law will have to specify when the group of neurons goes from producing consciousness to not producing consciousness. Unless these changes can be reduced to changes in a few basic physical variables, the linking law will end up involving a vast, if not infinite number, of independent variables, one for each type of change. Yet, as mentioned above, it does not seem there are any such variables to do the trick: certainly variables such as energy, temperature, and mass density will not work to distinguish conscious material systems from unconscious systems. This problem is greatly compounded when one considers that such parameters also have to be found for the linking laws for qualia — for example, there would need to be a few basic parameters that determined when a material state produces green qualia, yellow qualia, the smell of roses, and the like.

The problem is nicely illustrated by considering a concrete proposal (based on experimental evidence) that some neurologists have given for material conditions of conscious experience. As explained by neurologists R. Llinás, U. Ribary, D. Contreras, and C. Pedroarena,[10] the proposal is that conscious awareness occurs when there are resonant vibrations between the thalamic and cortical structures of the brain that are in the frequency range of 20 to 50 hertz. Based on their proposal, one could postulate a linking law according to which consciousness comes into existence if and only if the amplitude of such resonance vibrations is above a certain threshold. Although this proposal might seem to only involve a simple law, a problem arises regarding precisely specifying which neurological structures constitute a thalamic structure and which constitute a cortical structure; without such precise specification, the law will not be able to specify precisely when consciousness occurs. Although general descriptions can clearly be given (otherwise scientists could not distinguish such structures), the law will have to separate out all the borderline cases. One can therefore engage in the same thought experiment as above, in which one changes the interactions, compositions, and various other features of the neurons composing each of these structures. Thus, for instance, the linking law will have to specify precisely when a group of neurons constituting a thalamic structure goes from being a thalamic structure to a non-thalamic structure for every possible set of changes. Consequently, the problem of seeming to need an enormous number of independent variables in one's linking law will return.

One could attempt to evade this by introducing emergent properties or structures — that is, properties or structures that arise in complex systems but cannot be specified by a simple equation based on the configuration of the underlying particles. The introduction of emergent properties or structures, however, simply pushes the problem back to the laws specifying when those emergent properties or structures arise. This can be seen in the above concrete proposal, where the proposed emergent structures consist of the thalamic and cortical structures of the brain. Specifying these structures just pushes the problem of enormous complexity to another location.

As mentioned above, I have no proof that non-reductive materialists cannot find a simple linking law — one that only appeals to a few basic physical variables — that specifies those material states that give rise to consciousness. On the other hand, no one ever proved that the complexity of chemical and other laws could not be greatly reduced without the introduction of atoms; because atoms could be shown to do the trick, however, the burden was shifted to the other side to show how they could achieve such a reduction without such unseen entities. This chapter therefore, should be seen as showing that entity dualism has the promise of providing such a simplification, and thus as presenting a challenge to non-reductive materialists to find a way of doing the same.

THE DUAL ASPECT SOUL MODEL

Entity dualism can be defined as the claim that the experiencer is an immaterial entity. Further, entity dualists almost universally claim that the experiencer is a non-composite bearer of properties — that is, a *metaphysical simple*. This hypothesis avoids one problem related to the complex linking law problem for qualia, but only hinted at above: the need for a complex linking law to say which material composite is the experiencer. The reason is that since the metaphysical simple itself is the experiencer, no special linking law is needed to specify which of its states do, and do not, result in an experiencer. Further, postulating a metaphysical simple does not involve invoking a new metaphysical category or principle, since physics itself seems to need metaphysical simples: for instance, if one adopts a fundamental particle ontology, then the fundamental particles (such as electrons) are the non-composite bearers of properties; on the other hand, if one thinks fields are primary, then space-time points are considered metaphysical simples. So, at least with regard to its hypothesis that the experiencer is a metaphysical simple, this immaterial experiencer account does not add any new metaphysical category. Arguably, however, non-reductive materialists must add some new metaphysical principles or laws that have no precedent elsewhere: namely, those that specify that certain material systems are experiencers and others are not.

Merely hypothesizing such a metaphysical simple, however, does not itself solve the problem of linking brain states with the occurrence of conscious experience, or of specific qualia. For example, there would still need to be laws that linked states of the brain with the qualia experienced by the postulated metaphysical simple, with the same sort of thought experiment applying in this case as above: for any given quale, the laws have to specify all the possible configurations of particles that give rise to that quale and those that do not, thus once again seeming to require an enormous number of variables.

A potential solution to this problem is to postulate that this new metaphysical simple has two kinds of properties, *subjective* properties and *non-subjective* properties. Subjective properties are defined as those that explicitly or implicitly involve consciousness or awareness and non-subjective properties are defined as those that do not. For example, qualia are subjective properties whereas the various features of my desk — e.g. its weight, size, and shape — are non-subjective properties since they can be described without explicit reference to consciousness or awareness. Specifically, I postulate that there are linking laws that link these non-subjective properties with particular qualia or species of qualia. I then explicate how these non-subjective properties could serve as intermediaries that can account for the regularities linking states of the brain with qualia states using relatively few simple laws. I will call this model of the soul the *dual-aspect soul model*, since it ascribes two different sorts of properties to the soul.

This model further postulates that these non-subjective properties can be represented mathematically. This means that if one ignored its subjective properties, the hypothesis of such a soul would be equivalent to hypothesizing a new physical entity. The reason is that in modern physics, a physical entity can be defined as any entity that meets the following three criteria: (i) its states can be specified without reference to consciousness or awareness; (ii) its states can be described by some mathematical function; and (iii) the evolution of its states and their interaction with other material systems can be specified by a set of mathematical equations. The non-subjective properties of the soul are stipulated to meet all these conditions. Thus the primary way in which these dual-aspect souls differ from the commonly postulated material simples of physics (e.g. electrons) is that they have subjective properties in addition to non-subjective properties. Further, since the soul's non-subjective properties can be represented mathematically, an equation can be constructed that specifies how they are affected by the physical properties of other entities. This means that, in principle, there is no more difficulty in specifying the equations governing the evolution of a soul's non-subjective states and their interaction with other fields — e.g. standard material fields, such as those that occur in the brain or even the non-subjective states of other souls — than there would be with that of specifying the evolution and interaction of a newly hypothesized physical entity.

The primary motivation for such an account is to simplify the laws linking states of the brain with qualia and other subjective states. As explained above, the difficulty for non-reductive materialism is that there are good reasons to believe that there are an enormous number of irreducible independent variables in the linking laws, thus making the linking laws themselves enormously complex. This problem can be eliminated for qualia by requiring that there be relatively few, simply specifiable independent variables in the linking laws. Maximum simplicity will be achieved if there is one variable to determine the species of qualia, and another to determine the intensity of the qualia. Given that species of qualia are discrete (that is, they do not form a continuous spectrum), the specification of this variable would be maximally simple if it were also discrete — that is, if it were to come in integer multiples of some fundamental unit. The reason is that specifying an integer — for example, the number "three" — takes much less information than specifying a real number, which typically requires an infinite number of digits.

To see how such simplicity could be realized, I begin by considering a fictional "guitar-string soul" whose non-subjective states consist of the vibrational patterns on a guitar-string and whose subjective qualia are linked with the states of this guitar string by a postulated set of linking laws. This will help provide the basis for presenting a more realistic model of the soul in a following section.

THE "GUITAR-STRING" MODEL

Consider an idealized guitar string (i.e. one with absolutely uniform density, tension, and shape and no damping) fastened between two points a distance L apart. When plucked, the string will vibrate. The standing wave vibrations on the string form what is known as a *harmonic series* of wavelengths and corresponding frequencies. The lowest frequency wave is called the fundamental. The frequency of the kth harmonic is k times the frequency of the fundamental. So, for instance, the frequency of the third harmonic will be three times the frequency of the first. Each of these waves has two further attributes besides frequency: that of *amplitude* and *phase*.[11] Once these three attributes are specified, the exact waveform will be completely specified (see Figure 9.2).

First Harmonic

Second Harmonic

Third Harmonic

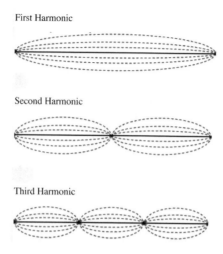

FIGURE 9.2: The wave patterns on the string for the first three harmonics. The wave in the first harmonic (the fundamental) vibrates back and forth with a frequency f, with the frequency of the second and third harmonics being twice and three times the fundamental, respectively. The amplitude is just the amount by which the string deviates from its resting position as it vibrates (as given by its height in the diagram).

Now suppose that a linking law assigned each of the first three harmonics a certain species of qualia: for example, it assigned waves falling under the first harmonic the qualia of tasting bitter; those under the second harmonic the qualia of seeing red; and those under the third harmonic, the experience of a certain type of pain. (For now, I neglect the fact that some of these qualia — such as color — are typically experienced as having spatial location.) Further, suppose that the law specified that the intensity of the quale was directly proportional to the amplitude of the corresponding wave falling under the relevant harmonics. For instance, this would imply that if one doubled the intensity of a wave falling under the first harmonic, the guitar-string soul would experience twice the intensity of the taste of bitterness. Such a law would be particularly simple. For example, the equation specifying the relation between the first harmonic and its corresponding qualia could be expressed by the simple equation $I_1 = C_1 A_1$, where I_1 is the intensity of the taste of bitterness, A_1 is the amplitude of the first harmonic, and C_1 is a constant of proportionality.[12] This equation has only one independent variable — that of the amplitude of the first harmonic — which can be specified by a simple description.

Linking laws like these are enough to determine the entire subjective experience of the soul. To see how, first note that any waveform on the string can be uniquely decomposed into its harmonics, by what is known as a Fourier series. Specifically, any waveform on the string can be decomposed into a combination of a wave of a certain amplitude and phase falling under the first harmonic, plus a wave of another amplitude and phase falling under the second harmonic, plus a wave of another amplitude and phase falling under the third harmonic, and so on. Further, the amplitude and phase corresponding to each harmonic is uniquely determined by the overall waveform on the string. Given any overall waveform, therefore, one can deduce the exact amplitude and phase of the wave falling under any of its harmonics, and hence the intensity of the qualia produced by that harmonic via the linking laws.[13] Consequently, this ability of waves to superpose and to be decomposable into a unique set of fundamental waveforms allows both the guitar-string soul to experience multiple qualia at the same time and for its qualia states to be determined by a few simple linking laws connecting the fundamental waveforms with qualia.[14] Finally, since the wave pattern on the string is determined by the laws of physics, this means that once the above linking laws are specified, the combination of qualia experienced by the soul will be determined by the standard laws of physics.

TOWARDS A MORE REALISTIC MODEL

Above, I presented a concrete illustration of how a dual-aspect model could greatly simplify the laws linking brain states with qualia. It is now time to turn to a more realistic version of the dual-aspect model based on ideas arising out of superstring theory. The model, however, should be only considered what physicists call a "toy" model — that is, a model presented for purposes of illustration and understanding — and not necessarily as the way the soul actually is. The primary purpose of the model is to show that the dual-aspect view has the potential of providing a framework for constructing a viable model of the soul that enormously reduces the complexity of linking laws. In some ways, the model below should be considered analogous to John Dalton's original hypothesis of atoms in the early 1800s. Although it took over a century to fully articulate the nature of atoms (with some modifications of his original proposal being made along the way), his hypothesis showed that the hypothesis of such entities held the promise of greatly reducing the number of fundamental chemical laws, a promise that was eventually fulfilled.

Superstring theory is widely considered the most plausible candidate for a truly fundamental theory of all physical reality. Superstring models in physics postulate that the fundamental entities in the universe are miniature strings of energy that vibrate in a ten- or eleven-dimensional space, six of which are compactified; in this way, they are analogous to miniature guitar strings with various fundamental modes of vibration. Although superstrings are postulated to have a fundamental length (e.g. 10^{-33} centimeters), the superstrings themselves should not be thought of as composed of a set of spatial points; rather, they are typically considered as non-composite entities — that is, as metaphysical simples. As stated by physicist Lesal Randall, "according to string theory, the most basic *indivisible* objects underlying all matter are strings — vibrating, one-dimensional loops or segments of energy."[15] She then goes on to stress that these strings are fundamental, not made of further parts.[16] For example, they are not made of spatial parts.[17] In this way, they are like the quantum mechanical wavefunction associated with an electron or other non-composite particle: although as typically represented, the electron's quantum wavefunction is spread out in space, no interpretation of quantum mechanics considers the electron as being composed of its spatial parts; at most, the wavefunction could be thought of as representing some physical disposition that determines the degree to which the electron is present at each spatial location — as for example, in some versions of the so-called "Heinsenberg interpretation" of quantum mechanics.

Finally, these strings have various modes of vibration — such as rotational modes — besides those given by their harmonic frequencies. An example of different vibrational modes from everyday physics is a steal beam, which can undergo vibrations perpendicular to its length ("up and down" vibrations) along with vibrations consisting of compression waves along its length. Because of the way in which the ten- or eleven-dimensional space is thought to be compactified in string theory, strings can have a wide variety of modes of vibration. Each mode is then postulated to correspond to the various families of fundamental particles — such as the leptons, a family that includes the electron and some other particles. Brane theory extends this idea to vibrating two- and higher-dimensional objects called *branes*, allowing for many additional modes of vibration. As with a guitar-string, each mode of vibration has well-defined harmonics, with each harmonic consisting of waves of definite frequency, but differing in amplitude and other features; further, the frequency of each harmonic is an integer multiple of some fundamental.

Taking inspiration from string theory, one could suppose that the soul itself is a miniature string (or brane) of energy, with its own dynamical equations. One could then postulate linking laws that link each mode of vibration with a particular genus of qualia, with each species of qualia under a given genus (such as taste) corresponding to a particular harmonic frequency of that mode, and with the intensity of the qualia falling under this species linked by some simple function to the amplitude of the wave (as in the guitar-string soul). Hence, the linking laws should display the same descriptive simplicity as they did for the guitar-string model. Further, higher-level groupings of vibrational modes could correspond to families of qualia, thereby providing a particularly elegant scheme of linking laws in which the structure of the higher-level groupings of the qualia corresponds to the structure of the different vibrational modes. Finally, since the non-subjective states would be mathematically represented like any other newly hypothesized physical states, in principle their equations of motion and the way they interact with other physical systems are no more problematic than that of a newly hypothesized fundamental physical entity — such as a superstring. For example, one could require conservation of energy in the same way that it is typically done in all other places in physics except gravity (see Chapter 5).

In the guitar-string soul, I developed the model for a soul that experienced three qualia and noted that I was ignoring the fact that some qualia — such as color qualia — have coordinate positions. It would be useful, however, to see whether the above model might be able to account for coordinate positions. One way of obtaining coordinate positions is in a similar way to TV. For example, in a standard black and white TV, the information in the TV signal causes temporal variations in intensity of the electron beam hitting the back of the screen. Since the electron beam sweeps the entire screen every sixtieth of a second (the standard refresh rate), these temporal variations are transformed into variations in intensity of the beam hitting over the two-dimensional rear surface of the screen. If at some time the beam is at a certain coordinate position in its sweep across the screen, the intensity of the beam hitting that coordinate position will be the intensity of the beam at that time. (The brightness of the screen at any point is proportional to the intensity of the beam at the point.) Thus variations of intensity in time are translated to variations of intensity in the two-dimensional space of the screen.

Following the example of the TV, one could postulate a law that maps temporal variations in qualia to spatial variations in the visual field, with some "refresh rate." This additional law would allow the production of qualia over coordinate positions in the visual field. A similar account could be given of the auditory and tactile qualia fields.[18]

Finally, the dual aspect model understands the complex neurological processing that is required for perception as the processing necessary so the brain can activate the requisite non-subjective states of the soul so as to produce an accurate representation of the environment. An analogy might help: the linking laws between the non-subjective states of the soul and the qualia are analogous to the mechanisms that link electrical signals on the back of a visual display — such as a computer monitor — with the visual image on the display. The systems in the brain are analogous to the highly complex systems that must translate the visual information picked up by a camera into the proper electrical signals required by the display being used, such as a display at mission control viewing information coming from a satellite orbiting Jupiter.

THE PRIMARY ADVANTAGE OF THE MODEL

The primary advantage of the dual-aspect model is that it offers the potential of constructing a model of the soul in which there are relatively simple laws that link non-subjective states with qualia states. Although it is possible that such laws could be constructed under a non-reductive materialist account, it is difficult to see how this could be done. Further, as pointed out above, the individual laws linking these non-subjective states with other material systems need not be any more complex than the normal laws of physics. Consequently, the total set of fundamental laws in a dual-aspect model has the potential of being much less complex than those most likely required by non-reductive materialism. Finally, although the dual-aspect soul theorist must hypothesize a new entity — an immaterial simple that has subjective properties along with other non-subjective properties — the non-reductive materialist also must hypothesize a new entity (a material composite) that has subjective properties. So, the non-reductive materialist will have a hard time arguing that despite the complexity of linking laws, their view is nonetheless to be preferred because it postulates fewer fundamental entities.

Despite the potential simplification afforded by the dual-aspect model, the set of linking laws would involve an unavoidable complexity given by the number of distinct species of qualia that cannot be put on a common scale (or other simply describable mathematical space), since effectively there will need to be a distinct linking law for each such species. (For example, the guitar-string model had effectively three linking laws, one for bitterness, one for redness, and one for pain.) Further, there will be a minimal, unavoidable arbitrariness for each linking law: e.g. it will be arbitrary why the k harmonic is associated with the particular species that it is, instead of some other species or none at all. All fundamental laws of nature, however, involve some arbitrariness. For example, if the fact that charges always repel each other were a fundamental law, then it could not be explained by a further law. One could attempt to eliminate the metaphysical arbitrariness by appealing to some underlying necessity in nature to account for the law — like charges repel each other because they *must* — but the epistemic arbitrariness will remain, since one cannot see why that necessity must hold (unless one builds into the concept of charge that it repels other charges, in which case the law tells us nothing). In this respect, laws connecting the mental and physical states are no more problematic than laws connecting physical states. The respect in which they are more problematic is that the effective number of such basic linking laws — one for each species of qualia — will likely be much larger than the number of fundamental laws of physics. The best one can hope for, therefore, is to minimize the complexity, not to eliminate it.[19]

At this point, one might wonder why non-reductive materialists could not follow the lead of the above dual-aspect model and propose a non-standard form of their view, one which postulates new non-subjective states as intermediaries, but ascribes them to a material composite instead of an immaterial entity. Although they could do this, the disadvantage of their account is that they will have to hypothesize an additional linking law to pick out which composite is the experiencer of the qualia.[20] When one experiences redness, for instance, what aggregate of particles is the experiencer? Some aggregate in the occipital lobe? The brain? The body? As Dean Zimmerman points out in Chapter 7, these sorts of entities are vague entities whose boundaries science does not specify. Yet, the experiencer has to be some specific aggregate (or set of aggregates); thus the linking law will have to specify which of the many possibilities it is — for example, in the case of the brain whether it includes the atoms in a particular highly deformed neuron at the edge of the skull, or in the case of the body, whether it includes the atoms at the edge of the calluses and toenails on one's feet. Even if non-reductive materialists could find a way to make this law relatively simple via the use of the postulated additional non-subjective properties, their view would likely be worse off than the dual-aspect soul view. Although both views require types of laws and entities not found in science (namely, the qualia linking laws and entities that have subjective properties), non-reductive materialism requires a new unprecedented type of fundamental irreducible law: one that specifies that a specific aggregate (or set of aggregates) is the bearer of some postulated set of properties. In contrast, throughout the physical sciences, only metaphysical simples (such as electrons) are postulated to be fundamental bearers of properties, with the properties of aggregates being assumed to be reducible to the intrinsic and relational properties of these simples. (Even if one believes in emergent entities, there are no fundamental laws in our current sciences that specify when they come into existence or their irreducible properties.) Thus, arguably, even in the best case scenario, non-reductive materialism cannot meet the scientific ideal of simplicity as well as the dual-aspect soul view. In any case, the above dual-aspect soul model presents a challenge for non-reductive materialists to sketch out a view that is as simple and elegant, especially if they want to claim the mantel of being more in accord with science.

Finally, the above model shows that even though one cannot offer a scientific account of the linking laws themselves — just as one cannot offer such an account of any fundamental laws of nature — the experiences of a dual-aspect soul could fall within the purview of science: once the linking laws are given, one can explain why the soul experiences the qualia it does, and predict its future qualia states using the standard laws of physics. This explicitly shows that entity-dualist accounts of the soul need not be antiscientific or merely appeal to mystery (or special acts of God), contrary to the claim made by many of its critics,[21] and even many of those sympathetic to some form of dualism.[22]

THE SOUL'S INTERACTION WITH THE BRAIN

I have already discussed in general terms how the non-subjective states of the soul could interact with the brain. Here I offer a physical analogy as to how this interaction could take place. The brain could be considered to provide energy to the soul, with specific brain systems — such as the occipital lobe — providing energy primarily to those vibrational modes of the soul with the same frequency, a phenomena known as *resonance*, which is pervasive throughout the physical world. Resonance is the reason radio or TV tuners pick up specific stations and why energy can be easily transferred between two tuning forks with the same frequency. Each of the five senses could have their own vibrational modes, with each species of qualia falling under one of the senses having its own harmonic frequency. This means that the soul would experience a given species of qualia only if the brain emitted the right frequency of energy (in perhaps the right mode). Further, higher-level abstract thinking could require activation of its own type of mode, also attuned to its own mode and overall frequency. Like TV signals, the waveform of these vibrational energies emanating from the brain to the soul — say from the occipital lobe — might also carry sensory and other kinds of information.

The interaction between the brain and the soul, and within the soul itself, need not be one way, however. There might be linking laws between certain specified subjective states and non-subjective harmonic states of the soul. For example, a linking law could specify that when a particular type of subjective state occurs, the amplitude (or energy) of the corresponding harmonic frequency of some specified vibrational mode will increase by an amount proportional to the intensity of that state and the time over which it occurred. This would allow the subjective states of the soul to influence its non-subjective states. Since the connection between the non-subjective states and other material states are specified by some set of equations, these subjective states can then affect the brain.[23]

One could also postulate the existence of various damping "mechanisms" in the soul, causing the energy of the vibrational modes to slowly dissipate, unless continually fed energy by the brain or something else. Almost all physical systems in the universe have these damping mechanisms; the only known possible exceptions are certain systems that exhibit specifically quantum mechanical behavior, such as superconductors. (Dualists who believe in survival of bodily death could hypothesize either that the damping mechanisms in the soul disappear at death, in analogy to how the resistance of a metal disappears when it goes into a superconducting state, or that some new energy source — such as a new body — continues to power its various modes.)

Of course, many other models could be proposed regarding how the brain and non-subjective states of the soul interact. The point here is that the dual-aspect framework allows one to build and potentially test more specific models of this interaction, and hence potentially make scientific progress on the nature of the interaction of the soul and the brain. For example, if one hypothesized that the occipital lobe emitted a particular kind of waves, one could then attempt to duplicate the material operation of the occipital lobe in some other material medium, place that material in its own sealed tiny container in the skull (so that it did not significantly interact with other neurons), and see if it affected the person's visual sensations without directly affecting the neurons in the visual areas of the brain. Such an experiment, even if it yielded negative results, would at least allow one to make progress on narrowing down the nature of the interaction between the brain and the non-subjective states of the soul. Thus, the dual-aspect framework could provide a fruitful scientific research program for understanding and explaining the relation between the mind and the brain.

EVOLUTION AND THE SOUL

How might the dual-aspect model fit with the theory of evolution and the existence of animal minds? For theists, one possibility is that God creates just one type of generic soul for all animals, but the structure of an animal's brain determines which non-subjective states of the soul are activated. As animal brains get larger (in the right ways) and have more of the right neurological subsystems, they are able to power those non-subjective states that must be activated for higher levels of consciousness — such as abstract thoughts — to occur.[24] Another possibility is that major groupings of animals, such as families, orders, or genera each have their own type of soul, with the variation among lower level groupings — such as species within a genus — being a result of the ability of their brains to activate and send appropriate signals to the various non-subjective modes.

Yet another possibility is to combine the dual-aspect model of the soul with some version of emergent entity dualism, such as that presented by William Hasker in Chapter 8. One way to do this takes its inspiration from modern quantum field theory, which views particles as *quanta* of their respective fields: for example, electrons are considered quanta of the electron field and photons are considered quanta of the electromagnetic field. From a field point of view, the quanta are merely excitations of the field, whereas from a particle point of view, the quanta are individual metaphysical simples.

Given that one accepts that some quanta are individual entities (as many philosophers are inclined to do for some types of quanta, such as the electron), one has a situation in which metaphysical simples are somehow produced out of the energy of the field, with the type of simples that are produced being dependent on the type of field in question. Since the energy of the individual quantum comes in discrete units, this means that in order for any quanta to be produced, the energy of the field must have at least the energy of a single quantum. For example, an electron has a fixed rest mass, which corresponds to a fixed energy as given by Einstein's famous equation $E = mc^2$. Thus, to produce an electron, the electron field must have at least this amount of energy. Applying this idea to the dual-aspect soul theory, souls could be considered analogous to quanta of an overarching "soul field." Hence, individual souls would only come into existence when enough energy is pumped into this soul field to produce at least one soul quanta — e.g. a single "soul string" in the toy model presented earlier. Just as only certain material structures can transmit and pump electromagnetic energy into a receiver (e.g. radio transmitters), it makes sense that only certain kinds of neurological structures are capable of pumping enough energy (of the right frequencies and of sufficient coherence) into the soul field to create a soul quanta. This implies that souls will only come into existence when animal brains reach sufficient size and complexity during the evolutionary process. Larger and appropriately structured brains could then be postulated not only to create souls, but to activate higher level modes of vibration of the soul-string, such as those required for abstract thought.

In one version of the above scenario, all souls would be the same type of entity, but with different modes of their souls being activated depending on brain structure and function. An alternative scenario is one in which there are distinct types of quanta of the soul field (just as in there are distinct types of quanta of material fields), some of which can only be created by sufficiently complex brains. Finally, one could hypothesize that the soul field obeys a rule that implies that normal brains have at most one soul quantum.[25] Whichever of the above views one adopts, the important thing to note is that they each allow the dual-aspect soul theory to provide a non-arbitrary dividing line between animals that have souls and those that do not (e.g. perhaps worms), along with non-arbitrarily accounting for the different levels of thought that various types of animals can achieve.[26,27]

CONCLUSION

I first argued that subjective states, such as what it is like to taste chocolate, cannot be reduced to purely physical states of the brain. Given this, one is left with the option of some form of non-reductive materialism (the view that the brain/body itself is the subject of experience and other conscious states) or some form of entity dualism (the idea that an immaterial entity is the subject of mental states). I then argued that if standard forms of non-reductive materialism are true, it is very likely that the laws linking physical states with subjective states would be enormously, if not infinitely, complex. Next, I proposed that what I called the dual-aspect view of the immaterial soul could potentially solve this problem. According to this view, the soul is a metaphysical simple that has both subjective and non-subjective states, the latter of which make no reference to consciousness and are describable mathematically. These additional properties allow one to construct a set of simple laws linking the non-subjective states of the soul with its subjective states. Further, because the non-subjective states are mathematically describable, potentially there could be simple equations that specified how these states interact with physical systems such as the brain. I then suggested how my account could be extended to subjective states influencing the brain, and how it might fit with the theory of biological evolution.

In closing, it should be stressed that although there are other motivations for entity dualism, the one pursued in this paper is based in the spirit of science itself: that of accounting for the known phenomena in the simplest possible way. Thus, reductive materialism was rejected because it could not account for the fact that we have subjective experiences. Second, non-reductive materialism was found wanting because it seemed to require enormously complex linking laws. Finally, the history of science suggests that to account for new phenomena in a simple way, often one must hypothesize new entities with new fundamental properties, as illustrated by the hypothesis of atoms. I then showed how introducing a new entity, the soul, that has both subjective and non-subjective properties could potentially provide a far simpler account of the observed correlations between brain states and subjective states. Along the way, we saw how this hypothesis has the potential of leading to a fruitful new research program.[28]

Afterword

Mark Baker and Stewart Goetz

The reader will have noticed that Collins' new version of the Soul
Hypothesis is inspired in part by an analogy with some fairly sophisticated modern physics — in particular by the fact that a vast amount of
content can be expressed in the different vibrational states of a simple
object, or in an electromagnetic wave. As such, there is nothing "old-
fashioned" or "out of touch" about this version of dualism. On the
contrary, it is possible, even beneficial, for a dualist to be as consistent
with and up-to-date on contemporary science as a materialist. Such
scientific knowledge will not inevitably refute his or her dualism, as
many seem to think, but may rather inspire it, and show new ways of
developing and expanding it.

Indeed, we offer this as the message not only of the last chapter, but of
the volume as a whole. By bringing together a set of essays by different
authors, with different perspectives and varied disciplinary expertise,
and knitting them together into a semi-unified whole, we have tried to
show that the Soul Hypothesis is still a very viable view for thoughtful
and scientifically-informed people to hold. The very basic features of our
experience which point toward dualism, such as our first-person experiences and our sense of acting freely, purposefully, and meaningfully,
cannot simply be denied or explained away. Many of the arguments that
are routinely trotted out against the existence of the soul are overblown,
or out of date, or beg the question. There are some interesting new arguments in favor of the existence of the soul to be considered carefully,
such as the argument from the vagueness of ordinary material objects.
Reductive neurological theories do not have all the answers that they
sometimes claim to have; on the contrary, they have some very suggestive
holes in them. Modern physics has not shut the door on a soul being able
to influence and be influenced by physical energy and matter. Dualistic
hypotheses can play a constructive role in scientific inquiry, all the way
from sorting out the types of linguistic aphasias people suffer from to

explaining why it is the observations of sentient beings that collapse the wave function in quantum mechanics. And there are different forms of dualism that may have different kinds of conceptual advantages. Indeed, there might be some which can both do the kind of explanatory work that souls have traditionally been asked to do, and also capture what is attractive about materialism when it comes to matters like evolution and the dependence of the mind on a functioning body of a certain kind. Adding these various contributions together, we claim that dualism is a living and healthy option, and deserves to be taken seriously in current discussions of the nature of human beings (and other animals).

We close this book with some discussion of one final question. If what we have claimed is true, then why isn't the Soul Hypothesis usually taken seriously? We observed in the Introduction that the seeming (near) consensus in favor of materialism in some circles could be something of an illusion. There seems to be little consensus in practice about the details of a purely materialistic account, and little sense of a converging research program. Rather, the community is held together largely by a negative slogan, which tacitly proclaims "Anything but dualism!" The question then arises, why can the intellectual community agree so readily on this, given that in other respects intellectuals are quite good at disagreeing, and (if we are right) the real facts of the case do not point unambiguously away from the existence of the soul?

One reason is, no doubt, the spirit of the age. Once a certain vocal critical mass of people has taken its stand against a certain idea, it is easy and comfortable for others to go along with the flow. More generally, there is a sense that science has progressed by demystifying and despiritualizing phenomena, reducing them to the operation of mindless physical forces. This is (roughly) how the reputations of the great scientific revolutionaries of the past were made. For example, Newton demystified and despiritualized celestial mechanics by showing that the planets and stars move according to the very same forces and equations as earthly objects do, namely gravity. Similarly, Darwin demystified and despiritualized biology, by showing that biological species are created by the same forces of descent with variation and natural selection that had been familiar to breeders of domestic animals for years. What then remains for more recent generations to demystify and despiritualize? One obvious answer is the (human) mind. If explanatory categories like spirit/soul, purpose, and agency can be expunged even from this domain — if one can remove crucially mental concepts even from our understanding of the mind — that would be the final frontier for this image of a reductionist, naturalizing science. Reputations could be made by accomplishing this new scientific revolution, or at least by contributing to it, or at least by heralding its accomplishment.

We can understand the allure of being part of such a project, and even how it might tempt one to claim success before it has fully been achieved. Still, much as a confident trash-talking athlete might well claim victory before a sports game is over — indeed, even before it has begun — we all realize that he still has to play the game through to the end . . . and for all his confidence, the result does not always turn out the way that he says it will. We hope that the more strident materialists will realize this as well, and play out the game.

But we suspect that the bias against the Soul Hypothesis has a bit more to it than scientific fashion and scientific ambition, factors that can be seen in how scientific questions of all kinds are pursued. The Soul Hypothesis has the additional fortune or misfortune of being strongly associated with traditional religious beliefs. For example, the monotheistic religions of Judaism, Christianity, and Islam have agreed that humans have a soul that survives the death of the body, will be judged by God, and will experience either punishment or reward in an eternal afterlife. Furthermore, the Eastern religions of Hinduism and Buddhism believe in the transmigration of souls, with each one being reborn into a new life depending on how it handled itself in its previous life. Although different in many ways, all of these religions clearly assume that humans (at least) have souls different from their bodies. Indeed, the belief in human souls and in greater spiritual powers go hand in hand in virtually all of the tribal religions known to anthropology, and together these beliefs form the universal basis for religious ritual and practice.[1] So it is very easy to see the Soul Hypothesis as a religious doctrine rather than as a theoretical hypothesis — especially for those conditioned to see these two categories as disjoint and fundamentally incompatible. So any unease or suspicion that one has about religious matters in general will quite naturally carry over to one's attitude toward the Soul Hypothesis.

But if one's ultimate interest is in the truth of the matter, whatever that may be, then one must be prepared to confront any of one's biases and habits of thought, however deep-set they may be. To be able to tell with some assurance whether the Soul Hypothesis is true or false, one needs to start by being open to some degree to each alternative, so that one can discern as impartially as possible what each might have going for it, and where the bulk of the evidence truly lies. As an aid to this, it behooves us to be as clear as we can about what really is the relationship between dualism and theism (the belief that God exists and acts in the world) and other related religious notions.

As best we can tell, the choice between dualism and materialism and the choice between theism and atheism are questions that are analogous to each other in many ways, but which are logically independent of each other. There is no contradiction between believing that God exists and believing that human beings are purely physical objects. There are some modern Christians who believe exactly this.[2] (This combination of views is made easier because of Christianity's emphasis on the resurrection of the body. Given this, Christians can plausibly believe in an afterlife without necessarily believing in a nonmaterial soul, even though prototypical Christianity holds to both.) Neither is there any contradiction between believing that human beings have an immaterial soul and believing that there is no God, as philosopher C.D. Broad did, for example. Of course, if one held to this combination of views one would need to have an idea about where individual human souls come from other than the traditional one that they are created individually by God. But there are certainly alternative dualistic views that would not hold this. For example, William Hasker's position that souls are generated by the right kinds of brains in accordance with natural laws in something like the way that magnetic fields are generated by the right kinds of iron bars is a sort of dualism that an atheist could perfectly well support (see Chapters 8 and 9). So the question of whether dualism is true and the question of whether theism is true are clearly separate questions, and they should be treated as such. Dualistic theories of human nature should not be discounted because they have religious associations.

But the two issues are not unrelated either; on the contrary, there are many parallelisms and assonances between the two. It so happens that all of the authors who have contributed to this volume are not only dualists but also theists of various kinds (indeed, all are Christians, although from very different backgrounds). This is presumably not a coincidence. There are many reasons why it is rather natural — although certainly not inevitable — to look at the two questions in a similar way. For example, if one is sympathetic to the hope of scientism, that all important truths are to be discovered by pursuing the scientific method in one of its narrower and more well-defined senses, then it is natural to look at dualism and theism with equal suspicion. After all, both involve affirming the existence of entities (God, the soul) that cannot be directly observed by the five senses or manipulated in a controlled experimental paradigm. On the other side, if one tends to think that ordinary folk understanding is likely to be approximately correct when it comes to things that are part of everyday human life and experience, then it is natural to look at dualism and theism with equal favor, since the two beliefs exist side by side in virtually every culture.

Even at a more detailed level, many similar considerations arise. For example, a dualist must come to grips with the question of how souls relate to chemical and physical events in the brain to produce voluntary actions, and the theist must come to grips with how God relates to natural laws when acting in the world in specific ways. The first is the problem of free will; the second is the problem of miracles; both can be seen as sub-cases of the problem of agency — the idea that physical events can be caused directly by mental events, not just by other physical events. The dualist-theist might well hope to solve or dissolve the two versions of the problem in the same way; the materialist-atheist might well hope to deny both problems in the same way. The parallelisms also hold for questions of interaction that go the other way. For example, the dualist will have views about how activity in the nervous system relates to perception and knowledge in the human soul, and the theist will have views about how God can perceive and know events that happen in the world. Here too parallel solutions might be attractive. Finally, at the most fundamental level, those who are attracted to spare ontologies across the board might never feel like there is enough evidence to posit a new category of thing; they will end up as both materialists and atheists. Those who put somewhat less intrinsic value on this as a theoretical priority might feel that both souls and God have met the necessary burden of proof; it will not be surprising if they end up as both theists and dualists (unless some difference in the kind of evidence found is encountered).

We can illustrate the nuances of these possibilities more fully by being a little more personal. The two editors of this volume both see a connection between their theism and their dualism, but they see it quite differently. For one of us, theism is the more certain truth, and the one that his pragmatic reasoning about these matters starts from. As a theist, he believes in a God that is distinct from the material universe, a God that is "a Spirit." Given this, he believes that there is a class of entities ("spirits"), which contains at least one member, such that those entities are not made up of matter or subject to physical laws but can interact causally with ordinary physical objects. But if there is one member of this class, the editor cannot automatically rule out the possibility that there are other members of this class — that human beings (created in the image of God) might also be things of this sort. He does not believe that this is entailed by his core Christian beliefs, but the possibility is raised by them. With this in mind, he looks at the evidence he can find from psychology and linguistics to see if there are observable phenomena that are better explained in this way, and concludes that there are. So for him, theism plus a consideration of relevant facts leads toward dualism.

For the other editor, the natural line of reasoning goes exactly the other way. To him, the more certain truth is dualism. It seems obvious to him that he cannot be simply a physical object, subject to all and only the laws of physics, given his first-person experience, his ability to reason, and his ability to make free choices guided by his purposes. It is also evident that, as a soul, he is able to cause events in his body, such as voluntary movements; agency is clearly possible. This then raises the possibility that there is some other, greater soul, who can in a free and purposeful manner cause events not only in one particular animal body, but anywhere in the material universe. Such a being would be God. With this possibility arising out of his dualism, he looks at the experiential evidence that points to the existence of such a being and concludes on the basis of this evidence that this being does exist. For him, dualism plus a consideration of relevant facts leads to theism.

What these two personal statements illustrate, we hope, is that there is a connection between dualism and theism, but it is neither an inevitable connection, nor a dogmatic one. The question about the existence of the soul and the question about the existence of God are parallel, but independent, and one can move back and forth between them in different ways — or not at all. The dualist and the theist face similar kinds of conceptual issues at various points, but the solutions needn't be the same, and the kinds of evidence that are relevant to deciding whether the two theories are true or false are different.

We have not revealed our beliefs with regard to theism until now, at the end of this book, so they would not distract the reader unduly from our reasons for holding to dualism, to which our theism is not directly or logically related. However, we have revealed our beliefs with regard to theism here, so that readers can judge for themselves whether we have distinguished the two topics properly, or whether our theism has led us to be too optimistic about the case for dualism. More than that, we want to challenge members of the materialist (near) consensus to be equally self-aware and up front about biases that they might have *against* the Soul Hypothesis, because they associate it with traditional religion rather than with rational/scientific inquiry. We claim that our theism has helped us to be open to considering the Soul Hypothesis within a cultural environment where many people simply are not open to considering this, but it does not account for our acceptance of that hypothesis. Our acceptance of it aspires to be based on evidence and

sound reasoning. We think that, if other people do the work of identifying their biases so as to assign them their proper role, and carefully
distinguish the Soul Hypothesis from other contentious (religious) ideas
with which it easily gets entangled, they will see virtues to the Soul
Hypothesis as well. We do not claim at this point to have yet established
the Soul Hypothesis beyond reasonable doubt, necessarily, but rather
that it still belongs in the discussion as a full partner, as we continue to
seek the truth about these matters. Just what bearing the truth about the
Soul Hypothesis may (or may not) have on the truth of other matters of
an obviously religious nature should be studied separately and should
not be allowed to confuse this matter.

Notes

Notes to the Introduction

1 This has been questioned by some with respect to at least the Hebrew scriptures, but see John Cooper's *Body Soul and Life Everlasting*, 2nd edn. (Grand Rapids, MI: Eerdmans, 2000) for an analysis.

2 Edward Burnett Tylor, *Religion in Primitive Culture* (New York: Harper, 1958).

3 Paul Murdock, "The Common Denominator of Cultures," in *The Science of Man in the World Crisis*, ed. R. Linton (New York: Columbia University Press, 1945), pp. 123–42.

4 Charles Francis Hockett, *Man's Place in Nature* (New York: McGraw-Hill, 1973), p. 133.

5 Ibid.

6 See also Donald Brown's *Human Universals* (New York: McGraw-Hill, 1991) for a discussion of "universal people."

7 Henry Wellman, *The Child's Theory of Mind* (Cambridge, MA: MIT Press, 1990), p. 50.

8 Paul Bloom, *Descartes' Baby: How the Science of Child Development Explains What Makes Us Human* (New York: Basic Books, 2004), p. 199.

9 Jesse Bering and David Bjorklund, "The Natural Emergence of Reasoning about the Afterlife as a Developmental Regularity," *Developmental Psychology* 40 (2004): 217–33.

10 Reported in Bloom's *Descartes' Baby*, pp. 199ff.

11 For example, see Paul M. Churchland, *Matter and Consciousness: A Contemporary Introduction to the Philosophy of Mind* (Cambridge, MA: MIT Press, 1988), p. 46; and Stephen Stich, *From Folk Psychology to Cognitive Science: The Case Against Belief* (Cambridge, MA: MIT Press, 1983), pp. 229–30.

12 This is not to say that there were no materialists (people who believe that anything that is real is material) before the beginning of the last century. Indeed, the belief that everything is made of atoms goes all the way back to some early Greek philosophers. However, materialism only became truly mainstream in intellectual circles in the last century.

13 For example, among philosophers of mind who deny the existence of the soul there is a huge divide between those who acknowledge the intrinsic hurtfulness of pain, what philosophers term a *quale* — property dualists, including the likes of David Chalmers (*The Conscious Mind: In Search of a Fundamental Theory* [Oxford: Oxford University Press, 1996]) and Thomas Nagel (*The View from Nowhere* [Oxford: Oxford University Press, 1986]) — and those who completely deny it, the eliminativists, such as Daniel Dennett (*Consciousness Explained* [Boston: Little, Brown and Company, 1991]) and David Papineau (*Thinking about Consciousness* [Oxford: Clarendon Press, 2002]). The philosopher John Searle says the following about one species of functionalists: "I believe you do not need refutation, you need help" (John Searle, *The Rediscovery of the Mind* [Cambridge, MA: MIT Press, 1992], p. 9). For a particularly spirited and entertaining exchange between Searle, Dennett, *et al.*, see Maxwell Bennett, Daniel Dennett, Peter Hacker, and John Searle, *Neuroscience and Philosophy: Brain, Mind, and Language* (New York: Columbia University Press, 2007).

14 For some of the things on this list — and a few more — and further discussion, see Colin McGinn, *Problems in Philosophy: The Limits of Inquiry* (Cambridge: Blackwell, 1993), and Steven Pinker, *How the Mind Works* (New York: W. W. Norton, 1997).

15 C. R. Gallistel and Adam Philip King, *Memory and the Computational Brain: Why Cognitive Science Will Transform Neuroscience* (Malden, MA: Wiley-Blackwell, 2009).

16 Gilbert Ryle, *The Concept of Mind* (New York: Barnes and Noble, 1949).

17 Another reason (perhaps not fully conscious) why people might want to discount this experiment as science could be the thought that the Soul Hypothesis did not initially enter the discussion as a scientific idea, but rather as a religious one. But the scientific status of an idea is not properly determined by its origins, but rather by the role that it comes to play within the practice of science. Thus, wild hunches out of the blue may well be as fertile a source of scientific hypotheses as anything is, although of course being wild and out of the blue is not what makes them scientific. For more discussion of the Soul Hypothesis as science and the Soul Hypothesis as religion, see the Afterword.

18 See Chapters 4 and 9 for more on the possibility of versions of the Soul Hypothesis being investigated empirically.

19 Wilder Penfield, *The Mystery of the Mind* (Princeton: Princeton University Press, 1975), p. 77.

20 Mario Beauregard, *A Neuroscientist's Case for the Existence of the Soul* (New York: Harper One, 2007), pp. 131–3.

21 Ibid., pp. 136–40.

22 Jeffrey Schwartz and Sharon Begley, *The Mind and the Brain: Neuroplasticity and the Power of Mental Force* (New York: Regan Books, 2002).

23 The authors thank Dean Zimmerman for helpful input on the writing of this Introduction.

Notes to Chapter 1: The Soul of the Matter

1 Frank Jackson, "A Priori Physicalism," in B. McLaughlin and J. Cohe (eds), *Contemporary Debates in Philosophy of Mind*, (Oxford: Blackwell, 2007), p. 186.

2 David Armstrong, *The Nature of Mind and Other Essays* (St. Lucia: University of Queensland Press, 1980), pp. 1–2. The emphasis is Armstrong's.

3 Richard Rorty, *Philosphy and the Mirror of Nature* (Oxford: Blackwell, 1980), p. 387.

4 Georges Rey, *Contemporary Philosophy of Mind* (Oxford: Blackwell, 1997), p. 29. The emphases are Rey's.

5 Paul M. Churchland, *Matter and Consciousness: A Contemporary Introduction to the Philosophy of Mind* (Cambridge, MA: MIT Press, 1988), p. 46.

6 Stephen Stich, *From Folk Psychology to Cognitive Science: The Case Against Belief* (Cambridge, MA: MIT Press, 1983), pp. 229–30.

7 Daniel C. Dennett, "Facing Backwards on the Problem of Consciousness," *Journal of Consciousness Studies* 3 (1996): 6.

8 Churchland, *Matter and Consciousness*, p. 11.

9 Daniel Dennett, *Consciousness Explained* (Boston: Little, Brown and Company, 1991), p. 36.

10 Ibid., p. 37.

11 Churchland, *Matter and Consciousness*, p. 15.

12 Ibid.

13 Dennett, *Consciousness Explained*, p. 29.

14 Ibid., p. 218.

15 Ibid., p. 134.

16 Susan Blackmore, *Consciousness: A Very Short Introduction* (Oxford: Oxford University Press, 2005), p. 81.

17 Ibid.

18 Drew V. McDermott, *Mind and Mechanism* (Cambridge, MA: MIT Press, 2001), p. 147.

19 Jeffrey Russell, *Inventing the Flat Earth: Columbus and Modern Historians* (Santa Barbara, CA: Greenwood Publishing Group, 1997).

20 John R. Searle, *The Mystery of Consciousness* (New York: The New York Review of Books, 1997), pp. 111–12. The emphases are Searle's.

21 Richard Swinburne, *The Evolution of the Soul*, rev. ed. (Oxford: Clarendon Press, 1997), p. 8. The emphases are Swinburne's.

22 Dennett, *Breaking the Spell: Religion as a Natural Phenomenon* (New York: Viking, 2006), pp. 239–40. The emphases are Dennett's.

23 Ibid., p. 130. The emphasis is Dennett's.

24 See Taliaferro, *Consciousness and the Mind of God* (Cambridge: Cambridge University Press, 1994).

25 Taliaferro, "The Virtues of Embodiment," *Philosophy* 76 (2001): 111–25.

26 Swinburne, *The Evolution of the Soul*, p. xi. I am deeply grateful to Stewart Goetz and Mark Baker for comments on an earlier version of this chapter.

Notes to Chapter 2: Minds, Brains, and Brains in Vats

1 See, for example, S. B. Buklina, "Clinical-neuroendocrinological syndromes due to lesions of the cingulate gyrus in humans," *Neuroscience and Behavioral Physiology* 28 (1998): 601–7; see also Marcel Kinsbourne, "The Mechanism of Confabulation," *Neuro-Psychoanalysis* 2 (2000): 158–62.

2 This has recently been shown by Sabine Borsutzky, *et al.* "Confabulations in Alcoholic Korsakoff Patients." *Neuropsychologia* 46 (13) (2008): 3, 133–43.

3 See for an example Daniel Dennett, "Two Contrasts: Folk Craft Versus Folk Science, and Belief Versus Opinion," in J. Greenwood (ed.), *The Future of Folk Psychology* (New York: Cambridge University Press, 1991), pp. 135–48.

4 A direct realist argues that the world as perceived is the world as it is. A representational realist argues that objects and events in the external world are not directly perceived but that some sort of representation of these is what is experienced. These are significantly different epistemological positions but both accept that perceptions are aspects of conscious experience as "folk psychology" understands it.

5 Actually, renal disease is associated with significant cognitive deficits. See Pankaj Madan, Om P. Kalra, Sunil Agarwal and Om P. Tandon, "Cognitive impairment in chronic kidney disease," *Nephrology Dialysis Transplantation* 22(2) (2007): 440–4.

6 I borrow the expression "brain in a vat" from Hilary Putnam's famous example, but not for the same purposes. For his use of the thought experiment see Hilary Putnam, "Brains in a Vat" in *Reason, Truth, and History* (Cambridge: Cambridge University Press, 1982), pp. 1–21.

7 Thomas Nagel, "What is it Like to be a Bat?," *The Philosophical Review* 83 (1974): 433–50.

8 Ibid, p. 435.

9 Unable to hold down any other position, the patient worked as a "mnemonist," one whose prodigious memory could be presented as a form of entertainment.

10 A. R. Luria, *The Mind of a Mnemonist: A Little Book About a Vast Memory*, trans. Lynn Solotaroff (Cambridge, MA: Harvard University Press, 1968/1987).

11 The technique includes drilling through the cranial bone to relieve pressure. See K. W. Alt, *et al.*, "Evidence for Stone Age Cranial Surgery," *Nature* 387 (1997): 364.

12 James Henry Breasted, *The Edwin Smith Papyrus* (New York: New York Historical Society, 1922).

13 For an interesting discussion of Galen's priority, see Charles Gross, "Galen and the Squealing Pig," *The Neuroscientist* 4 (1998): 216–21.

14 H. von Staden, ed. and transl., *Herophilus: The Art of Medicine in Early Alexandria* (Cambridge: Cambridge University Press, 1989).

15 For an informing review of Lorber's still disputed conclusions see Roger Lewin, "Is Your Brain Really Necessary?", *Science* 210 (1980): 1,232–4. There is no question, however, that brain mass in the hydrocephalic does not reliably predict IQ.

16 Gall's system was presented in six volumes translated into English as *On the Functions of the Brain and of Each of Its Parts* and published in 1835 by Marsh, Capen & Lyon. Portions of this and related works are readily available on internet sites.

17 See Paul G. Firth and Hayrunnisa Bolay, "Transient High Altitude Neurological Dysfunction: An Origin in the Temporoparietal Cortex," *High Altitude Medicine & Biology* 5(1) (2004): 71–5.

18 Rita Sloane Berndt, Charlotte C. Mitchum, and S. Wayland. "Patterns of Sentence Comprehension in Aphasia: Consideration of Three Hypotheses," *Brain & Language*, 60 (1997), 197–221; and Yosef Grodzinsky, "The Neurology of syntax: Language Use Without Broca's Area," *Behavioral and Brain Sciences* 23 (2000): 1–71.

19 See, in this connection, Judit Druks and John C. Marshall, "When Passives are Easier than Actives: Two Case Studies in Aphasic Comprehension," *Cognition* 55 (1995): 311–31.

20 Barry Horwitz, *et al.*,"Activation of Broca's Area During the Production of Spoken and Signed Language: a Combined Cytoarchitectonic Mapping and PET Analysis," *Neuropsychologia* 41(14) (2003): 868–76.

21 Malcom Macmillan, *An Odd Kind of Fame* (Cambridge, MA: MIT Press, 2002), p. 189.

22 Ibid., p. 190.

23 See Claudio Cantalupo and William D. Hopkins, "Asymmetric Broca's area in great apes," *Nature* 414 (2001): 505.

24 Macmillan, *An Odd Kind of Fame*.

25 Hanna Damasio, *et al.*, "The Return of Phineas Gage: Clues About the Brain from The Skull of a Famous Patient," *Science* 264 (1994): 1,102–5.

26 Macmillan, *An Odd Kind of Fame*, p. 81.

27 Ibid., p. 87.

28 An example of this is Antonio Damasio's *Descartes' Error: Emotion, Reason and the Human Brain* (New York: Grosset/Putnam, 1994), which makes use of just these arguable factors in fashioning what turns out to be a far more orderly and coherent scheme than anything in the Phineas Gage record warrants.

29 Macmillan, *An Odd Kind of Fame*, p. 333.

30 Gary Lynch and Richard Granger, *Big Brain* (New York: Palgrave-Macmillan, 2008).

31 Ibid., p. 157.

32 Ibid., p. 10.

33 Ibid., p. 154.

34 Ibid., p. 203.

35 Ronald Singer, "The Boskop 'Race' Problem," *Man* 58 (1958): 173–8.

36 Max Bennett and P. M. S. Hacker, *Philosophical Foundations of Neuroscience* (Oxford: Blackwell, 2003).

37 I mean not to underestimate the rich conceptual texture of "action theory." A good collection of thoughts on the matter is Alfred Mele, ed., *The Philosophy of Action* (Oxford: Oxford University Press, 1997).

38 Aristotle, *On the Soul*, trans. J. Smith (Stilwell, KS: Digireads.com Publishing).

Notes for Chapter 3: Brains and Souls; Grammar and Speaking

1 Steven Pinker, *The Blank Slate: The Modern Denial of Human Nature* (New York: Viking, 2002), p. 41. The emphases are Pinker's.

2 Noam Chomsky, *Syntactic Structures* (Mouton: The Hague, 1957) and "Review of Skinner: Verbal Behavior," *Language* 35 (1959): 26–58.

3 Noam Chomsky, *Cartesian Linguistics* (New York: Harper and Row, 1966).

4 Chomsky, "Review of Skinner."

5 Chomsky, *Syntactic Structures.*

6 René Descartes, *A Discourse on Method*, trans. John Veitch (London: Dent, 1912), pp. 44–5.

7 Dorothy Cheney and Robert Seyfarth, *How Monkeys See the World* (Chicago: University of Chicago Press, 1990), Chapters 4 and 5.

8 Alan Turing, "Computing Machinery and Intelligence," *Mind* 65 (1950): 433–60.

9 There is an interesting lesson to learn from current attempts at running approximations to Turing's famous test in connection with the Loebner prize. Stuart Shieber ("Lessons from a Restricted Turing Test," *Communications of the Association for Computing Machinery* 37 [1994]: 70–8) observes that the programs that people rate as most human-like succeed almost entirely because they find ways to avoid the expectation that conversation should be appropriate

in the sense intended in the CALU. The semi-successful programs pose as a psychoanalyst, or as a paranoid schizophrenic, or as a whimsical conversationalist, or as a seven-year-old child — all people for which we are willing to suspend to some degree our normal expectations concerning coherent and rational conversation. So our "most human-like" computers do not succeed by duplicating the CALU capacity, but rather by side-stepping it.

10 Willem Levelt, *Speaking: from Intention to Articulation* (Cambridge, MA: MIT Press, 1989).

11 Ibid., p. 157.

12 See Cheney and Seyfarth's *How Monkeys See the World* for some striking examples from monkeys and apes.

13 David Caplan, *Neurolinguistics and Linguistic Aphasiology* (Cambridge: Cambridge University Press, 1987); Harold Goodglass and Edith Kaplan, *The Assessment of Aphasia and Related Disorders* (Philadelphia: Lea and Febiger, 1972); and Andrew Kertesz, *Aphasia and Associated Disorders: Taxonomy, Localization, and Recovery* (New York: Grune and Stratton, 1979). Also see Chapter 2 in this volume for some discussion.

14 D. F. Benson and N. Geschwind, "Aphasia and Related Cortical Disturbances," in A. B. Baker and L. H. Baker (eds), *Clincal Neurology*, vol. 1, (New York: Harper and Row, 1971), chapter 10, pp. 6–13.

15 Caplan, *Neurolinguistics and Linguistic Aphasiology*, p. 55.

16 Goodglass and Kaplan, *The Assessment of Aphasia and Related Disorders*, p. 59.

17 Ibid., p. 59.

18 Ibid., p. 55.

19 Ibid.

20 For some comments on the not-so-often discussed Transcortical Motor Aphasia (also called Dynamic Aphasia; (Mariusz Maruszewski, *Language, Communication and the Brain* [Mouton: The Hague, 1975], pp. 111–15), which comes closest to this imagined profile, see Baker, ("The Creative Aspect of Language Use and Nonbiological Nativism," in Peter Carruthers, Stephen Laurence, and Stephen Stitch (eds), *The Innate Mind: Foundations and the Future* (Oxford: Oxford University Press, 2007), p. 248, n. 6. The relationship between the location of a brain lesion and a particular kind of deficit is often messier and more complex than simplified textbook accounts would have us think; see Robinson (Chapter 2 of this volume) for some discussion. But the argument I am exploring here does not depend on any strong claim that a mental function (like the CALU) must be realized neurologically in exactly the same place or in exactly the same way in all people — only that there is some physical (hence localizable) neurological realization. Robin Collins (in a personal communication) called to my attention the existence of savant syndromes, in which people with abnormal brains actually have increased mental abilities in some specific

domain (mathematics, music, etc.), which further complicates the relationship between brains and abilities. Despite this, I do subscribe to the weak and uncontroversial view that it is generally bad to have a brain injury, and different sorts of brain injuries have different sorts of effects from which we might hope to learn something.

21 Caplan, *Neurolinguistics and Linguistic Aphasiology.*

22 Dorothy Bishop, "Specific Language Impairment: Diagnostic Dilemmas," in Ludo Verhoeven and Hans von Balkom (eds), *Classification of Developmental Language Disorders: Theoretical Issues and Clinical Implications*, (Mahwah, NJ: Lawrence Erlbaum Associates, 2004), pp. 309–26.

23 I. Rapin and D. Allen, "Developmental Language Disorders: Nosologic Considerations," in U. Kirk (ed.) *Neuropsychology of Language: Reading and Spelling*, (New York: Academic Press, 1983), pp. 155–84.

24 Bishop, "Specific Language Impairment: Diagnostic Dilemmas," p. 321.

25 Rapin and Allen, "Developmental Language Disorders: Nosologic Considerations," p. 174.

26 Ibid., p. 175.

27 Sue Savage-Rambaugh, *Kanzi: The Ape at the Brink of the Human Mind* (New York: Wiley, 1994).

28 See also Chenney and Seyfarth's *How Monkeys See the World* on the properties of primate communication in the wild.

29 Jerry Fodor, *The Mind Doesn't Work That Way* (Cambridge, MA: MIT Press, 2000).

30 See also John Heil ("Does Cognitive Psychology Rest on a Mistake?," *Mind* 90 [1981]: 321–42) for an even more general critique of a purely computational model of the mind. He questions whether the expression of "premises" in the mind seen as a computational medium could even have meanings in themselves, say by virtue of representing something about the world. He argues that the states of a computer do not represent/mean anything in themselves, apart from a meaning that is assigned to them in a partially arbitrary way by the computer's programmer. If the human mind is thought of as a computer, then it is not clear what within a purely materialistic framework could play the role of the programmer to extrinsically assign meanings to our various brain states over a suitably general and abstract range.

Notes to Chapter 4: Making Things Happen: Souls in Action

1 Selena Roberts, "Freedom Does More than Improve a Swing," *New York Times*, August 11, 2005.

2 Ibid.

3 William Lyons, *Matters of the Mind* (New York: Routledge, 2001), p. 9.

NOTES TO PAGES 100-104

4 John Searle, *The Rediscovery of the Mind* (Cambridge, MA: MIT Press, 1992), p. 91.

5 John Horgan, "In Defense of Common Sense," *New York Times*, August 12, 2005.

6 Francis Crick, *The Astonishing Hypothesis: The Scientific Search for the Soul* (New York: Scribner, 1994), p. 10.

7 Daniel Dennett, *Elbow Room* (Cambridge, MA: MIT Press, 1984); and *Freedom Evolves* (New York: Viking, 2003).

8 Owen Flanagan, *The Problem of the Soul* (New York: Basic Books, 2002), p. 3. Andrew Melnyk says that "unless . . . intuitions [that mental events . . . are completely different from physical events] are turned into arguments, they are worthless." "Some Evidence for Physicalism," in Sven Walter and Heinz-Dieter Heckmann (eds), *Physicalism and Mental Causation: The Metaphysics of Mind and Action*, (Charlottesville, VA: Imprint Academic, 2003), p. 166, footnote 12. Whether or not these intuitions are worthless depends upon the argumentative context in which they are raised. On the one hand, they are pretty much worthless in an argumentative context where a dualist is trying to argue for dualism against a non-dualist opponent. On the other hand, in an argumentative context where a non-dualist (like Melnyk) is trying to show that dualism is deeply problematic, it is perfectly appropriate for a dualist to make use of these intuitions in establishing the initial plausibility of dualism. The argumentative context of this paper is of the latter kind.

9 An earlier version of the material in this section appears in Stewart Goetz and Charles Taliaferro, *Naturalism* (Grand Rapids, MI: Eerdmans, 2008), Chapter 2.

10 Richard Taylor, *Metaphysics*, 4th edn. (Englewood Cliffs, NJ: Prentice Hall, 1992), pp. 20–2.

11 Jaegwon Kim, *Philosophy of Mind* (Boulder, CO: Westview Press, 1996), pp. 131–2, 147–8.

12 In fairness to Kim, it is important to note that he too recognizes the counterintuitive nature of the conclusion of the argument from causal closure, which is that our mental lives have no explanatory role to play in accounting for events in the physical world (our mental lives are explanatorily epiphenomenal). Hence, in order to preserve an explanatory role for the mental, he believes that we should be committed to a reduction of the mental to the physical:

Mind-to-body causation is fundamental if our mentality is to make a difference to what goes on in the world. If I want to have the slightest causal influence on anything outside me — to change a light bulb or start a war — I must first move my limbs or other parts of my body; somehow, my beliefs and desires must cause the muscles in my arms and legs to contract, or cause my vocal cords to vibrate. Mental causation is fundamental to our conception of mentality, and to our view of ourselves as agents; . . . any theory of mind that is not able to accommodate mental causation must be considered inadequate, or at best incomplete. . . . Does this mean that we are committed willy-nilly to reductionism? The answer is no: what we have established . . . is a *conditional* thesis, "If mentality is to have any causal efficacy at all — it must be physically reducible." Those of us who believe in mental causation should hope for a successful reduction. *Physicalism, or Something Near Enough* (Princeton: Princeton University Press, 2005), pp. 152–3, 161.

According to Kim, then, physical reduction (reduction of the mental to the physical) enables us to preserve our belief that mentality makes a causal explanatory difference. Notice, however, the price that must be paid to embrace this "solution" to the problem of causal closure. Mentality can make such an explanatory difference, only if we give up both the idea that mental actions are ultimately and irreducibly explained by purposes and the view that we have free will. While Kim is correct when he insists that none of us wants to give up on the idea of mental causation, some of us also do not want to give up the idea that mental causation itself occurs only because mental events such as choices are indeterministic events that are ultimately and irreducibly explained by purposes. Given the high price that must be paid to endorse Kim's "solution" to the problem of causal closure, it is imperative to examine whether there is a good reason to believe in the principle of the causal closure of the physical world.

13 In maintaining that a neuroscientist as an ordinary human being would surely refer to my purposes in an explanation of my typing, I am not claiming that we are always right when we provide a teleological explanation of another person's behavior. We might sometimes be wrong. But it is a huge step to conclude from "some teleological explanations of behavior are false" that "there is ultimately no role for teleological explanations of behavior." Moreover, while I might be mistaken about whether your behavior was merely reflexive or purposeful, I am in a far better epistemic position to know whether my own behavior was purposeful or not. The following words of Alfred North Whitehead are apropos: "Scientists [and, I would add, philosophers] animated by the purpose of proving that they are purposeless constitute an interesting subject for study." *The Function of Reason* (Boston, MA: Beacon Press, 1958), p. 16.

14 Wilder Penfield, *The Mystery of the Mind* (Princeton: Princeton University Press, 1975).

15 Karl Popper says that "the physicalist principle of the closedness of the physical [world] . . . is of decisive importance, and I take it as the characteristic principle of physicalism or materialism." Karl R. Popper and John C. Eccles, *The Self and Its Brain* (New York: Routledge, 1977), p. 51. Popper adds, and then argues for the view, that "there is no reason to reject our prima facie view [that the physical world is open to mental, purposeful explanations]; a view

that is inconsistent with the physicalist principle." Ibid. The biologist J. B. S. Haldane writes "My practice as a scientist is atheistic. That is to say, when I set up an experiment I assume that no god, angel or devil is going to interfere with its course . . . I should therefore be intellectually dishonest if I were not also atheistic in the affairs of the world." From Haldane's "Fact and Faith" and quoted in Lawrence M. Krauss "God and Science Don't Mix," *The Wall Street Journal*, June 26, 2009. Haldane is mistaken when he claims that his atheism in his experimental work must, lest he be intellectually dishonest, carry over into his daily life outside the laboratory. What is true is that he would be intellectually dishonest in failing to carry his atheism from the laboratory into his daily life, if he were a naturalist. But his practice as a scientist does not require that he be a naturalist.

16 Penfield, *The Mystery of the Mind*, pp. 76, 80.

17 Richard Feynman, *The Meaning of It All* (Reading, MA: Perseus Books, 1998), pp. 16, 45.

18 David Chalmers, *The Conscious Mind: In Search of a Fundamental Theory* (New York: Oxford University Press), p. 153.

19 Ted Honderich, *How Free Are You?: The Determinism Problem* (New York: Oxford University Press, 1993), Chapter 3.

20 Ibid., p. 37. The emphases are Honderich's.

21 Ibid., pp. 7–11. The emphases are Honderich's.

22 Ibid., p. 11.

23 Keith Campbell, *Body and Mind* (Notre Dame, IN: University of Notre Dame Press, 1980), p. 17.

24 See Barry Loewer's "Review of *Mind in a Physical World: An Essay on the Mind-Body Problem and Mental Causation*, by Jaegwon Kim," *The Journal of Philosophy* 98 (2001): 315–24.

25 Jaegwon Kim, "Book Symposia: *Mind in a Physical World*," *Philosophy and Phenomenological Research* 65 (2002): 674–7.

26 Kim's response on behalf of the reality of mental causation appears puzzling until one remembers that he believes mental causation is ontologically reducible to physical causation. Cf. Kim, "Book Symposia: *Mind in a Physical World*," p. 642.

27 Ibid., p. 676. One might add that the concept of the mass of an object, when expressed numerically, is typically interpreted as a function of that entity's resistance to acceleration by a force.

28 Taylor, *Metaphysics*, p. 20.

29 C. D Broad makes this point in his *The Mind and Its Place in Nature* (Paterson, New Jersey: Littlefield, Adams & Co., 1960), p. 107.

30 Thomas Nagel, "Brain Bisection and the Unity of Consciousness," in *Mortal Questions* (Cambridge: Cambridge University Press, 1979), pp. 147–64.

31 Penfield, *The Mystery of the Mind*, p. 76.
32 Ibid., p. 77.
33 Dennett, *Elbow Room: The Varieties of Free Will Worth Wanting*, pp. 76–7.

Notes to Chapter 5: The Energy of the Soul

1 This chapter is a condensed and simplified version of my article, "Modern Physics and the Energy Conservation Objection to Mind-Body Dualism" originally published in *The American Philosophical Quarterly*, 45 (2008): 31–42. I would like to thank the John Templeton Foundation for support of this work as part of a group grant *"The Soul Hypothesis: Developing Non-Supervenience Views of the Mental"*; several members of the group (Mark Baker, Stewart Goetz, Charles Taliaferro, William Hasker, and Dean Zimmerman) for reading over an earlier draft, and Richard Swinburne, Marc Lange, William Lane Craig, and an anonymous referee for providing helpful comments.

2 Daniel Dennett, *Consciousness Explained* (Boston: Little, Brown and Company, 1991), p. 35. The italics are mine.

3 Owen Flanagan, *The Science of the Mind*, 2nd edn. (Cambridge, MA: MIT Press, 1991), p. 21.

4 Jerry Fodor, "The Mind-Body Problem," in R. Warner and T. Szubka (eds) *The Mind-Body Problem* (Oxford: Blackwell, 1994), p. 25.

5 Although this chapter will only be concerned with the energy conservation objection to substance dualism, this objection is of more general interest: it can be raised against most views in which the human person is claimed to causally influence the brain in a way that cannot be explained by current physics, such as views that state that choices and/or intentions causally produce brain events.

6 E. J. Lowe, "Causal Closure Principle and Emergentism," *Philosophy* 75 (2000): 574.

7 Ibid.

8 C. J. Ducasse, *Nature, Mind, and Death* (La Salle, IL: Open Court, 1951), p. 241.

9 For illustrative purposes, we neglect the motion and curvature of the Earth itself, which makes all these frames non-inertial.

10 Robert Wald, *General Relativity* (Chicago: University of Chicago Press, 1984), p. 70, n. 6.

11 Ibid., p. 286.

12 Ibid.

13 Ibid.

14 Carl Hoefer, "Energy Conservation in GTR," *Studies in the History and Philosophy of Modern Physics* 31 (2000): 194.

15 Insofar as they discuss the issue, physicists specializing in general relativity

agree that there is no adequate definition of local energy in general relativity: for example, Wald (*General Relativity*, p. 70, n. 6; p. 286–7), C. Misner, K. Thorne, and J. Wheeler, (*Gravitation* [San Francisco: W. H. Freeman and Company, 1973], pp. 457–70), and Roger Penrose (*The Emperor's New Mind: Concerning Computers, Minds, and the Laws of Physics* [Oxford: Oxford University Press, 1989], p. 220; and *The Road to Reality: A Complete Guide to the Laws of the Universe* [New York: Alfred A. Knopf, 2004], p. 467). Penrose, however, has attempted to retain some global conception of the conservation of energy by claiming that general relativity shows that gravitational energy is non-local (*The Emperor's New Mind*, pp. 220–1). Even this move, however, would require that the total energy of the universe be well defined, which it is not. Further, if Penrose is right, the total mass-energy of the brain is not entirely confined to any local region, but at least in part involves the entire universe. Such a non-local conception of the mass-energy of the brain, however, makes it difficult even to formulate the energy-conservation objection, thus undermining almost all of its purported force.

To practically deal with this problem of the lack of any definition of local energy in general relativity, physicists often define a *pseudo-tensor* that they identify with the stress-energy of the gravitational field for purposes of doing calculations. For example, such a pseudo-tensor can be defined for the weak field limit of general relativity and the predictions based on this conform to experiment for at least one binary star system. (See, for example, Sean Carroll, *Spacetime and Geometry: An Introduction to General Relativity* [San Francisco: Addison Wesley, 2004], p. 315; and Penrose, *The Road to Reality*, pp. 467–8.) Such pseudo-tensors, however, cannot be treated as providing the real stress-energy of a system since they are not frame invariant. The pseudo-tensors typically used, for instance, imply that in some frames of reference, flat space-time has gravitational energy, even though by definition flat space-time contains no gravitational fields!

16 Hoefer, "Energy Conservation in GTR," p. 196.

17 The above discussion shows that when a system interacts with a gravitational field, the boundary version of energy conservation no longer even applies to the non-gravitational fields — such as the various matter fields composing the systems. Mathematically, the reason this non-applicability occurs can be understood by considering how the boundary version of the principle of energy conservation is derived in the absence of gravitational fields (that is, in flat space-time). Whether or not gravitational fields are present, the divergence of the stress-energy tensor for a system must equal zero: $L^2T = 0$, where L represents the four-divergence and T the stress-energy tensor. In flat space-time, the boundary version of energy conservation follows from $L^2 T = 0$ by Gauss's theorem (cf. Wald, *General Relativity*, pp. 62–3, eqs. 4.2.11 and 4.2.18). Consequently, in flat space-time it is legitimate to think of the divergence equation $L^2T = 0$ as

equivalent in flat space-time to energy conservation. Accordingly, in texts on general relativity this equation is typically presented as the way of summarizing the law of energy and momentum conservation in non-quantum physics (see, for example, Carroll, *Spacetime and Geometry*, pp. 35–6, eqs. 1.115 and 1.120). In curved space-time, however, there is no way of deriving the boundary version of the principle of energy conservation from this divergence equation. Hence, even though this divergence equation is assumed to hold for non-gravitational fields whether or not gravitational interactions are present, the same is not true for energy conservation (Wald, *General Relativity*, pp. 69–70). Because the divergence equation is often treated as though it is the same as the boundary version of the principle of energy conservation (which is only legitimate for flat space-time) and because it is easy to forget that stress-energy is not defined for gravitational fields, even students of general relativity can be easily misled into thinking that energy conservation is universally applicable.

18 P. J. E. Peebles, *Principles of Physical Cosmology* (Princeton: Princeton University Press, 1993), p. 139. This non-conservation of energy is also exploited by the widely-discussed inflationary cosmological models. In inflationary cosmology, the entire mass-energy of the universe is postulated to be blown up ("inflated") out of a minuscule region of pre-space (e.g. less than 10^{-30} centimeters in diameter) with a minuscule total energy. Some popular treatments — such as that of Alan Guth (*The Inflationary Universe: The Quest for a New Theory of Cosmic Origins* [New York: Helix Books], 1997, pp. 9–12, 170-4) — try to claim that the total energy of the universe remains constant in this blowing-up process since the gravitational field produced by the matter in the universe contributes a negative total energy; but this could not be correct since the total energy of the universe is undefined in general relativity (except in the special case mentioned above). Rather, as other textbooks recognize (e.g. see G. Börner, *The Early Universe: Facts or Fiction?* [New York: Springer-Verlag, 1988], p. 298), inflationary cosmology exploits the non-conservation of energy in general relativity. Indeed, according to one textbook, the postulated inflation field acts as a "reservoir of unlimited energy, which can supply as much as is required to inflate a given region to any required size at constant energy density" (John Peacock, *Cosmological Physics* [Cambridge: Cambridge University Press, 1999], p. 26); no energy conservation here!

19 Hoefer, "Energy Conservation in GTR," p. 188.

20 Ibid., pp. 189–91. The principle of energy conservation — often called the first law of thermodynamics — goes back to the 1840s. For example, Julius Robert von Mayer published a paper in 1842 proposing this law, on which basis he claimed priority (P. M. Harmon, *Energy, Force, and Matter: The Conceptual Developments of Nineteenth-Century Physics* [Cambridge: Cambridge University Press, 1982], p. 63). The principle was at least in part

motivated by the proposal that heat was really a form of mechanical energy, instead of some special fluid. (Without a proposal like this, energy does not appear to be conserved: a dropped iron ball appears to entirely lose its normal kinetic and mechanical energy upon impact.) Thus the tenure of this principle was at most around 70 to 80 years, from the 1840s to the development of Einstein's theory of general relativity in 1915.

21 Hoefer, "Energy Conservation in GTR," p. 195. It should be noted that since energy and momentum are united in relativity, if no adequate stress-energy tensor can be found for the gravitational field, then the momentum of a gravitational field or wave cannot be defined (see, for example, Misner, Thorne, Wheeler, *Gravitation*, pp. 463-9). This means that there cannot be an applicable principle of momentum conservation in general relativity, although this is often not discussed.

22 A reader familiar with the literature might wonder why we are considering quantum mechanics for cases of interaction without energy exchange instead of simpler cases from classical mechanics often presented in response to the energy conservation objection. The reason is that they fail upon closer inspection. For example, a commonly used example (e.g. by C. D. Broad, *The Mind and Its Place in Nature* [London: Kegan Paul, Trench, Trubner & Co., 1925], Chapter 3; and Keith Campbell, *Body and Mind*, 2nd edn. [Notre Dame, IN: University of Notre Dame Press, 1984], pp. 52-3) is that of a frictionless pendulum in which the string causally influences the motion of the bob, yet imparts no energy to it since the force the string exerts is always perpendicular to the direction of motion. Thus it is pointed out, as long as a "mental force" acting on a particle in the brain is perpendicular to the direction of motion of the particle, it would causally influence the motion of the particle without any exchange of energy occurring. Such forces, however, do impart momentum to the objects under consideration because of Newton's Second Law, $F = ma$. This type of response to the energy conservation objection, therefore, fails when the full conservation law of energy and momentum is considered. The only way to conserve both energy and momentum in these cases is to have an equal force in the opposite direction act on another particle, thus causing the two changes in momentum to cancel. Even this scenario, however, would violate the boundary version of energy-momentum conservation as applied to any region that only contained one of the particles.

23 This is true whether or not one adopts a realist interpretation of quantum mechanics. Even if one thinks that quantum mechanics is merely a useful instrument of prediction, these correlations occur between the results of measuring apparatuses, and Bell's theorem rules out any explanation of them in terms of local causation.

24 Hoefer, "Energy Conservation in GTR," p. 196.

Notes to Chapter 6: The Measure of All Things: Quantum Mechanics and the Soul

1 For a discussion of background, or "control" beliefs, see Nicholas Wolterstorff, *Reason within the Bounds of Religion* (Grand Rapids, MI: Eerdmans, 1984).

2 See Nick Herbert's *Quantum Reality: Beyond the New Physics* (New York: Anchor Books, 1987) for a nice non-technical exposition of some of these experiments.

3 Not every linear mapping is unitary, but we will not need to draw that distinction in this discussion.

4 D. Z. Albert, *Quantum Mechanics and Experience* (Cambridge, MA: Harvard University Press, 1992), pp. 76–7.

5 Ibid., Chapter 7.

6 D. Bohm, "A New Theory of the Relationship of Mind and Matter," *Philosophical Psychology* 3 (1990): abstract.

7 Albert, *Quantum Mechanics and Experience*, Chapter 5.

8 Hugh Everett, "On the Foundations of Quantum Mechanics" (PhD thesis, Princeton University, 1957).

9 D. Z. Albert and Barry Loewer, "Two No-Collapse Interpretations of Quantum Theory," *Nous* 23 (1989): 169–86.

10 For further discussion of these issues, I highly recommend Jeffrey Barrett's book *The Quantum Mechanics of Minds and Worlds* (New York: Oxford University Press, 1999).

11 See especially D. Wallace, "Everett and Structure," *Studies in History and Philosophy of Modern Physics*, 34 (2003): 87–105.

12 For example, Descartes' famous dream argument (in the first Meditation) is supposed to show that his mental state is logically consistent with the physical facts being quite different than what they actually are. Similarly, David Chalmers' zombie argument is supposed to show that the physical state of a person's body and brain is logically consistent with that person having no mental states whatsoever.

13 A similar idea — viz. the non-superposability of mental states solves the measurement problem — is mentioned in David Chalmers, *The Conscious Mind* (New York: Oxford University Press, 1996) and "Consciousness and Its Place in Nature," in S. P. Stich, and T. A. Warfield (eds), *Blackwell Guide to the Philosophy of Mind* (Boston: Blackwell, 2003), pp. 102–42. Chalmers claims that such a view needs to be elaborated, and I do so in the following section.

14 For example, see H. P. Stapp, (2001), "Quantum Theory and the Role of Mind in Nature," *Foundations of Physics* 31(10) (2001): 1,465–99; and *Mindful Universe: Quantum Mechanics and the Participating Observer* (New York: Springer, 2007).

15 Albert and Loewer, "Two No-Collapse Interpretation of Quantum Theory."

16 Thanks to colloquia audiences at Maryland, Notre Dame, and Princeton

who provided feedback on the ideas in this paper. A special thanks to the co-authors and editors of this book who provided absolutely invaluable help with dialectical and expository issues. The graphics in this chapter were generously released by their creators into the public domain, and may be downloaded from www.wikimedia.org.

Notes to Chapter 7: From Experience to Experiencer

1 Franz Brentano, *Psychology from an Empirical Standpoint* (London and New York: Routledge, 1995), p. 159.
2 George Graham, "Self-Consciousness, Psychopathology, and Realism about the Self," *Anthropology and Philosophy* 3 (1999): 533–9.
3 Given certain metaphysical views, they *might* affect such a shift, but not just any change in one's self-conception is guaranteed to bring about a change in the thing to which one refers using first-person pronouns.
4 Thomas Nagel, *The View From Nowhere* (New York and Oxford: Oxford University Press, 1986), pp. 41–2. The emphasis is Nagel's.
5 René Descartes, *The Philosophical Writings of Descartes*, vol. 2, trans. by John Cottingham, Robert Stoothoff, and Dugald Murdoch (Cambridge: Cambridge University Press, 1984), p. 13.
6 See Roderick M. Chisholm, "Which Physical Thing Am I? An Excerpt from 'Is There a Mind-Body Problem?'," in Peter van Inwagen and Dean Zimmerman (eds), *Metaphysics: The Big Questions*, 2nd edn. (Malden, MA: Wiley-Blackwell, 2008), pp. 328–33; and Philip L. Quinn, "Tiny Selves: Chisholm on the Simplicity of the Soul," in Lewis Hahn (ed.), *The Philosophy of Roderick M. Chisholm*, (LaSalle, IL: Open Court, 1997), pp. 55–67.
7 I suppose one *could* say that the presence of a soul in our case acts as a sort of "consciousness magnet," pulling mentality away from the physical substance — say, the brain — to which it would otherwise be "attracted."
8 William Hasker, *The Emergent Self* (Ithaca, NY: Cornell University Press, 1999).
9 Richard Swinburne, *The Evolution of the Soul*, rev ed. (Oxford: Clarendon Press, 1986), chapter 10.
10 Hasker, *The Emergent Self*, Chapter 8; and Swinburne, *The Evolution of the Soul*, chapter 15.
11 I know of only one line of thought that would support such a bizarre view: the idea that persons are to their bodies as programs are to the computers that run the programs. Now there may be more and less plausible ways to understand this idea. But, on one way of construing the nature of a *program*, it is a set of rules, independent of the particular computers running them. Programs, so understood, are more like mathematical entities: abstract objects, existing outside space and time. But it is hard to take this picture seriously. If programs

are abstract things, like functions defined over numbers, then they are unchanging, and they exist no matter what the world is like. But surely *persons* are not unchanging things that exist no matter what the world is like.

12 I express my reservations about one traditional argument for dualism in "Two Cartesian Arguments for the Simplicity of the Soul," *American Philosophical Quarterly* 28 (1991): 217–26.

13 Paul M. Churchland, *Matter and Consciousness* (Cambridge, MA: MIT Press, 1985), pp. 12–13.

14 An extreme form of act-object theory is presupposed in G. E. Moore's "The Refutation of Idealism", in *Mind* 12 (1903): 433–53. For defense of the act-object theory, see Frank Jackson's *Perception* (Cambridge, MA: Cambridge University Press, 1977).

15 Classic defenses of adverbialism are found in C J. Ducasse, *Nature, Mind, and Death* (La Salle, IL: Open Court, 1951), Chapter 13; and Roderick M. Chisholm, "The Theory of Appearing," in Max Black (ed), *Philosophical Analysis* (Englewood Cliffs, NJ: Prentice-Hall, 1963), pp. 97–112.

16 Jackson, *Perception*, p. 59.

17 C. D. Broad, *Scientific Thought* (London: Routledge and Kegan Paul, 1923), pp. 245–55.

18 I say more in defense of these claims in "From Property Dualism to Substance Dualism," *Proceedings of the Aristotelian Society*, supplementary volume 84: (page numbers missing). The kind of argument that I think leads the act-object property dualist to sense data can be found in Howard Robinson, *Perception* (London: Routledge, 1994), Chapter 6, pp. 119–50.

19 Here, I slightly repurpose a comparison due originally to Peter van Inwagen; see his *Material Beings* (Ithaca, NY: Cornell University Press, 1990), p. 238.

20 For important versions of such a theory, see Kit Fine, "Vagueness, Truth and Logic," *Synthese* 30 (1975): 265–300; and Van McGee and Brian McLaughlin, "Distinctions without a Difference," *Southern Journal of Philosophy* (Supplement) 33 (1994): 203–50. David Lewis endorses such an account in his *On the Plurality of Worlds* (Oxford: Basil Blackwell, 1986), p. 244.

21 See William Robinson, *Understanding Phenomenal Consciousness* (Cambridge: Cambridge University Press, 2004), pp. 207–26.

22 See David Chalmers, *The Conscious Mind* (New York: Oxford University Press, 1996),

23 For criticisms and questions, I am grateful to participants in conferences hosted by the Ursinus College, University of Nottingham, and the University of Geneva, and to the Metaphysics and Philosophy of Religion reading group at Rutgers. Special thanks are due to Mark Baker, John Hawthorne, Philipp Keller, Daniel Nolan, Ted Sider, Timothy Williamson, and Leopold Stubenberg. Also, in retrospect, I can see that I owe a great debt to Peter

Unger's book, *All the Power in the World* (New York: Oxford University Press, 2005).

Notes to Chapter 8: Souls Beastly and Human

1 For my account of this case I am relying on Aram Vartanian, "Trembley's Polyp, La Mettrie, and Eighteenth-Century French Materialism," in Philip P. Wiener and Aaron Noland (eds), *Roots of Scientific Thought: A Cultural Perspective* (New York: Basic Books, 1957), pp. 497–516. Page references in the text are to this essay.

2 "Along with its powers of locomotion, contraction and extension, eight or ten arm-like projections at its mouth-end could seize whatever prey came their way, which was then conveyed to the stomach and digested." Ibid., p. 497.

3 Ibid.

4 Ibid., p. 498.

5 Ibid., pp. 504–5.

6 Ibid., p. 503.

7 For more on the background for Trembley's discovery, see Aram Vartanian, *Diderot and Descartes: A Study of Scientific Naturalism in the Enlightenment* (Princeton: Princeton University Press, 1953), Chapter 4; and John P. Wright and Paul Potter (eds), *Psyche and Soma: Physicians and metaphysicians on the mind-body problem from Antiquity to Enlightenment* (Oxford: Clarendon, 2000), Chapters 10 and 11.

8 Vartanian, "Trembley's Polyp, La Mettrie, and Eighteenth-Century French Materialism," p. 508.

9 Ibid.

10 Our science today only partly agrees with this. Modern biology does see plants and animals as differing at a fundamental level; polyps are unambiguously animals, and there are no "animal-plants." But the common ancestry of all living things is affirmed, which readily lends itself to interpretation in terms of a single "scale of nature" if we are so inclined.

11 Vartanian makes a strong case for the importance of the polyp to La Mettrie and to later French materialism.

12 Jaegwon Kim, *Physicalism, Or Something Near Enough* (Princeton: Princeton University Press, 2005).

13 I should state that Kim would not necessarily agree with the reasons I am giving here; for his reasons his own writings should be consulted.

14 Nor is this limited to contemporary materialism; remember La Mettrie's reference to "certain physical causes . . . to which the whole chain of this vast universe is so necessarily bound and subjected that anything that occurs could not have not occurred."

15 There is a theory of mind called *functionalism*, according to which such "intentional states" as desiring, intending, and the like are whatever plays a certain causal role in explaining an organism's behavior. This causal role, it is asserted, is actually played by brain states, and so the intentional states can be incorporated into a thoroughly materialist view of the mind. For a variety of reasons, I do not think this functionalist view is correct. However, even if functionalism is accepted, it remains true that a person's behavior is to be explained entirely in terms of the physical structure and function of the brain and nervous system; subjective experience as such plays no role in these explanations. In view of this, the criticisms developed in this section still apply.

16 Alternatively, it may be held that mental events are distinct from physical events but are "supervenient" on physical events; this means that every mental event is completely determined by the corresponding brain-event. The arguments given in the text apply to this case also.

17 Only a general and approximate correspondence is in question; our color and sound perceptions, for example, do not literally represent what is going on in the physical world. But physicalism is at a loss to explain even the degree of accuracy in representation that we actually find to be the case.

18 It may occur to some readers that there doesn't need to be anything that "has" the experiences; the experiences themselves might just exist, without being had by anything. I do not believe this is a satisfactory view, all things considered. But the important thing for present purposes is this: the experience itself is not a physical thing, so a view which postulates such experiences existing all on their own is not and cannot be a materialist view.

19 For more discussion of these arguments see William Hasker, "On Behalf of Emergent Dualism," in Joel B. Green and Stuart Palmer (eds), *In Search of the Soul: Four Views of the Mind-Body Problem* (Downers Grove, IL: InterVarsity Press, 2005), pp. 75–100; also, *The Emergent Self* (Ithaca, NY: Cornell University Press, 1999), Chapters 3 and 5. An excellent discussion of the argument from reason will be found in Victor Reppert, *C. S. Lewis's Dangerous Idea* (Downers Grove, IL: InterVarsity Press, 2003). Reppert presents this and some related arguments in a way that is philosophically responsible yet readable and accessible.

20 Vartanian, "Trembley's Polyp, La Mettrie, and Eighteenth-Century French Materialism," p. 502.

21 Some of the material in the remainder of this essay is taken from William Hasker, "On Behalf of Emergent Dualism."

22 Some of the reasons for this assertion are found in the argument from reason.

23 Part of the philosophical motivation for making this move can be found in the unity-of-consciousness argument presented earlier.

24 For more extensive accounts of emergent dualism, see *The Emergent Self* and "On Behalf of Emergent Dualism."

25 Keith Yandell's critique does press the analogy beyond its proper limits, and beyond anything I have said about it; see his "Mind-Fields and the Siren Song of Reason," in *Philosophia Christi* 2:2 (2000), pp. 183–95. For my reply, see my "Response to My Friendly Critics," pp. 197–207 of the same issue.

26 Wilder Penfield, *The Mystery of the Mind* (Princeton: Princeton University Press, 1975), p. 215.

27 See Kip Thorne, *Black Holes and Time Warps: Einstein's Outrageous Legacy* (New York: Norton, 1994), p. 263.

28 Roger Penrose, "Black Holes," in Laurie John (ed.), *Cosmology Now* (New York: Taplinger, 1976), p. 124. Kip Thorne agrees: "A black hole is made from warped space and time. It may have been created by an imploding star. But the star's matter is destroyed at the hole's center, where space-time is infinitely warped. There's nothing left anywhere but warped space-time" (interview in *Discover Magazine*, November 2007, p. 51). And see Thorne, *Black Holes and Time Warps*, p. 30.

29 There is an interesting problem here which has been raised by several critics, most persistently by Kevin Corcoran (see his comments in *In Search of the Soul*, p. 112). If God creates a new body, would not that body immediately generate a soul of its own, thus frustrating the aim of providing re-embodiment for the soul of the deceased person? Previously I have stated that "we must imagine the new body created from the very beginning *as the body of this very soul*; the renewed self must be 'in charge' of the resurrection body right from the start" (*The Emergent Self*, p. 235). But perhaps this was not sufficiently explicit. Consider, then, the following (admittedly far-fetched) analogy. A large hurricane is building in the Gulf of Mexico and is threatening New Orleans. God in his mercy desires to spare the Gulf coast a repetition of the horrors of Hurricane Katrina. But for some reason God wishes this particular hurricane to run its natural course rather than being stilled instantly, as was the storm on the Sea of Galilee. So instead of quelling the storm, God transports it to a location in the Pacific Ocean, moving the top thirty meters of ocean water together with the atmosphere up to a height of 15,000 meters. At the same time, he transfers a similar mass of water and atmosphere from the Pacific to the Gulf. The cooler Pacific waters quickly cause the weather in the Gulf to calm down. The surrounding waters and atmosphere in the Pacific, however, are supernaturally heated and put in motion in such a way as to sustain the activity of the hurricane that is already under way. Now, here is the point: the waters and atmosphere in the Pacific, given their present temperature, currents, wind flow, etc., would naturally tend to generate a "new" hurricane in that region. But this hurricane-generating tendency is as it were pre-empted by the transplanted Atlantic hurricane, and we have as a result only one hurricane in the Pacific rather than two. The application of the example to the emergent soul is left as an exercise for the reader.

Notes to Chapter 9: A Scientific Case for the Soul

1 Daniel Dennett, *Consciousness Explained* (Boston: Little, Brown and Company, 1991), pp. 35–7; and John Searle, *The Rediscovery of the Mind.* (Cambridge, MA: MIT Press, 1992), p. 4.

2 There are other severe problems with reductive materialism which I do not discuss, such as the problem of how thoughts could be meaningful or how they could be *about* things. For example, since under materialism the only properties and relations in the world are physical, how could the thought "there are extraterrestrials somewhere in the universe" be about the universe, when there is no plausible material relation one has to the entire universe that could corresponds to this "aboutness"? (The relation could not be that of causality, for instance, since many parts of the universe are causally isolated from us.) In philosophy, this problem regarding "aboutness" goes under the name of the *problem of intentionality.*

3 Michael Tye, "Qualia," in the *Stanford Encyclopedia of Philosophy*, online at http://plato.stanford.edu/entries/qualia, 2007, Section 1. Accessed July 22, 2009.

4 David Chalmers has developed this argument in detail in a major book on the subject (*The Conscious Mind: In Search of a Fundamental Theory* [Oxford, UK: Oxford University Press, 1997]), along with a series of articles and responses to critics, many of which are available on the internet. Many others have presented similar arguments, such as Colin McGinn (*The Mysterious Flame: Conscious Minds in a Material World* [New York, NY: Basic Books, 2000]) and Thomas Nagel ("What is it Like to Be a Bat?," *The Philosophical Review* 83, 4 [October 1974]: 435–50).

5 Given that this is a conceptual truth, it will be true even if, following the reductive materialist, experiences are merely brain states. Therefore, one must either deny that it is a conceptual truth or deny the existence of subjective experiences.

6 A standard version of non-reductive materialism is one that does not invoke any additional physical entities or properties not found in the physical sciences. What a non-standard version would look like will become clear below.

7 Thomas Nagel, "The Psychophysical Nexus," in Thomas Nagel, *Concealment and Exposure and Other Essays* (New York, NY: Oxford University Press, 2002).

8 Mathematically, $F = Gm_1m_2/r^2$, where F represents the amount of force, m_1 and m_2 the masses of the first and second objects, r the distance between the centers of gravity of the two objects, and G is the gravitational constant.

9 Often by rewriting an equation expressing a law of physics one can change what are considered the independent variables and dependent variables, but this does not affect my overall argument.

10 R. Llinás, U. Ribary, D. Contreras, and D. Pedroarena, "The Neuronal Basis for Consciousness," *Philosophical Transactions of the Royal Society of London B* 353 (1998): 1,847.

11 The amplitude of the wave is given by the maximum displacement of the string from its resting position for a complete cycle of oscillation. To understand the idea of phase, first note that since all the waves falling under the kth harmonic will be vibrating with a frequency fk, all points on the string except the nodal points will move from maximum positive displacement, to zero displacement, to maximum negative displacement, and then back again to maximum positive displacement with frequency fk. The phase of the wave specifies where it is in this cycle relative to some reference time — say at time t = 0. Mathematically, the waveform of the kth harmonic is given by the equation $h_k(x, t) = A_k \sin(kx\pi/L)$ $\cos(2\pi f_k t + {}_k)$, where x is the position along the length of the string (with one end fixed at 0 and the other end fixed at L), t is the time, A_k is the amplitude, $_k$ is the phase, and *sin* and *cos* are the sine and cosine functions, respectively.

12 Like all constants in physics, C_1 would be expressed in some chosen system of units. For example, if one used *bit* to denote some standard unit for the experienced intensity of bitterness and *amp* to denote some standard unit for amplitude, then C_1 would be expressed in terms of bit per amp. So, for instance, if C_1 = 5.12 bit/amp, and the first harmonic had an amplitude of 2.1 amp, then the intensity of experienced qualia of bitterness would be $I_1 = C_1 A_1$ = 5.12 bit/ amp x 2.1 amp = 10.752 bits. Notice the similarity between this law and some laws in science: for example, the distance that light travels in a vacuum is given by d = ct, where d is the distance, t is the time, and c is the speed of light — approximately 30,000,000 meters/second.

13 Specifically, the mathematician Daniel Bernoulli (1700–1782) showed that a waveform on an ideal string of the type described above can be decomposed into a unique weighted sum of the waves falling under each individual harmonic as given by the following equation: $W(t) = A_1(t)h_1(\theta_1) + A_2(t)h_2(\theta_2) +$ $A_3(t)h_3(\theta_3) + \ldots$ where for any given time t, W(t) is the total waveform on the string, h_1, h_2, h_3, etc., are the waveforms of the first, second, third, etc., harmonics with phases θ_1, θ_2, θ_3 etc., and $A_1(t)$, $A_2(t)$, $A_3(t)$, etc., are the effective amplitudes of the first, second, and third harmonics, etc. Put differently, if one superposed a waveform of the first harmonic with amplitude A_1 and phase θ_1 with a waveform of the second harmonic with an amplitude A_2 and phase θ_2, and so on, one would obtain the total waveform W(t).

14 This ability of states to superpose and be decomposed into more fundamental states is a feature of all attributes in quantum mechanics, and hence is a pervasive underlying feature of the physical world. This opens up a much greater range of models for the soul than those that specifically appeal to harmonic states.

15 Lisa Randall, *Warp Passages: Unraveling the Mysteries of the Universe's Hidden*

Dimensions (New York: Harper Perennial, 2005), p. 283. The italics are mine.

16 Ibid.

17 Although a single string can divide into two strings (and two strings can interact to form one string), this does not mean the string is composed of two strings. As an analogy, a free neutron will decay into an electron, proton, and a neutrino, even though in the Standard Model of Particle Physics it is not composed of any of these entities, but rather of three quarks. Similarly, the muon — the heavy sister of the electron — is considered a non-composite particle, yet it decays into an electron and two neutrinos.

18 One might also wonder how the above model could account for different hues and saturations of color qualia. One way of accounting for these differences begins by distinguishing between qualitative versus quantitative differences in color qualia. Each kind of qualitative difference corresponds to a distinct species of qualia. For each of these species of qualia, a linking law links a harmonic with that species in the same way as in the guitar-string model; further, any quantitative differences in the qualia are then linked with quantitative differences (such as that of amplitude) in the waves falling under each harmonic. The brain is then postulated to process visual stimuli and interact with the soul in such a way that it only activates the harmonic corresponding to the perceived color qualia — in analogy to how a TV transmitter will only activate a TV tuner set to the same frequency. Finally, since normal individuals do not experience a superposition of colors — for example, when one looks at a surface that emits both red and green light, one does not experience both a red quale and green quale but rather a new color (yellow) — there needs to be some mechanism that keeps this from happening. This could simply be the result of the brain only significantly activating one harmonic, in which case the soul would only experience one color per coordinate patch. Or, there could be a further law that requires that the soul experience only one species of color qualia per coordinate patch. The former, but not the latter, would allow one in principle to modify someone's brain in such a way (such as by putting some device in the brain) that the person would experience a superposition of colors in one coordinate patch. This possibility is one way in which the dual-aspect model could be further developed via scientific experiments.

19 Further, it seems that any metaphysical account of physical laws can be given for linking laws: e.g. if one claims that physical laws hold because of some underlying necessity or causal power, one could claim the same for the linking laws.

20 For an outstanding treatment of the problem of specifying which material aggregate is the experiencer along with various metaphysical problems surrounding the existence of composite material entities, see Peter van Inwagen's *Material Beings* (Ithaca, NY: Cornell University Press, 1990).

21 See Dennett, *Consciousness Explained*, pp. 35–7 and Searle, *The Rediscovery of the Mind*, p. 4.

22 Robert Adams, "Flavors, Colors, and God," in Robert Adams, *The Virtue of Faith and Other Essays in Philosophical Theology* (Oxford: Oxford University Press, 1987), chapter 16, pp. 243–62.

23 The above account does not include agency and the ability to choose. To do this, one must just hypothesize that the soul has the power to affect subjective states. How the soul — as a "metaphysical agent" — is able to affect these states, however, remains a mystery, falling outside of any sort of law-like account.

24 One could even postulate that the modes corresponding to abstract thought have a certain minimum level of energy — that is, that they are quantized (as the various fields of physics are). As a result, they could only be activated by a brain that is large enough to generate the minimum level of energy.

25 Similar rules, called "superselection rules" occur throughout quantum mechanics. An example is the Pauli-exclusion principle, which dictates that not more than one electron can occupy a quantum state; since each orbital in an atom has two possible quantum states corresponding to the two different directions of electron spin, this rule implies that each orbital can have at most two electrons.

26 Some might wonder if the arbitrariness is just pushed to the conditions necessary to create soul-quanta. The answer is that there is an arbitrariness in the value of the parameter that determines the minimum energy of a soul quanta; this sort of arbitrariness, however, is no greater than that of the parameters that determine the energy of individual quanta in standard physics — e.g. the value of the rest energy of the electron in the case of the electron field. Further, although the non-reductive materialist could hypothesize the existence of a quantized energy field such that the experiencer comes into being with the first quanta produced, it is still likely that complex linking laws would be required to determine which aggregate of particles compose the experiencer, as argued previously.

27 Some might wonder how survival of bodily death could occur under the dual-aspect theory without invoking a new body for the soul to interact with. First, note that even if one thinks the soul is generated by the brain, there is no reason to think that it could not continue to exist after the brain dies; as an analogy, if photons of light are produced by shining one's flashlight into empty space, they will continue to exist even if one were to destroy the flashlight. Significant life after death, however, would require perceptions of the environment, memory, and the like. Something corresponding to vision might be able to occur by the sensory non-subjective modes of the soul being directly stimulated by the electromagnetic field that exists at every point in space; this would allow the soul to not only "see" using the normal visible spectrum, but also using other parts of the electromagnetic spectrum such as the infrared and X-rays.

Another possibility is that the soul has the equivalent of radar, sending out its own vibrations, which are reflected back from objects in its environment with corresponding information about them. As for memory, special non-subjective modes of the soul — or some associated field — could record all of one's experiences, in analogy to how many of today's computers come with a second hard drive that automatically backs up all one's programs and data. Indeed, in modern field theory, all material structures —and hence all storage of memory — consist of fields that retain their basic form for a long period of time. For example, a stable arrangement of electrons, protons, and neutrons consists of particular stable states of the electron, proton, and neutron fields.) This memory might be only accessible when the brain dies, much like rebooting a computer from the second hard drive. Another possibility is that the information regarding the past of the entire universe is stored somewhere, which after death each soul has partial access to, in analogy to how some computers backup their data to external mass storage sites.

28 I would like to thank all the contributors to this book for comments on an earlier version of this paper, particularly Mark Baker, Stewart Goetz, and Dean Zimmerman. I would also like to thank Richard Swinburne, David Schenk, and Caleb Miller for comments.

Notes to the Afterword

1 Edward Burnett Tylor, *Religion in Primitive Culture* (New York: Harper, 1958).
2 Indeed, the bulk of modern academic theologians seem to have this view, in contrast to some Christian philosophers. Others include Peter van Inwagen (*Material Beings* [Ithaca, NY: Cornell University Press, 1990]) and Nancey Murphy (*Whatever Happened to the Soul* [Minneapolis, MN: Fortress Press, 1998]).

Bibliography

Adams, Robert. 1987. "Flavors, Colors, and God." In Robert Adams (ed.), *The Virtue of Faith and Other Essays in Philosophical Theology*. Oxford: Oxford University Press. pp. 243–62.

Albert, D. Z. 1992. *Quantum Mechanics and Experience*. Cambridge: Harvard University Press.

Albert, D. Z. and Barry Loewer. 1989. "Two No-Collapse Interpretations of Quantum Theory." *Nous* 23: 169–86.

Alt, K. W., *et al.* 1997. "Evidence for Stone Age Cranial Surgery." *Nature* 387: 364.

Aristotle. 2006. *On the Soul*. J. A. Smith (trans.). Stilwell, KS: Digireads.com Publishing.

Armstrong, David. 1980. *The Nature of Mind and Other Essays*. St. Lucia: University of Queensland Press.

Barrett, Jeffrey. 1999. *The Quantum Mechanics of Minds and Worlds*. New York: Oxford University Press.

Beauregard, Mario and Denyse O'Leary. 2007. *A Neuroscientist's Case for the Existence of the Soul*. New York: Harper One.

Bennett, Maxwell, Daniel Dennett, Peter Hacker, and John Searle. 2007. *Neuroscience and Philosophy: Brain, Mind, and Language*. New York: Columbia University Press.

Bennett, Maxwell, and P. M. S. Hacker. 2003. *Philosophical Foundations of Neuroscience*. Oxford: Blackwell.

Benson, D. F. and Norman Geschwind. 1971. "Aphasia and Related Cortical Disturbances." In A. B. Baker and L. H. Baker (eds), *Clinical Neurology*, vol. 1. New York: Harper & Row, pp. 6–13.

Bering, Jesse and David Bjorklund. (2004). "The Natural Emergence of Reasoning about the Afterlife as a Developmental Regularity." *Developmental Psychology* 40: 217–33.

Berndt, Rita Sloan, Charlotte C. Mitchum, and Sarah Wayland. 1997. "Patterns of Sentence Comprehension in Aphasia: A Consideration of Three Hypotheses." *Brain & Language* 60: 197–221.

Bishop, Dorothy. 2004. "Specific Language Impairment: Diagnostic Dilemmas." In L. Verhoeven and H. von Balkom (eds), *Classification of Developmental Language Disorders: Theoretical Issues and Clinical Implications*. Mahwah, NJ: Lawrence Erlbaum Associates, pp. 309–26.

Blackmore, Susan. 2005. *Consciousness: A Very Short Introduction*. Oxford: Oxford University Press.

Block, Ned. 1980. "Troubles with Functionalism." In Ned Block (ed.), *Readings in Philosophy of Psychology*, vol. 1. Cambridge: Harvard University Press, pp. 268–305.

Bloom, Paul. 2004. *Descartes' Baby: How the Science of Childhood Development Explains what Makes us Human*. New York: Basic Books.

Bohm, David. 1990. "A New Theory of the Relationship of Mind and Matter." *Philosophical Psychology* 3: 271–86.

Börner, Gerhard. 1988. *The Early Universe: Facts or Fiction?* 1st edn. New York: Springer-Verlag.

Borsutzky, Sabine *et al.* 2008. "Confabulations in Alcoholic Korsakoff Patients." *Neuropsychologia* 46(13): 3,133–43.

Breasted, James Henry. 1992. *The Edwin Smith Papyrus*. New York: New York Historical Society.

Brentano, Franz. 1987. *On The Existence of God*. Susan F. Krantz (ed. and trans.). Dordrecht: Martinus Nijhoff Publishers.

———. 1995. *Psychology from an Empirical Standpoint*. London and New York: Routledge.

Broad, C. D. 1923. *Scientific Thought*. London: Routledge and Kegan Paul.

———. 1925. *The Mind and Its Place in Nature*. London: Kegan Paul, Trench, Trubner & Co.

———. 1960. *The Mind and Its Place in Nature*. Paterson, NJ: Littlefield, Adams, & Co.

Brown, Donald. 1991. *Human Universals*. New York: McGraw-Hill.

Brown, Warren, Nancey Murphy, and H. Newton Malony, (eds). 1998. *Whatever Happened to the Soul?* Minneapolis, MN: Fortress Press.

Buklina, S. B. 1998. "Clinical-neuroendocrinological Syndromes due to Lesions of the Cingulate Gyrus in Humans." *Neuroscience and Behavioral Physiology* 28: 601–7.

Butler, Bishop. 1961. *The Analogy of Religion*. New York: Frederick Ungar Publishing Company.

Campbell, Keith. 1980. *Body and Mind*. Notre Dame, IN: University of Notre Dame Press.

———. 1984. *Body and Mind*. 2nd edn. Notre Dame, IN: University of Notre Dame Press.

Cantalupo, Claudio and William D. Hopkins. 2001. "Asymmetric Broca's Area in Great Apes." *Nature* 414: 505.

Caplan, David. 1987. *Neurolinguistics and Linguistic Aphasiology*. Cambridge: Cambridge University Press.

Carroll, Sean. 2004. *Spacetime and Geometry: An Introduction to General Relativity*. San Francisco, CA: Addison Wesley.

Chalmers, David. 1996. *The Conscious Mind: In Search of a Fundamental Theory*. New York: Oxford University Press.

———. 2003. "Consciousness and its Place in Nature." In S. P. Stich and T. A. Warfield (eds), *Blackwell Guide to the Philosophy of Mind*. Boston, MA: Blackwell, pp. 102–42.

Cheney, Dorothy, and Robert Seyfarth. 1990. *How Monkeys See the World*. Chicago: University of Chicago Press.

Chisholm, Roderick M. 1963. "The Theory of Appearing." In Max Black (ed.),

Philosophical Analysis. Englewood Cliffs, NJ: Prentice Hall, pp. 97–112.

————. 1976. *Person and Object*. La Salle, IL: Open Court.

————. 1978. "Which Physical Thing Am I? An Excerpt from 'Is There a Mind-Body Problem?'." *Philosophical Exchange* 2: 25–34. Reprinted in Peter van Inwagen and Dean Zimmerman (eds), *Metaphysics: The Big Questions*. 2nd edn. 2008. Malden, MA: Wiley-Blackwell, pp. 328–33.

Chomsky, Noam. 1957. *Syntactic Structures*. The Hague: Mouton.

————. 1959. "A Review of B. F. Skinner's *Verbal Behavior*." *Language* 35: 26–58.

————. 1966. *Cartesian Linguistics*. New York: Harper and Row.

Churchland, Paul M. 1988. *Matter and Consciousness: A Contemporary Introduction to the Philosophy of Mind*. Cambridge, MA: MIT Press.

Collins, Robin. 2008. "Modern Physics and the Energy Conservation Objection to Mind-Body Dualism." *American Philosophical Quarterly* 45(1): 31–42.

Cooper, John. 1989. *Body, Soul, and Life Everlasting*. Grand Rapids, MI: Eerdmans.

Crick, Francis. 1994. *The Astonishing Hypothesis: The Scientific Search for the Soul*. New York: Scribner.

Damasio, Antonio. 1994. *Descartes' Error: Emotion, Reason, and the Human Brain*. New York: Grosset/Putnam.

Damasio, Hanna *et al.* "The Return of Phineas Gage: Clues About the Brain from The Skull of a Famous Patient." *Science* 264: 1,102–5.

Dennett, Daniel. 1984. *Elbow Room*. Cambridge, MA: MIT Press.

————. 1991. *Consciousness Explained*. Boston: Little, Brown and Company.

————. 1991. "Two Contrasts: Folk Craft Versus Folk Science, and Belief Versus Opinion." In J. Greenwood (ed.), *The Future of Folk Psychology*. New York: Cambridge University Press, pp. 135–48.

————. 1996. "Facing Backwards on the Problem of Consciousness." *Journal of Conscious Studies* 3: 4–6.

————. 2003. *Freedom Evolves*. New York: Viking.

————. 2006. *Breaking the Spell: Religion as a Natural Phenomenon*. New York: Viking.

Descartes, René. 1912. *A Discourse on Method*. John Veitch (trans.). London: Dent.

————. 1984. *The Philosophical Writings of Descartes*, vol 2. Cambridge: Cambridge University Press.

Druks, Judit, and John C. Marshall. 1995. "When Passives are Easier than Actives: Two Case Studies in Aphasic Comprehension." *Cognition* 55: 311–31.

Ducasse, C. J. 1951. *Nature, Mind, and Death*. La Salle, IL: Open Court.

Everett, Hugh. 1957. "On the Foundations of Quantum Mechanics." Unpublished doctoral dissertation. Princeton University.

Feynman, Richard. 1998. *The Meaning of It All*. Reading, MA: Perseus Books.

Fine, Kit. 1975. "Vagueness, Truth, and Logic." *Synthese* 30: 265–300.

Firth, Paul G., and Hayrunnisa Bolay. 2004. "Transient High Altitude Neurological

Dysfunction: An Origin in the Temporoparietal Cortex." *High Altitude Medicine & Biology* 5(1): 71–5.

Flanagan, Owen. 1991. *The Science of the Mind.* 2nd edn. Cambridge, MA: MIT Press.

———. 2002. *The Problem of the Soul.* New York: Basic Books.

Fodor, Jerry. 1994. "The Mind-Body Problem." In R. Warner and T. Szubka (eds), *The Mind-body Problem.* Oxford: Blackwell, pp. 24–40.

———. 2000. *The Mind Doesn't Work That Way.* Cambridge, MA: MIT Press.

Foster, John. 1991. *The Immaterial Self.* London: Routledge.

Gall, Franz Josef. 1835. *On the Functions of the Brain and of Each of Its Parts.* Boston: Marsh, Capen & Lyon.

Gallistel, C. R., and Adam Phillip King. 2009. *Memory and the Computational Brain: Why Cognitive Science Will Transform Neuroscience.* Malden, MA: Wiley-Blackwell.

Gillett, Carl, and Barry Loewer, (eds). 2001. *Physicalism and its Discontents.* Cambridge: Cambridge University Press.

Goetz, Stewart and Charles Taliaferro. 2008. *Naturalism.* Grand Rapids, MI: Eerdmans.

Goodglass, Harold, and Edith Kaplan. 1972. *The Assessment of Aphasia and Related Disorders.* Philadelphia: Lea & Febiger.

Graham, George. 1999. "Self-Consciousness, Psychopathology, and Realism about the Self." *Anthropology and Philosophy* 3: 533–9.

Grodzinsky, Yosef. 2000. "The Neurology of Syntax: Language Use without Broca's Area." *Behavioral and Brain Sciences* 23(1): 1–71.

Gross, Charles. 1998. "Galen and the Squealing Pig." *The Neuroscientist* 4: 216–21.

Guth, Alan. 1997. *The Inflationary Universe: The Quest for a New Theory of Cosmic Origins.* New York: Helix Books.

Hasker, William. 1999. *The Emergent Self.* Ithaca, NY: Cornell University Press.

———. 2000. "Response to My Friendly Critics." *Philosophia Christi* 2(2): 197–207.

———. 2005. "On Behalf of Emergent Dualism." In Joel B. Green and Stuart L. Palmer (eds), *In Search of the Soul: Four Views of the Mind-Body Problem.* Downers Grove, IL: InterVarsity Press, pp.75–100.

Harmon, P. M. 1982. *Energy, Force, and Matter: The Conceptual Development of Nineteenth Century Physics.* Cambridge: Cambridge University Press.

Heil, John. 1981. "Does Cognitive Psychology Rest on a Mistake?" *Mind* 90: 321–42.

Herbert, Nick. 1987. *Quantum Reality: Beyond the New Physics.* New York: Anchor Books.

Herophilus. 1989. *The Art of Medicine in Early Alexandria.* by H. von Staden. (ed. and trans) Cambridge: Cambridge University Press.

Hockett, Charles Francis. 1973. *Man's Place in Nature.* New York: McGraw-Hill.

Hoefer, Carl. 2000. "Energy Conservation in GTR." *Studies in the History and Philosophy of Modern Physics* 31(2): 187–99.

Honderich, Ted. 1993. *How Free Are You? The Determinism Problem.* New York: Oxford University Press.

Horgan, John. 2005. "In Defense of Common Sense." *New York Times*, August 12.

Horowitz, Barry *et al.* 2003. "Activation of Broca's Area During the Production of Spoken and Signed Language: A Combined Cytoarchitectonic Mapping and PET Analysis." *Neuropsychologia* 41(14): 1,868–76.

Jackson, Frank. 1977. *Perception.* Cambridge: Cambridge University Press.

———. 1982. "Epiphenomenal Qualia." *Philosophical Quarterly* 34: 127–36.

———. 2007. "A Priori Physicalism." In B. McLaughlin and J. Cohen (eds), *Contemporary Debates in Philosophy of Mind.* Oxford: Blackwell, pp. 186–99.

Kant, Immanuel. 1965. *Critique of Pure Reason.* Norman Kemp Smith (trans.). New York: St. Martin's Press.

Kertesz, Andrew. 1979. *Aphasia and Associated Disorders: Taxonomy, Localization, and Recovery.* New York: Grune & Stratton.

Kinsbourne, Marcel. 2000. "The Mechanism of Confabulation." *Neuro-Psychoanalysis* 2: 158–62.

Kim, Jaegwon. 1996. *Philosophy of Mind.* Boulder, CO: Westview Press.

———. 2002. "Book Symposia: *Mind in a Physical World.*" *Philosophy and Phenomenological Research* 65: 674–7.

———. 2005. *Physicalism, or Something Near Enough.* Princeton: Princeton University Press.

Krauss, Lawrence M. 2009. "God and Science Don't Mix." *The Wall Street Journal,* June 26.

Levelt, Willem. 1989. *Speaking: From Intention to Articulation.* Cambridge, MA: MIT Press.

Lewin, Roger. 1980. "Is Your Brain Really Necessary?" *Science* 210: 1,232–4.

Lewis, David. 1986. *On the Plurality of Worlds.* Oxford: Basil Blackwell.

Llinás, Rodolfo, U. Ribary, D. Contreras, and D. Pedroarena. 1998. "The Neuronal Basis for Consciousness." *Philosophical Transactions of the Royal Society of London B* 353: 1,841—9.

Loewer, Barry. 2001. "Review of *Mind in a Physical World: An Essay on the Mind-Body Problem and Mental Causation* by Jaegwon Kim." *Journal of Philosophy* 98: 315–24.

Lotze, Hermann. 1894. *Microcosmus: An Essay Concerning Man and his Relation to the World,* vol. 1. Elizabeth Hamilton and E. E. Constance Jones (trans). New York: Charles Scribner's Sons.

Lowe, E. J. 2000. "Causal Closure Principles and Emergentism." *Philosophy* 75: 571–85.

Luria, A. R. 1968/1987. *The Mind of a Mnemonist: A Little Book About a Vast Memory.* Lynn Solotaroff (trans.). Cambridge: Harvard University Press.

———. 1976. *Basic Problems of Neurolinguistics.* The Hague: Mouton.

Lynch, Gary, and Richard Granger. 2008. *Big Brain.* New York: Palgrave-Macmillan.

Lyons, William. 2001. *Matters of the Mind.* New York: Routledge.

Macmillan, Malcolm. 2002. *An Odd Kind of Fame.* Cambridge, MA: MIT Press.

Madan, Pankaj, Om P. Kalra, Sunil Agarwal, and Om P. Tandon. 2007. "Cognitive

Impairment in Chronic Kidney Disease." *Nephrology Dialysis Transplantation* 22(2): 440–4.

Maruszewski, Mariusz. 1975. *Language, Communication and the Brain*. The Hague: Mouton.

McDermott, Drew. 2001. *Mind and Mechanism*. Cambridge, MA: MIT Press.

McGee, Van, and Brian McLaughlin. 1994. "Distinctions without a Difference." *Southern Journal of Philosophy* 33: 203–51.

McGinn, Colin. 1993. *Problems in Philosophy: The Limits of Inquiry*. Cambridge: Blackwell.

———. 2000. *The Mysterious Flame: Conscious Minds in a Material World*. New York: Basic Books.

Mele, Alfred, (ed.). 1997. *The Philosophy of Action*. Oxford: Oxford University Press.

Melnyk, Andrew. 2003. "Some Evidence for Physicalism." In S. Walter and H. D. Heckmann (eds), *Physicalism and Mental Causation: The Metaphysics of Mind and Action*. Charlottesville, VA: Imprint Academic, pp. 155–72.

Misner, C., K. Thorne, and J. Wheeler. 1973. *Gravitation*. San Francisco: W.H. Freeman and Company.

Moore, G. E. 1903. "The Refutation of Idealism." *Mind* 12: 433–53.

———. 1922. *Philosophical Studies*. London: Routledge and Kegan Paul.

Murdock, Paul. 1945. "The Common Denominator of Cultures." In R. Linton (ed.), *The Science of Man in the World Crisis*. New York: Columbia University Press, pp. 123–42.

Nagel, Thomas. 1974. "What is it Like to be a Bat?" *The Philosophical Review* 83: 435–50.

———. 1979. *Mortal Questions*. Cambridge: Cambridge University Press.

———. 1986. *The View from Nowhere*. New York: Oxford University Press.

———. 2002. *Concealment and Exposure and Other Essays*. New York: Oxford University Press.

Papineau, David, 2002. *Thinking about Consciousness*. Oxford: Clarendon Press.

Peacock, John. 1999. *Cosmological Physics*. Cambridge: Cambridge University Press.

Peebles, P. J. E. 1993. *Principles of Physical Cosmology*. Princeton: Princeton University Press.

Penfield, Wilder. 1975. *The Mystery of the Mind*. Princeton: Princeton University Press.

Penrose, Roger. 1976. "Black Holes." In Laurie John (ed.), *Cosmology Now*. New York: Taplinger, pp. 103–126.

———. 1989. *The Emperor's New Mind: Concerning Computers, Minds, and the Laws of Physics*. Oxford: Oxford University Press.

———. 2004. *The Road to Reality: A Complete Guide to the Laws of the Universe*. New York: Alfred A. Knopf.

Pinker, Steven. 1997. *How the Mind Works*. New York: W.W. Norton.

———. 2002. *The Blank State: The Modern Denial of Human Nature*. New York: Viking.

Popper, Karl R., and John C. Eccles. 1977. *The Self and Its Brain*. New York: Routledge.

Price, H. H. 1932. *Perception*. London: Methuen.

Putnam, Hilary. 1982. *Reason, Truth, and History*. Cambridge: Cambridge University Press.

Quine, W. V. 1973. *The Roots of Reference*. La Salle, IL: Open Court.

Quinn, Phillip L. 1997. "Tiny Selves: Chisholm on the Simplicity of the Soul." In Lewis Edwin Hahn (ed.), *The Philosophy of Roderick M. Chisholm*. Chicago: Open Court, pp. 55–67.

Randall, Lisa. 2005. *Warp Passages: Unraveling the Mysteries of the Universe's Hidden Dimensions*. New York: Harper Perennial.

Rapin, I. and Allen, D. 1983. "Developmental Language Disorders: Nosologic Considerations." In U. Kirk (ed.), *Neuropsychology of Language, Reading, and Spelling*. New York: Academic Press, pp.155–84.

Reppert, Victor. 2003. *C.S. Lewis's Dangerous Idea*. Downers Grove, IL: InterVarsity Press.

Rey, Georges. 1997. *Contemporary Philosophy of Mind*. Oxford: Blackwell.

Roberts, Selena. 2005. "Freedom Does More than Improve a Swing." *New York Times*, August 11.

Robinson, Howard. 1994. *Perception*. London and New York: Routledge.

Robinson, William. 2004. *Understanding Phenomenal Consciousness*. Cambridge: Cambridge University Press.

Rorty, Richard. 1980. *Philosophy and the Mirror of Nature*. Oxford: Blackwell.

Russell, Bertrand. 1917. *Mysticism and Logic*. London: George Allen and Unwin.

Ryle, Gilbert. 1949. *The Concept of Mind*. New York: Barnes and Noble.

Savage-Rumbaugh, Sue. 1994. *Kanzi: The Ape at the Brink of the Human Mind*. New York: Wiley.

Schwartz, Jeffery, and Sharon Begley. 2002. *The Mind and the Brain: Neuroplasticity and the Power of Mental Force*. New York: Regan Books.

Searle, John. 1992. *The Rediscovery of the Mind*. Cambridge, MA: MIT Press.

———. 1997. *The Mystery of Consciousness*. New York: The New York Review of Books.

Shieber, Stuart. 1994. "Lessons from a Restricted Turing Test." *Communications of the Association for Computer Machinery* 37(6): 70–8.

Shoemaker, Sydney and Richard Swinburne. 1984. *Personal Identity*. Oxford: Blackwell.

Sider, Theodore. 2001. *Four-Dimensionalism*. New York: Oxford University Press.

Singer, Ronald. 1958. "The Boskop 'Race' Problem." *Man* 58: 173–8.

Smythies, J. R. 1956. *The Analysis of Perception*. London: Routledge and Kegan Paul.

Stapp, Henry Pierce. 2001. "Quantum Theory and the Role of Mind in Nature." *Foundations of Physics* 31(10): 1,465–99.

———. 2007. *Mindful Universe: Quantum Mechanics and the Participating Observer*. New York: Springer.

Stich, Stephen. 1983. *From Folk Psychology to Cognitive Science: The Case Against Belief*. Cambridge, MA: MIT Press.

Swinburne, Richard. 1997. *The Evolution of the Soul*. Rev. edn. Oxford: Clarendon Press.

Taliaferro, Charles. 1994. *Consciousness and the Mind of God*. Cambridge: Cambridge University Press.

————. 2001. "The Virtues of Embodiment." *Philosophy* 76(1): 11–25.

Taylor, Richard. 1992. *Metaphysics*. 4th edn. Englewood Cliffs, NJ: Prentice Hall.

Thorne, Kip. 1994. *Black Holes and Time Warps: Einstein's Outrageous Legacy*. New York: Norton.

————. 2007. "Interview". *Discover Magazine*. November, p. 51.

Turing, A.M. 1950. "Computing Machinery and Intelligence." *Mind* 65: 433–60.

Tye, Michael. 2007. "Qualia." *Stanford Encyclopedia of Philosophy*. Available online at http://plato.stanford.edu/entries/qualia.

Tylor, Edward Burnett. 1958. *Religion in Primitive Culture*. New York: Harper.

Unger, Peter. 2006. *All the Power in the World*. Oxford: Oxford University Press.

van Inwagen, Peter. 1990. *Material Beings*. Ithaca, NY: Cornell University Press.

————. 1995. "Dualism and Materialism: Athens and Jerusalem?" *Faith and Philosophy* 12: 475–88.

Vartanian, Aram. 1953. *Diderot and Descartes: A Study of Scientific Naturalism in the Enlightenment*. Princeton: Princeton University Press.

————. 1957. "Trembley's Polyp, La Mettrie, and Eighteenth-Century French Materialism." In Phillip P. Wiener and Aaron Noland (eds), *Roots of Scientific Thought: A Cultural Perspective*. New York: Basic Books, pp. 497–516.

von Staden, H. (ed. and trans.) 1989. *Herophilus: The Art of Medicine in Early Alexandria*. Cambridge: Cambridge University Press.

Wald, Robert. 1984. *General Relativity*. Chicago: University of Chicago Press.

Wallace, David. 2003. "Everett and Structure." *Studies in History and Philosophy of Modern Physics* 34(1): 87–105.

Wellman, Henry. 1990. *The Child's Theory of Mind*. Cambridge, MA: MIT Press.

Whitehead, Alfred North. 1958. *The Function of Reason*. Boston: Beacon Press.

Wolterstorff, Nicholas. 1984. *Reason within the Bounds of Religion*. Grand Rapids, MI: Eerdmans.

Wright, John P. and Paul Potter (eds). 2000. *Psyche and Soma: Physicians and Metaphysicians on the Mind-Body Problem from Antiquity to Enlightenment*. Oxford: Clarendon Press.

Yandell, Keith. 2000. "Mind-Fields and the Siren Song of Reason." *Philosophia Christi* 2(2): 183–95.

Zimmerman, Dean. 1991. "Two Cartesian Arguments for the Simplicity of the Soul." *American Philosophical Quarterly* 28: 217–26.

————. 2004. "Should a Christian be a Mind-Body Dualist?" In Michael Peterson and Ray van Arragon (eds), *Contemporary Debates in Philosophy of Religion*. Malden, MA: Basil Blackwell, pp. 314–27.

————. 2010. "From Property Dualism to Substance Dualism." *Proceedings of the Aristotelian Society* Supplementary Volume 84: pp. 119–50.

Index